A PASSPORT
TO
AMERICA

Rene' B. Vesery

ACKNOWLEGEMENTS

I want to thank my dear wife Anne of fifty three years for all her help and encouragement in putting this book together. Her computer knowledge was instrumental in the organization of my novel.

I would especially like to thank my grandson Dakota and my good friend Arthur for being the first to read and critique my manuscript.

PROLOGUE

It was late in the summer of 1918, somewhere on the Steppes of the Ukraine. Shots rang out again from the church yard cemetery. It was getting late now. The sun had set in the west. Jacques lay quietly under the thick bramble bushes. His face and hands were scratched and bleeding from the thorns of the blackberry bushes, but he lay there face down partially concealed in natures debris of leaves and dirt under the bushes. He could hear voices in the distance shouting in Russian as other shots rang out. Then again, the chattering rat-a-tat of a machine gun confirmed that the remaining prisoners who did not escape were filling the open graves that each man had dug for himself. All who were left that did not escape in the confusion were paying the price now for Jacques' life and his freedom. There was nothing he could do but pray for their souls and hope that those Bolshevik bastards would not find him.

When it was dark, maybe they would give up the search. His captors were not well equipped and not very dedicated either. Thank God, they had only a few guns among the group, one of which was the machine gun set up for their assignation. Jacques doubted that the couple of lanterns his captors were using would be sufficient illumination to find all of the escapees in the darkness of the night. He lay there wondering how many of his fellow prisoners had made it into the forest and how many had been shot or re-captured. He was the first over the wall and didn't look back to see how many others made it. The group was made up of foreigners in Ukraine. There were Greeks, Germans, a Frenchman, an Italian, an Armenian, a Pole and a Czech soldier who was fighting against the Bolshevik's for the Tsar. They all desired the freedom to return to their respective homelands.

As darkness fell, only the sound of the crickets chirping remained. The mosquitoes buzzing in Jacques' ears and sucking his blood was of little consequence compared to the fate he shared with his fellow prisoners only an hour or so ago. He knew that those mosquitoes smelled the blood from the bramble scratches and were eager to feast upon him. Patience was of the utmost importance so he lay there motionless for, what seemed like, well over an hour. Then rising quietly from the brush in the darkness, he listened carefully for sounds of his comrades. Thankfully, the night was pitch black and moonless. Though his eyes were adjusted to the darkness, it was still difficult to find his way through the thick forest. Jacques tried a soft whistle but there was no response. Were some of the other prisoners still silently hiding in the woods, or was he the only one who escaped?

CHAPTER ONE

It was a beautiful October day. The sky was azure blue. They were to meet in front of the photography studio at 10:00 AM on Wednesday morning and his mother was rarely late. Jacques arrived five minutes early because he knew that Maman did not like to be kept waiting. Jacques was dressed in his usual gray business suit with a starched collared white shirt. He wore the cufflinks that his brother Michael had given him before he left for France. They were a gift from their Uncle Gustaf Tomasini, Maman's older brother. He also wore the silk tie that Maman brought back for him on her last visit to Milan where her family still lived. Jacques knew that wearing these would please his mother. He carried a cane as was fashionable for a gentleman to carry in Europe in 1914. Jacques' birthday had just passed. He was twenty-three and still a bachelor.

Maman arrived on the dot at ten o'clock. She was dressed in a brown dress with a matching jacket with two large leather buttons on each sleeve. The peach colored frilly blouse had a high turtle necked collar. A cameo broach that was her Grandmothers adorned her neck. Her hair was tucked up under a very large brimmed hat that was embellished with lace and a few small silken flowers. Maman insisted that they meet at Atelier Francis de Jongh at 6, Avenue du Theatre for photographs of her with her son. She had had pictures taken of herself with Michael and each of the three girls and did not want to leave Jacques out. He was the hardest to coral these days because of the added obligations at the family owned Wheat Exchange, cast upon due to his father's illness and his brother's decision to leave for France and join the fight for their father's homeland. After all, their grandparents, uncles, aunts, and cousins still lived there. Michael always seemed to be more attached to his French roots than was Jacques.

This was the war to end all wars and Michael Vesery had to be a part of it. He was a lieutenant in the Swiss Army and felt that his expertise and leadership could in some way help defeat the Kaisers German Army.

Michael had attended the University in Lausanne and was qualified to be an officer in the Swiss Army whereas Jacques had gone straight into the family business. He was very good with numbers and Papa trained him well. Papa was born in France and they lived in a French speaking Canton in Switzerland but Jacques learned to count in Italian from his Maman. That always annoyed his Papa. "Will you please count in French, so I can understand what you are talking about," Papa would say.

Jacques was also a member of the Swiss Army as are all male residents of Switzerland from the age of fifteen to forty nine. However, Jacques as an enlisted member of the militia felt an obligation to stay in Lausanne and protect the country of his birth in these troubled times of war, in spite of Switzerland's neutrality. Besides, Maman could not handle running the family business on her own. So when the memo came from the newly appointed wartime General of the Swiss Army, General Ulrich Wille, which stated that all French speaking members of the Army were invited to join the French Army, Michael was one of the first to volunteer.

Now it was picture taking time. The photographer took many different poses. Several pictures were taken with Maman's hat on and others with her hat removed, each time taking a moment to fix her hair or deciding whether her hat was on just so. Maman was to return to the studio in several days to choose the portraits she wanted. It would not be an easy choice especially for the photographer who was very patient. The Vesery family was one of the prominent families in the community and the photographer's fees were more than sufficient to cover the extra time spent in the selection process.

After the photo shoot was over, Jacques was happy to return to the office a few blocks away and leave Maman to her shopping before she returned home. The office of the family business, the Wheat Exchange, was in a loft on the second floor of a building that overlooked a small family burial plot that had seventeen head stones and one larger monument with the family name 'Breher' on it. There was a very large sycamore tree that shaded the plot which was enclosed with a wrought iron fence and a gate on the far side. The Wheat Exchange was a business that his father Michael Vesery Senior started as a young man. Born in the Loire valley of France, Michael Sr. was the youngest son of Valerie and Anton Vesery, a family of wheat farmer's whose land had been in the family's possession for many generations. Most of the wheat that was grown on the family farm in Chemille in the Provance of Pays de La Loire (the low country of the Loire River) was shipped to Switzerland by river barge or by train through the Saint Marie Railroad tunnel to Vallorbe then on to Geneva, Lausanne and many other cities in this beautiful mountainous country. Switzerland was a dairy country so they had to import most of their wheat. Jacques' father took advantage of this fact and moved to Lausanne on beautiful Lake Leman to start his business. As the business grew and demand became greater, the Wheat Exchange began importing their wheat from the Ukraine in Russia. The vast Steppes of the Ukraine produced an abundance of wheat at a much cheaper price than that of the French.

Now Jacques' father was not well and with his brother Michael off to war to fight for France, the burden fell on Jacques' shoulders. Not that there was anything physical to the job; it was all sales and bookkeeping. Orders would arrive for so many metric tons of wheat and the shipments would be directed to the customer's warehouses to be processed into flower. Jacques' job was to keep the paper work straight and the shipments of wheat flowing from the Ukraine. For this there were three office workers; one to handle the customs forms for the transportation of the wheat, one for accounts receivable and the third person did accounts payable. Jacques was the salesman who saw customers and suppliers which involved some traveling in Switzerland and an occasional trip to the Ukraine.

The most common way to travel to the Ukraine in normal times was by train to Constantinople on the Orient Express. The celebrated Orient Express left from the rail station Gare de l`Est in Paris, made a regular stop in Bern, traveled through Switzerland, Austria-Hungary, Bulgaria and ended in Constantinople; a trip of over two thousand kilometers with several days spent on the train. From Constantinople it was most convenient to book passage on one of the many ships that sailed the Black Sea to the port of Odessa in the Russian Empire. However, these were not normal times. There was a war going on in Europe. The German alliance of Germany, Austria-Hungary and Bulgaria had declared war on France, Belgium, Russia and Serbia. Turkey was a non participating partner in the alliance with Germany and Great Britain entered the war as an ally of Belgium because it was invaded by the Kaiser's German army. It was now 'World War I'.

After a full day of work, Jacques returned home where his three younger sisters were all a buzz about the up-coming wedding of Emile, the oldest, to Yuri Vladimiorvich Bek, a Ukranian that she had met on a trip to Odessa with her mother and father in the summer of 1914. Yuri's father was in the shipping business. The Bek family owned a fleet of small cargo ships that plied the Black Sea and some parts of the Mediterranean and now as far west as France; mostly with shipments of wheat from the Ukraine. It was no coincidence that these two young people met because both families were in favor of the marriage even though it was not arranged. Jacques' parents did not believe in arranged marriages although it was still common practice throughout Europe.

Preparations were being made for the wedding ceremony to be held on the first Saturday in November. Yuri`s family was to arrive several days before the wedding. They were sailing from Odessa to Marseille on one of the family ships that brought a shipment of wheat. It was a small group. Yuri`s mother, father, two younger sisters and a younger brother along with his grandmother on his mothers side were to attend the wedding. Jacques made the arrangements for them to stay at a chateau on the Avenue de Beaumont one kilometer from the Vesery family home in Lausanne.

When Jacques entered the family home, the girls and their mother were in the library making plans for the upcoming event. It sounded like they were all talking at once.

"What is all this chatter about?" Jacques said, laughing as he entered the room.

"We are discussing the details of the wedding," Maman said. "Would you like to join us? A male opinion might be interesting, especially from someone who is as detail oriented as you are my son." "Oh, what would an aging bachelor like Jacques know about weddings anyway Maman," countered Lilly, his youngest sister who was sixteen.

Then his three sisters began to tease Jacques about the girls he knew and the ones who they thought were just right for him to marry. Then Olga entered the fray.

"Jacques, why not tell us about the girl you used to visit across the lake in Evian? Was she pretty? You made an awful lot of trips on the ferry that summer. Tell us what she looked like. Does she still live there in Evian?"

"That girl in Evian was just a casual acquaintance. Yes, she was pretty," Jacques said. Then he added, "Well, maybe I should have married Evette," said Jacques jokingly, knowing that his sisters did not like her.

"No!" exclaimed Olga, "Evette is such a snob." Olga was the middle sister of the three and the most outspoken. She was eighteen. Maman immediately corrected her.

"Olga, you must not say derogatory things about someone like that. It is impolite and improper for a young lady to discuss other people in that manner.

"Yes, but Maman, you did not get to know her like we did." Olga returned.

"Do not answer me back. Remember, I am your mother."

"Maman, you are too easy on these girls of yours. Had I answered in that manner, I would have received the back of your hand across my face, posthaste. You girls are spoiled." Jacques said, with a touch of humor in his voice and a wink at his sisters.

They giggled. Jacques was their favorite brother, because he was so adventurous and fun to be with. Michael, their oldest brother was quiet and just too serious. Not that they loved him any less. They thought he was very brave to join the French Army. Mother replied,

"You were a boy and needed harsher treatment. And look at you now. I think I did a fairly good job of raising you".

"Thank you, Maman. I think that I will decline the invitation to join you in your discussions of the wedding details and see how Papa is doing." As he left the room, he quietly closed the library doors behind him.

His next stop was the kitchen to see what they were going to have for dinner this evening. The smell of fresh baked bread, as he approached the kitchen, enlivened his curiosity. Other delicious smells joined that of the bread as he opened the door. Margarette was putting the finishing touches on a roast that looked delicious. Margarette Cogny had been the family housekeeper and cook for the past fourteen years. She was a small, rather round, fifty-seven year old widow whose husband had passed away fifteen years earlier. She had two children that ventured out into the world when their father had died and was basically alone when she came to work for the Vesery family. They provided quarters for her on the third floor where there were two very comfortable rooms facing the rear of the house overlooking the small vegetable and flower garden, the carriage barn and the chicken coop. It was a pleasant view. Margarette was happy there and was considered by all to be a member of the family.

Jacques and Margarette had a very special relationship. As a boy of ten, he had the job of collecting the eggs from the chicken coop every morning while his older brother Michael cared for the family horse. When collecting the eggs, Jacques would always select one egg, puncture a small hole in the end and suck out the raw egg, then replace the empty shell in the basket with all of the good ones. Upon counting the eggs in the basket for whatever she planned to cook there was always one short. At first this would infuriate her but eventually she accepted it as the boyish prank that it was and Jacques eventually became her favorite person in the house because of his fun loving nature and his willingness to help her in the kitchen. He also recognized that Margarette was an excellent French cook and he did love good food. The menu in the house often favored the likings of her special young friend. The girls always teased him about the influence he had on what came from their kitchen.

After giving his favorite chef a hug and stealing the end slice of the freshly baked bread, he went upstairs to the sitting room where his father was resting in a lounge chair. Father was not feeling well for the past few months; the doctor had diagnosed his condition as 'consumption'. With rest, he had gotten better but it was not easy for his father to rest. Papa was not the kind of man to sit around doing nothing. He was feeling better now. The coughing had subsided and the night sweats were no longer as frequent as they had been.

"How are things going at the Exchange?" Papa asked, as Jacques entered the room.

"Going well," Jacques replied as he sat at his father's feet on the end of the lounge chair. "How are you feeling today?"

"Much better, but your mother still refuses to let me out of this prison until the doctor tells her that I am well enough to live a normal life."

"Maman is only looking out for your best interests," Jacques said, not allowing his father to reply. "The latest wheat shipment has been delivered to the warehouse in Geneva and payment has been sent to our bank. The next boat will arrive in Marselle soon, and we expect it to be bringing the Bek family here for the wedding." Jacques sighs! "The last shipment of this growing season has left Dnipropetrovsk and should be somewhere in the Black Sea. That delivery will fill our warehouse for the coming winter."

"Good," said Papa "And what is going on with Boris Zaitzev in Kiev?"

"There has been no reply to the wire that I sent last Friday, but with the war going on, things are very unstable out there. I will give them time to reply" said Jacques.

"By the way, it takes a very elusive character to avoid that beehive of activity downstairs in the library".

"Yes, Papa, I am as aware as you are of the danger involved in lingering by the library lately. And I noticed that you have avoided the library also." They both laughed.

"I don't want to bother you with all of the day's trivialities from the office, so let me go and change out of my business clothes and into something more comfortable before dinner. Will you be joining us for dinner this evening, Papa?"

"Yes, I will be along shortly."

"Good, then I will see you at dinner" With that, Jacques left the room.

At dinner that evening, the whole family was gathered at the dining room table with the exception of Michael who was away fighting for the Republique Francaise. Michael was the oldest son and his place at the table was at the right hand of their father who sat at the head. Jacques sat to the left of Papa and Emile sat next to Jacques. She was the next oldest to Jacques and on the quiet side; although tonight she was extremely talkative. She was also the center of most conversation because of her upcoming wedding to Yuri and his arrival within the next few days. Olga occupied the place next to Michael's empty chair at the table. Olga was very talkative and straightforward. She had an opinion about everything and never was afraid to share it with anyone. Jacques liked to bait her to keep the dinner conversations lively and it worked. Lilly, the baby, sat next to Olga at the left hand of Maman. Lilly was on the frail side but that was really only her mothers opinion. At sixteen, she was still giggly and enjoyed being the 'baby' of the family. It did give her some extra privileges.

Emile was continuing the conversation about Yuri and his family and her upcoming wedding and honeymoon that had started earlier in the library.

"I hope Yuri`s family will all like me," Emile said finally.

"Well, we all know that Yuri likes you enough to travel all the way here from Odessa to marry you," Olga retorted.

"How could anyone not like you, our dear sweet sister? I will miss you so much when you go back to Odessa with Yuri," Lilly added. When the wedding conversation dwindled and all were addressing their food, Lilly said,

"We haven't had a letter from Michael in a long while. I hope he is safe and well." Everyone remained silent for several moments until Papa said,

"Sometimes it is better that we do not hear from the war. I am sure Michael is safe and well, but just too busy to write."

"I try to write to Michael every day but I miss a day here and there," Lilly admitted. Emile and Olga added that they wrote him on alternate weeks, so he would always have mail from home. At the end of the meal, the girls cleared the table and went to the kitchen to help Margerette. Jacques and Papa went to the library to talk about business and the war and Maman retired to her room to read or write to Michael.

Maman insisted that the three girls do their share of work in the house. It taught them responsibility. After all, Margarette was their cook; the one who prepared their meals, not a laborer who was hired to clean up after them. One of their assigned tasks in the house was to clear the table, wash the dishes, dry them and put them away. On occasion, arguing could be heard coming from the kitchen about who washed the dishes last, or whose turn it was next. On the whole, the girls accepted their responsibilities willingly and did not complain.

In the library, Papa was telling Jacques

"I cannot emphasize enough the importance of keeping up the value of our family name in business and in the community. We also need to maintain good relationships with our customers as well as with our suppliers. Boris Zaitzev at the Ukraine Wheat Co-operative is a good man and a good friend. He would bend over backwards to keep us happy and we must do the same for him. Boris sends us the best quality of wheat. Better than what he sends north to feed the Tsars' people. He gives us only the grain from the Cossack farmer's fields. I am telling you this again so that you do not forget. I have no control over the business any more so it is your responsibility and your duty to keep things running smoothly. I built up this business from nothing and I expect that you and your brother will make it grow to support your children and even your grandchildren. I know that I have told you all of this before but now I am sick and God knows how much longer I will be here to remind you."

"Do not talk that way Papa. There is nothing to worry about. You have trained your boys to be responsible men. You know that Michael and I will always do the right thing." Then Jacques went outside the house to smoke a cigarette. He did not want to smoke in the house because he knew that the smoke would irritate his father's condition.

CHAPTER TWO

A few days later, a message came to the Wheat Exchange office that Yuri had arrived alone in Geneva and he would arrive at the train station (Place de La Gare) in Lausanne on the 3:30 PM train from Geneva. Jacques was shocked to hear that Yuri was alone! He knew that Emile would be very happy to see Yuri but upset to hear that he is arriving alone. After all the wedding was only two weeks away.

At noon Jacques left the office after explaining the situation to his office manager Marie and for her to tell anyone who asked that he had gone out for lunch. Marie LaManna was Jacques first cousin on his mother's side and the expert on Swiss Customs Forms and Regulations. Her four grown children had left Switzerland to take up residence in other countries in Europe and America as they were encouraged to do. Switzerland is a very small country and did not want to become over populated. Marie and her husband Roberto lived in a cottage in Pully and Roberto worked in a small local chocolate shop.

Jacques surprised his mother when he arrived home for lunch. As he was explaining the situation Emile entered the room. She was also shocked to see Jacques at this hour. It was just not like him to come home for lunch.

"I have good news," Jacques said as he reached for Emily's hands. "Yuri is here."

Emile squealed as she hugged her older brother.

"Don't squeeze me to death or I won't be able to pick him up at the train station."

In her excitement, Emile screamed, "When?"

"Today. On the 3:30 PM train from Geneva."

Now Maman chimed in, "Calm down my dear. We do not have much time to prepare for the arrival of the Bek family. There is much to do."

"Wait! Wait!" Jacques interrupted. "Yuri will be arriving here alone! His family is not arriving with him. I am sure there is an explanation. Maybe Yuri is so anxious to see my beautiful sister that he left his family standing at the docks in Marselle. I am sure he will clear all of this up when we greet him at the train station this afternoon. Emile, you and I will take the Renault down to meet him. So get yourself ready. We will leave here at three o'clock. That will give us plenty of time to enjoy lunch and get to the station early in case the train arrives ahead of schedule", 'which it never does', Jacques said under his breath. Swiss trains run like clockwork; exactly on time.

Maman said, "Let us have a bite to eat before we start getting ready."

"I can't! I'm too excited to eat" Emile said as she turned and ran up the stairs to her room.

A few minutes before three o'clock, Jacques called from the bottom of the stairs, "Emile, are you ready?"

Then he turned to exit through the rear of the house. Before the door closed behind him, Emile was right on her brothers heels and looked radiant. Jacques started up the Renault and pulled it out of the small barn where Emile climbed into the front seat. The 1909 Renault BH was very powerful and the family's first automobile. This auto had to be powerful to cope with the extremely hilly terrain of Lausanne. However, the Vesery family kept the horse carriage even though the horse was replaced by the Renault they purchased in the fall of 1909. They drove past Our Lady of Faith Catholic Church on Avenue de Bethusy, number 54 where the wedding was scheduled to take place; past the Palace Saint Francois then turned left on Rue de Petit Chene. This cobbled-stoned street wandered downhill at a particularly steep grade and ended directly in front of the railroad station. Jacques had to shift down into first gear and let the engine hold the Renault from speeding downhill as he did not relish the thought of burning out the brakes.

They arrived early. The train pulled into the station at exactly 3:30 PM. As the passengers disembarked, they could see Yuri's blond head above the crowd. He was a tall and handsome Cossack with high cheekbones and blue eyes. He carried a duffel bag over one shoulder and a box with gifts tied up with cord in his left hand. He was dressed for travel. Emile dashed into the oncoming crowd and jumped into his arms, knocking the duffel from his shoulder and the box from his hand. It was so good to see his sister so happy and excited. When Yuri took her in his arms, her feet came off the ground and he spun her around clearing the immediate area of passing pedestrians.

Jacques then made his way through the thinning crowd to greet his soon-to-be brother-in-law. Speaking in Russian, he shook Yuri's hand and said,

"Welcome to our family and our beautiful city of Lausanne."

"Spacibo bolshoye," (thank you very much) Yuri replied. Then Yuri continued the conversation in French because he felt it to be rude not to speak the language of the country. Yuri began,

"It was a long trip. We had some bad weather at sea and some delays with our shipment entering the port at Marselle but I will go into those details later. How are you, my love Emile?"

"I am so happy that you are here. And where are your mother and father?"

Yuri replied apologetically,

"I regret that they will not be coming to our wedding because we all agreed that the trip would be too dangerous and there was a chance that they would not be able to return to Odessa, but we will talk about this later."

Retrieving Yuri's bag and box, Jacques led the way to the Renault with the two lovers trailing behind and holding on to each other. Jacques placed Yuri's belongings in the front passenger seat, opened the rear door and motioned for the two lovers to sit together in the rear seat. When Jacques settled into the driver's seat, Yuri said, "This is a beautiful automobile. I would bet that it goes fast."

"Very fast!" Jacques replied. "I had it up to fifty-three kilometers per hour on the shore road to Montreux a few weeks ago." He then drove the big auto onto the Avenue De la Gare. Then Yuri turned his attention to his future bride and they spoke softly to each other for the remainder of the trip back to the Vesery home.

When they arrived at the house they were greeted warmly by the whole family. Olga and Lilly had never met Yuri so introductions were made. Olga shook Yuri's hand while Lilly kissed him on the cheek then turned a bright shade of red. Yuri gave Lilly a hug and said, "No cause to be shy, we will be related soon." And all chuckled, easing Lilly's embarrassment.

"When will your family arrive," Maman asked?

"They will not be coming because of the danger in traveling these days, Maman," Jacques inserted. "Yuri will explain it all over dinner."

"Very well then, I guess some plans will have to be changed," Maman ordered. "You must cancel the arrangements for the chateau on Avenue de Beaumont, Jacques. Yuri will stay with us in Michael's room. Olga, go see to it that Michael's room is in order. Lilly, go to the kitchen and inform Margarette that we have a guest for dinner and give her all the help she needs. We will sit in the library until Olga reports that the room is ready."

Yuri protested, "I don't want to put you out like this."

"Nonsense, you are a member of the family, Yuri. What would your mother think of us if we sent you to a hotel?" Yuri laughed, and nodded his acceptance.

"When your room is ready you may go and freshen up for dinner. Jacques will show you where your room is, Yuri." With that Maman left the room to make sure that all was going as planned.

That evening, at dinner Jacques sat in Michaels chair giving Yuri his seat that was between Papa and Emile. After Papa said grace, he turned to Yuri and said, "We are all very anxious to hear the events of your trip, my Son."

"Yuri is not your son, Papa" Olga piped up.

"But he soon will be and I am happy and proud to call Yuri 'Son' because he is a fine young man and very smart to marry your sister Emile," Papa said pointedly.

"Thank you! I am proud to be a member of your family and happy that Emile will be a member of mine. Where shall I begin? I would like to say that my mother and father and all of my family are extremely disappointed about not attending the wedding. Please accept their apologies. On September 17th, I sailed on our ship, the 'Hero Potyomkinsty' to Dnipropetrovs`k where her hull was loaded with wheat. Then we returned to Odessa to pick up additional crew members for the voyage. The news was not good. Our newest ship the 'Grand Duchesses Anastasia' had returned from Athens with a report that two German war ships were anchored at the Golden Horn of Constantinople. The war between Russia and Germany meant that our ships may be in peril. Father suggested that we postpone the wedding, to which I objected. Then my father went over all of the reasons why it would be foolish to attempt this trip. The worst scenario being that the Germans could sink our ship with the whole family aboard or that we could be stranded in Switzerland and not be able to return home. It was my idea to sail with the wheat shipment and not disappoint my dear Emile." She smiled. "The 'Hero' sailed from Odessa the next morning and approached the Bosporus cautiously. There were other ships passing through in both directions and some were flying the flag of Russia, so we proceeded. At the Golden Horn there were two German Cruisers, the Geoben and the Breslau anchored in mid-channel and both were flying Turkish ensigns. When we approached the Dardanelles, all ships were guided to one side by German patrol boats and the area they were protecting was being saturated with mines. At the lower end of the Dardanelles they were deploying anti-submarine nets. So, when we arrived in Athens we were advised that the Germans had closed the Dardanelles to all shipping. I would guess that the 'Hero' was one of the last ships to get through. I am a lucky man to be here today and luckier to be here with my love, Emile," Yuri explained.

"We are grateful for having you here and for bringing us Swiss our much needed wheat" Papa said. And all agreed.

"It was very wise of Vladimir, your father, not to chance coming here with this war going on. Yuri, you may have to remain with us for as long as the war lasts and that may be years. I pray for your family in Odessa and that we Swiss will not become involved. War is a terrible thing."

CHAPTER THREE

The first order of business for the young couple was to meet with Monsignore Deruaz and receive permission to be married in Our Lady of Faith Church. Yuri and the Bek family were members in good standing of the Russian Orthodox Church and the church the Vesery family attended was Roman Catholic. This created somewhat of a problem because the Catholic Church was not authorized to marry couples outside of the Catholic Faith. However, Emile was aware that some exceptions were permitted after she had spoken with the Monsignore on several occasions. Luckily, Yuri had brought with him a letter of recommendation from the Bishop of his church in Odessa, his original birth certificate and a small donation that gained him permission to be married at the alter rail, but not with the traditional wedding Mass. In addition, Emile and Yuri were required to meet several times with Monsignore Deruaz for instructions in 'The Faith' and to sign an affidavit that they would raise their children as Catholics, which they did. The wedding ceremony was then confirmed for Saturday, November 7th at 3:00 PM.

After each meeting with Monsignore Deruaz, Emile and Yuri would tour a different section of the city. The first place they visited was the fishing village of Vidy on Lake Leman. This was Emily's favorite place. She enjoyed strolling along the lake shore in summer under the shade of the tall pines and sycamore trees and even in winter when the same trees were shrouded in icicles. It was a brisk day with the air crisp and the skies clear. The two lovers sat on a bench holding hands. They watched a paddlewheel lake steamer gracefully glide into the adjoining dock to dismiss the passengers that were bound for Lausanne and take on those that were bound for the other cities along the lake. Later they strolled out on another pier and looked down to see the lake trout swimming many meters below the surface in the crystal clear water. Then they decided to take the ferry across the lake to Evian, on the French side of Lake Leman. There was a small restaurant along the lakefront where they stopped for coffee and chatted until it was time to board the ferry for the return trip to Lausanne. From the ferry you could see the snow capped mountains beyond the lake to the south-east. They took in the view as they snuggled together on the deck.

On another day, the young couple climbed to the hilltop of the old medieval town to visit the Cathedral that seemed to tower above the city. Slightly out of breath, they paused in front of the thirteenth century Cathedral to look down and inhale some of the crisp air that was blowing in from the mountains past Lake Leman. After visiting the inside of the stark Cathedral, Yuri's curiosity got the better of him and he asked,

"Is this where the crier calls out the hour from the bell tower to wake me through the night?"   "Yes,"   Emile   laughed. "Does the watchman's cry disturb you? His hourly call from the tower is a tradition that has been carried on for hundreds of years."

"I must be a light sleeper, but I have only had to endure your watchman's call for a few nights. Perhaps I will get used to it in time." He paused and thought for a moment.

"Your brother Michael had to live with this all of his life? Michael's room does face in that direction! Perhaps that is why Michael is so serious. He has never had enough sleep!"

This outrageous statement put Emile into such a fit of laughter that Yuri had to help her from falling. When Emile regained her composure Yuri wiped the tears of joy from her beautiful face and held her closely as they continued their journey toward home.

"Michael certainly is the serious one in our family, but we

love him dearly," Emile admitted. "Both of your brothers are true gentlemen, even though they each have totally different personalities," Yuri admitted as they continued their walk home.

On the morning of the wedding, Jacques the 'best man' woke up early and escorted Yuri from the house. They had breakfast in a small restaurant, and then went directly to the Wheat Exchange office to wait for the hour when they would go to the church. This allowed the women space to prepare the bride for her special day. It also allowed the two men time to discuss the crisis that both of their businesses were experiencing due to the war. Jacques also thought that their discussion would take Yuri`s mind off of the impending wedding at three o'clock that afternoon. However, Yuri was not nervous at all.

Excitement in the house was at a fever pitch. The only one who seemed to be calm and in control was Emile, the bride. The girls all seemed to be getting ready in Emile`s room. Papa could hear the endless chatter as he knocked on the door.

"May I come in?" Papa called.

"Come in," they replied in unison.

The girls were all busy and no one noticed that Papa entered the room with shaving cream on his face. He immediately went to an unsuspecting Emile and gave her a peck on the cheek leaving a smudge of shaving cream on her face. Emile screamed and jumped away.

"Papa!" Emile cried. "Now I have to fix my face all over again!"

Papa scurried from the room laughing while all three girls scolded him. When Maman found out what was going on she said to the girls,

"You know your father, always the tease." Then she went to reprimand him for the prank.

By the time Papa drove Maman, the bride, Olga and Lilly to the church all had been forgiven. It was good that the groom and Jacques arrived very early because it was discovered that the wedding ring had been left at the office and Jacques had to run back and retrieve it. Thank God the office was not far from the church. The bride was beautiful in her white long sleeved taffeta gown with a long train. Emile wore her mother's veil for something old; something new was her wedding gown;

something borrowed was her cousin Marie's handkerchief and something blue was a ribbon on her garter. The ceremony was very nice. Monsignore Deruaz read from Corinthians chapter thirteen about love, "Love is patient, love is kind." He elaborated on that reading; then they recited their vows and he pronounced Yuri and Emily man and wife. After the ceremony everyone went back to the Vesery home where Margarette had prepared food and champagne for the guests. As the party progressed Jacques drove the newlyweds to the train station where they boarded the train that would take then to Zermatt for their honeymoon, a view of the Matterhorn and maybe a little skiing.

Two weeks later, when the newlyweds arrived home, they found that Emily's room had been remodeled to accommodate the couple with a double bed and an additional armoire for Yuri's clothes. Although Yuri was anxious to return to Odessa with his new bride there were many arrangements to be made before they could do so in these unsafe times. The route by ship was cut off by the German blockade of the Dardanelles. A land route was also dangerous because of the fighting between Bulgaria and Serbia, also between the Germany Alliance versus Russia. All routes seemed to be cut off. There was much planning to be done before that return trip would be possible.

Meanwhile word came from the Bek family suggesting a route that could be taken to bring Yuri and Emile back to Odessa safely. The plan was to have one of the Bek ships pick up the couple at Marselle and take them to Athens. Two of the Bek's ship's were being forced to use Athens as their home port now because the Germans had blocked off their route through the Dardanelles. These plans were made for some time in early spring and the remainder of the journey would be arranged when they arrived in Athens. Olga and Lilly were happy that their married sister and Yuri would spend the holiday at their home this year. With Michael away at war it would be terrible for their sister and brother-in-law to leave so soon after the wedding. Christmas would not be the same without them.

It was the beginning of December, when a long awaited letter came from Michael. Family tradition dictated that Maman hold the letter unopened until she could read it out loud to the whole family at the evening meal. Margarette had the meal prepared much earlier than usual and the whole family was gathered in the library anxiously awaiting the news. When all were seated at the dining room table Maman opened the letter and read.

Twenty-forth day of November 1914

Dearest Family:

I want to congratulate Emile and Yuri on their wedding. I am so sorry that I was not able to attend but I wish you all the luck in the world and many beautiful babies.

Please forgive me for not writing sooner. As you know, after I arrived in Paris they sent me for Officers Evaluation and Indoctrination. They promoted me to Captain because of my experience in the Swiss Army and gave me five days leave before assigning me to the front. I took this time to visit Grandmaman and Grandpapa in Chemille. Thank God they are not in the path of the war as yet. It was wonderful to visit with them and our uncles, aunts and cousins, although some of the boys are off to fight for their country. I enjoyed the visit with your side of the family immensely, Papa. When I returned, they assigned me to the British Second Battalion as Liaison Officer because of my knowledge of the English language. Thank you Maman for insisting I learn English. This war is appalling. The Kaiser has sent a regiment of untrained school boys against our unit of well trained British soldiers, only to be slaughtered by the thousands. The waste of lives is hard to comprehend and the beautiful medieval city of Ypres that we are fighting for has been completely destroyed. But enough of the bad news! I am well and grateful for my family who keeps up my moral with all of the letters that I receive. God bless all of you. Pray for me and victory for the Republique Francaise.

My love to all, Michael

Papa said grace and each person added a special prayer for Michael including Margarette who stood by the kitchen door for the reading of Michael's letter. After dinner, Papa, Jacques and Yuri retired to the library to work on a plan to keep the wheat flowing from the Ukraine. Many suggestions were mulled over. Then Yuri suggested,

"Would it be possible to register one or two of our ships under Swiss Registry?" That got Papa and Jacques' attention.

"Let me think. If I know my history, under the Treaty of Paris of 1815, the Swiss were guaranteed neutrality for all time. Isn't that correct? Do you think that the Germans would honor that 'Neutrality' and let Swiss ships through their blockade?"

"That is an excellent suggestion. It might work, but I would not ask you to place your ships in our name so we can continue doing business. That would be presumptuous on our part," Jacques replied and Papa agreed.

"What would be the harm in doing that? We are one family now. And if it makes you uncomfortable to do that, we could transfer the ships back to Russian registry when the war ends. I think we should draw up the papers of transfer and apply to the Swiss Maritime Office to see if it is possible," Yuri proposed.

"Yes, but will your father agree to this?" Papa said.

"I believe my father will realize the wisdom of the transfer" Yuri added.

Both Jacques and Papa sensed that their new in-law had good insight and was very clever even though he was more than a year younger than Jacques.

Papa said, "My boy, you have wisdom beyond your years and you are a good businessman. Let's proceed with this plan, but first you must get permission from your father. Vladimir Sergeyevich must be very proud of his son, the heir to his family business.

"Thank you sir," Yuri said.

Papa put his hand on Yuri's shoulder and said, "Please call me Papa."

CHAPTER FOUR

The next day a wire went off to the Bek Shipping Company in Odessa and several days later a return wire was received at the Wheat Exchange. Marie handed Jacques the message from the wireless office. The message read: Congratulate Son – STOP - Proceed with plans –STOP- Take 2-GDT and HP –STOP- Germans confiscate Alexander Pushkin – STOP- Zaitzev wants payment- STOP- VS Bek –STOP - End of message. Jacques read the message several times. He decoded it in his mind. Yes, Yuri needed to be congratulated on both his marriage and the brilliant idea of the ships transfer of registry. Vladimir thinks it is a good idea. The Germans have confiscated the Bek ship Alexander Pushkin with all of our wheat aboard. And last but not least, the wheat wholesaler in Kiev, Boris Zasitzev, who we buy from wants to be paid for the confiscated wheat. The only part of the message that he was unsure of was (Take 2-GDT and HP). Jacques would have to ask Yuri; he would know what his father's message meant.

That evening, before dinner, Jacques met with Papa and Yuri in the library. He read the wire and looked at Yuri?

"That is not good news," Yuri proclaimed. "What my father is telling us is that we should transfer two ships to your name and put them in Swiss registry. The two ships are the Grand Duchesses Tatiana and the Hero Potyomkinsty. Their home port is Athens, now that they can't get through to our Black Sea ports. If I know my father, the paper work on the two vessels is already on its way." Yuri said,

"If you are right that will speed up the process. I will draft a formal complaint to the German Government to return our shipment of wheat along with the Bek`s ship. That wheat belongs to Switzerland, a neutral country. Then I will explain the situation to Boris Zaitzev and assure him that he will receive payment as soon as I can forward it to him, even if I have to bring it to him myself. Boris knows that we are men of our word. Then we will file a claim with Lloyds of London who insures our wheat shipments. It will take some time but Zaitzev will have to be patient."

Then Papa said, "Jacques, when you have the papers drawn up I will take them to Bern to see if some of my friends in the Government can help us in any way. I will present the complaint to the German Ambassador if necessary."

"I do not think you are well enough to travel to Bern, Papa?"

"I am fine and we need to do this. I will go."

When Papa made up his mind to do something, not even Maman could hold him back.

Several days passed before Jacques had finalized the formal complaint to the German Government. Then he sent off the claim to Lloyds of London. He gave copies of both to his father to read and approve. Papa read the documents that were properly notarized and said,

"I will leave tomorrow to take this one to the Capitol in Bern and see what kind of help I can get holding up the complaint to the German Ambassador. On the other hand, I am worried that Lloyds of London will not honor our claim because it may view our loss as an 'act of war'."

The train ride to Bern would only take a little more than an hour but Maman protested vehemently and the three girls and Jacques agreed with her.

"This trip is too much for you. You are a sick man and have no right to put your life in jeopardy for a shipment of wheat! Think of us for once! Stay home for your wife and family and let your son go. He is very capable."

Papa argued, "I know many more people in the Government than Jacques does. Mary Anne, my dear wife, I must do this to provide for my family. The survival of our family business depends on the success of this mission to the Capitol. I will not die a happy man if we do not succeed. I am feeling fine now, so I must go."

The next morning, Jacques reluctantly drove Papa to the train station in the Renault. He took the short cut route down the Rue du Petit Chene. Papa was rather surprised at the steepness of the street when riding down it in an automobile and the way it wound from one side to the other. On foot it was a steep grade but it did not seem to wiggle like a snake. Papa commented to Jacques, "I don't ever want to ride down this street in an automobile again!"

"Papa, your age is stealing your adventurous spirit. Remember when you made that very large elaborate kite with the basket fixed under it? We went up in the mountains where the wind was strong. You put me in the basket and flew the kite with me in it! You told me that some day I would fly like that in an airplane. How old was I?"

Papa laughed, "You were about three years old and you were less than four meters off the ground before I brought you down. That was probably my biggest and best kite. And you remember that?"

"How could I forget? When we returned home, and you told Maman what we had done, she was furious. I also remember how she scolded you and made you promise never to do that again."   "Yes." Papa laughed. "Your mother was angry."

Reminiscing had relieved Papa's anxiety from the ride down the steep grade. By that time, they had arrived at the train station. They parked the Renault and Jacques escorted his father into the station to wait for the train. Papa said, "This may take a few days. So tell Maman not to worry if I am not home by this evening."

Then he boarded the train to Bern.

On the way home, Jacques stopped at Our Lady of Faith Church, parked the car in front and went inside. The church was empty so he sat in one of the rear pews to pray. He was worried about Papa. While he was deep in prayer, Monsignore Deruaz appeared on the altar. He did not notice Jacques until he finished lighting the candles. Then he quietly walked down the center isle and almost in a whisper he said, "Jacques Vesery?"

Jacques' head popped up when he heard his name being called. He was unaware that the priest was in the church.

"Good morning Monsignore!"

"I was not sure that it was you kneeling with your head down, Jacques. Is there a problem?" asked Monsignore.

"I am worried about my father. As you know he has not been well lately. We have a business problem and Papa insisted that he had to go to Bern to straighten things out. The Germans have confiscated one of our wheat shipments in the Black Sea and Papa went to see the German Ambassador with a formal complaint. I wanted to go but Papa insisted that he knew the Ambassador and that he was the only one who could accomplish the intended mission. Papa has been feeling a little better lately but he is still weak from the sickness. That worries me."

Monsignore knelt in the pew next to Jacques. He said,

"Let us pray together to Saint Christopher, the 'Patron Saint of Travelers'. He will bring your father home safely. He is the 'Christ Carrier'. I know that your Papa is a stubborn man, but I am surprised that your Maman was not able to stop him. She is a very strong woman." Then they prayed. Jacques thanked the Monsignore and asked him to continue praying for his father's health and his safe return home.

Papa returned two days later having completed his excursion to the Capitol. All in all, it was a successful trip but it had taken a toll on Papa's health. Maybe it was the soot from the coal fired steam engine or the anxiety of dealing with the German Embassy but his cough had returned and he looked drained. However, Papa did find out who to contact at the Maritime Office in Geneva and what paper work was required to register and transfer the two ships to Swiss registry. Papa also partitioned the German Ambassador to allow Swiss ships free passage through their blockade of the Dardanelles. To emphasize the plea, Papa added, "Switzerland needs our wheat as much as Germany depends on Swiss banking."

The Ambassador agreed to seek help on behalf of Swiss ships but could make no promises.

Eventually, word came that the 'Grand Duchesses Tatiana' was arriving in Marselle within the week. Yuri and Emile traveled to Marselle to retrieve the ownership papers of the 'Tatiana' and the 'Hero Potyomkinsty'. Jacques met them in Geneva and they went to the Swiss Maritime Office on Rue de la Gabella to start the process going forward. The wheels of government do not move particularly fast and the Christmas season was upon them and that meant even more delays.

Christmas was rather quiet in the Vesery house this year because of Michael's absence and the deteriorating health of Papa. It was pleasant to have Yuri here to celebrate the holidays with them, even though he was used to celebrating the Russian Orthodox Christmas on January seventh. So the Vesery family extended Christmas to make Yuri feel at home. One day soon after the holiday season was over Lilly came rushing into the house.

"It is a letter from Michael" Lilly said excitedly!

It was late in the afternoon and everyone was in the house so Maman agreed to read Michael's letter immediately in the library as long as Margarette was available and not too busy preparing dinner. After they were all gathered, Maman read:

January 1, 1915

Dearest Family:

I am well and in good spirits and I hope this letter finds everyone at home in good health as well. This war has become a stalemate. We have been mired down in trenches in the cold, the wet and the mud in freezing temperatures for over a month now. Neither side is able to move forward. The Germans have attacked us with mustard gas and some times the bombardments go on all night from both sides. The brave men of the British Expeditionary Force have withstood the shortage of food, the dysentery, the rats and trench foot. Some of the less fortunate soldiers had to have their feet amputated because gangrene set in. When I die I know I will go to heaven because I have already been to hell. The distance between our lines and the Germans we call 'No Mans

Land', is pock marked with shell holes and littered with the bodies of the brave soldiers that ventured out into it from both sides. Late in the afternoon of December 24th it was decided that we would attempt a truce for Christmas Day. The truce was accepted and it seemed to spread along the front. Both sides went about collecting their dead and wounded in peace. In the evening, we heard strains of 'Oh Tannenbaum' and 'Silent Night' coming from the German lines and our troops began to join in the singing. By midnight soldiers from both sides of the war were out in 'No Mans land' sharing smokes and conversation between the Brits and the Germans. Christmas Day was peaceful and quiet and the next day we resumed shooting at each other. Oh, the foolishness of war. I can't wait to get home to our warm house and my wonderful family.

I love you all, Michael

Olga was the first to speak after a long silence.

"I feel so guilty being here in the comforts of home with people that love me while Michael is out there fighting in a war."

"It was his choice," Papa replied, "And I pray for him constantly."

Then Papa went into a fit of coughing and Maman escorted him upstairs to their bedroom where he remained for the rest of the evening.

In February of 1915, they received approval from the Maratime office for the transfer of the 'Grand Duchesses Tatiana' and the 'Hero Potyomkinsty' to Swiss Registry but they require that new names accompany the returned documents. Another requirement was to file the transfer with the Russian Maritime office in Kiev. Permission was granted to fly the Swiss Ensign on both ships with the new names. It was decided that the 'Hero Potyomkinsty' would be re-named the 'Angelique' and the 'Grand Duchesses Tatiana' would be called the 'Valerie'. It was agreed that French sounding names on Swiss ships would be more in keeping with their country of origin. They could have used Germanic names but thought better of that idea because the

Mediterranean Sea was controlled by French and British ships of war.

CHAPTER FIVE

In the beginning of March, the 'Hero Potyomkinsty' arrived in Marselle, was partially re- painted and renamed the 'Angelique'. A Swiss Ensign flew from its flag staff. When it was ready to sail, Emile and Yuri said their tearful good-byes and left Lausanne by train bound for Marselle. They were welcomed aboard the newly refurbished 'Angelique' by her Captain Leo Suslov, a long time employee of the Bek Shipping Company. Captain Suslov was extremely happy that his ship had become a woman because he believed that the sea treated female ships with much more respect than ships with masculine names. He had worked his way up through the ranks to become Captain and was a very good one. Yuri had often sailed under Captain Suslov`s tutelage as a teenager and up to his twenties while he was learning the business. The Captain treated Yuri like a son and greeted him with a big Russian hug, then turned to Emile, bowed and kissed her hand.

"I am honored to meet the bride of my favorite sailor," he said with a toothy grin on his jolly face.

"May you have a long and happy life together and many healthy children."

After chatting for awhile, he escorted them to the largest of the two passenger cabins on the ship and left them to settle in.

On the voyage, Yuri met with the four trusted sailors that his father had chosen to guide them over land the rest of the way from Athens to Odessa. The easy way was by sea but that was impossible. British and French war ships were now bombarding Turkish fortifications along the Dardanelles and British and Australian forces had just invaded the Gallipoli Peninsula which comprises the western bank of the Dardenelles.

Two of the sailors had recently made the overland trip from Burgas, Bulgaria to Dedeagatch in Greece on horseback to deliver the documents of the two ships that were transferred. So Misha and Stamos were familiar with the terrain. Misha said, "The trip is about 300 kilometers and it took us two weeks. Can your bride ride a horse?"

"Yes, Emile is good with horses, even though her family now owns an automobile."

"Oh! An automobile! What kind is it?" Stamos chimed in. "I would love to try driving one of those."

"It is a French Renault and I did get to drive it and it does go fast," added Yuri.

Then he asked, "What route do you plan to take from Dedeagatch? And is it safe?"

Misha explained, "We will go to the river that is the border of Turkey, go north, and then cross into Turkey for several miles before we reach Bulgaria. The border guards are easy to bribe. We had no trouble. Then we will go on to Burgas where a fishing boat will be waiting to take us to Odessa."

"Very good Misha. I shall make arrangements for the six of us to leave from Athens by train. We can get horses and supplies for the trip when we get to Dedeagatch. Good, then it is settled."

They all agreed to the plan.

Emile enjoyed watching the sunset over the Mediterranean each evening from a secluded place near the stern of the ship where she was usually joined by her husband. Occasionally, the married couple would retire to their cabin during the long days at sea to make love. Yuri explained all of the plans to Emile and answered all of her questions so she would not feel anxious about the journey. As the ship turned north into the Sea of Crete, they encountered war ships flying flags of France and Britain. Emile became worried seeing the ships of war and ventured to the bridge to seek the assurance of Captain Suslov. He greeted her warmly and asked,

"What can I do for you today my dear? Are you enjoying the voyage?"

"Yes, I am. But the war ships are making me a little nervous."

"Ah, pay no attention to them. They have their own business to attend to. They will not bother us merchant ships. In fact, they protect us," said the Captain.

That seemed to set Emile's mind at ease. He did not mention about the German submarines that also lurked in these waters. He did not want to make her more nervous. Then after a thoughtful pause, she asked,

"When will we arrive in Athens?"

"Tomorrow morning. God willing. But we will not actually dock in Athens. We will go ashore in Piraeus, only about ten kilometers from Athens. You must come up to the bridge tomorrow morning when we approach the harbor. I will have time then to point out all of the important sights. We will have a harbor pilot on board to bring us into port. I will show you where the young Greek men dive for the famous golden cross on January 6th as part of the observation of the Epiphany. We have just missed the celebration of 'Ploiaphesia' on the fifth of March. For hundreds of years the people of Piraeus honor 'Isis the Goddess of Navigation.' This is the time that the seas become calm in the spring and trade can begin after the winter storms."

"Thank you, Captain Suslov. I promise I will be here bright and early tomorrow morning for your guided tour," Emile said with a smile as she left the bridge.

After they arrived in Athens, it took Yuri a few days to make all of the arrangements for the trip to Dedeagatch. In between, the newlyweds spent some time enjoying the ancient city and the Greek food. Yuri had previously spoken with the sailors who were familiar with the territory and would guide them through the mountains and into Bulgaria. The train ride was slow and not as comfortable as those of Western Europe. In Dedeagatch, they purchased six horses and supplies for the journey. Stamos suggested that Emile might be more comfortable if she dressed as a boy and that she would attract less attention while traveling with five men. Emile, with her easy-going personality, agreed. She dressed as a boy, tucked her long hair up under her cap and saddled up to ride. With much good natured teasing and laughter the group set out for the Turkish border.

When they came near the bridge that crossed the river, Misha told the group to wait. "Stamos and I will cross first and the four of you will give us some time to persuade the Turkish guards to let all six of us cross into their country. You will have no trouble on the Greek side because you are leaving their country."

All five men carried concealed pistols in the event that trouble did occur. Hopefully they would not have to use them. Misha and Stamos stopped on the Greek side of the river and told the guards that there were four more in their party but they were to hold them at the border until they signaled for them to cross. The Greek border guards agreed and they were rewarded at the expense of Yuri's father. There was no love lost between Greeks and Turks. They would be just as happy to cut each others throats in the middle of that bridge. The two men proceeded, were recognized, and were greeted warmly by the Turks on the other side. They dismounted and produced a bottle of Ouzo for each of the two guards. Then the Turks invited them inside the meager guard house to collect their bribe and share some drinks from their newly acquired bottles. When the guards began to feel their Ouzo, Misha and Stamos gave them each four Russian gold coins and asked if it was alright for their four friends to come across.

The Turk said, "Russian gold is as good as any other. Gold is gold. Bring your friends, but we will not share our Ouzo with them!"

A signal was given for the others to proceed. The Turkish guards didn't even come out of the guard house to see how many people crossed the border into their country.

The group traveled dirt farm roads, avoiding the larger towns, heading northeast. Streams were still high with runoff from winter snow but none were impassable. At the Bulgarian border, the procedure was reversed, bribing the Bulgarian 'Pomak' guards to let the six of them into their country. Now the landscape was a bit more tolerable with rolling hills as they approached Burgas on the coast of the Black Sea. As promised, a fishing boat was waiting for them. Stamos and Yanni said goodbye. They were going to return to their homeland Greece, while Misha and Aleksey accompanied Emile and Yuri on the small fishing boat to Odessa. This time the voyage was not so pleasant. The weather was bad. The seas were rough and the fishing boat was much, much smaller than the 'Angelique'. Emile became sea sick at the onset and had to remain in a bunk until they reached Odessa.

Even though the weather was dreary when they reached Odessa, the Bek family was gathered on the pier to greet them. Yuri had been away from home for over seven months and it was almost a year since Emile had come to visit with her mother and father. Yuri`s two sisters Svetlana, who was seventeen and Galina at fifteen were anxious to renew their friendship with their new sister-in-law and young Nikita missed his big brother who he idolized. Angelena and Vladimir Bek were just happy that Emile and their son had arrived safely with all of the terrible things that are going on in the world these days. As they got off of the fishing boat, Yuri carried his bride onto the pier and put her down.

Angelena rushed over to Emile and blurted out, "Dochka moya' my poor child you look terrible."

With that, Emile burst out in tears. "Mother!" Yuri scolded "The weather was bad and Emile became sea sick."

"I am so sorry," Angelena said, cradling Emile in her arms.

You will feel much better when we get you back to our nice warm house on solid ground.

Between Angelena`s chicken soup and some black bread, Emile felt fine in no time.

CHAPTER SIX

Back in July of 1914, all of the talk around Paris was of the assassination of Austria's Archduke Franz Ferdinand by a Serbian on June 28th of that year. This was not a great concern of André Basic, the eighteen year old ballet dancer. His only concern was how and if he would be able to travel to Odessa, Russia by September first to start his apprenticeship at the Odessa Opera Theatre Ballet Company. He had just received notice in the mail last week that he was accepted as an apprentice and would be studying under one of the masters of the Russian Ballet, Alexander Gorsky. After struggling for the past five years to learn the skills of a male ballet dancer, he was thrilled and excited to receive such good news. André grew up in the Latin quarter of Paris. His parents were not rich. Their small apartment was on the second floor overlooking Rue Saint Jacques and from their front window one could see Rue des Ecoles. Across the quay was the famous Cathedral of Notre-Dame.

André was very athletic and loved to ride his bicycle. When he was 9 years old his father bought him a used bicycle for his birthday. His Father purchased the bicycle from a co-worker in the factory where he toiled for the few meager francs he was paid to support his wife Amelia and their son André. The co-workers son had outgrown the bicycle and it was just the right size for Andre. Unfortunately, the bike was not in great working order but it was only a few francs and that was all his father could afford. André's father was handy and knew he could fix what was wrong with it. In the process of fixing the bicycle André's father Jon made the wheel bearings a little tighter than they should have been, but what did André know about bicycles at nine years old. He learned to ride and loved cycling around the city for hours. Little did André know how his rather obstinate bicycle would prepare him and his young legs for his future of dancing on the stage of a ballet theatre.

In the summer of 1909 André's mother obtained two tickets to the ballet. She was a former dancer in the Moulon Rouge but she always admired the beauty of the ballet. On the other hand his father was not particularly interested in the ballet so his Mother Amelia asked André to accompany her. André was thrilled to be his mother's escort for the evening. It made him feel so grown up that he would accompany and protect his beautiful mother on this outing. He knew that his mother loved to dance. She would sing and prance around the house while cleaning or while preparing their meals. This would make his mother so happy. "Les Sylph ides" was the name of this ballet performed by Serge de Diaghileffs of the "Ballet Russe" and choreographed by the visionary Russian dancer Michel Fokine. Fokine had choreographed "The Dying Swan" for Anna Pavlova which brought them both great acclaim. Vaslav Nijinsky was the featured male dancer in this ballet and he was magnificent, especially in the eyes of young André. It was this beautiful ballet that inspired him to become a dancer. So at the age of thirteen he started his career by enrolling in a local ballet school. His parents were not able to afford ballet lessons for André so he found a job delivering produce with his bicycle for the grocer on the next block. Working after school made him feel very independent and paid for his ballet lessons.

André was a handsome young man. His dark hair, high cheekbones and muscular body made him stand out among the other young male students. But it was his heart and his dedication that made him the envy of his peers. The Ballet Master of his school thought highly of André and his ability as an accomplished dancer and pursued an apprenticeship with the Odessa Opera Theatre Ballet Company which Andre gladly accepted. Now as Andre was making arrangements for the long journey to Odessa, he had to worry about the political situation in Europe. Would this silly business with the Archduke place the continent in turmoil or perhaps even start a war? If a war broke out, it is possible that he would be stranded there and not be able to return home to Paris? If need be or even worse, he may be called to join the Army and fight in this silly war. He wondered, 'why must people kill each other when there was such beauty in the world?' But this opportunity was too great to pass up so he went to the rail station to purchase his tickets for the 2300 kilometer rail trip to Odessa on the famous Orient Express. With his passport secured he was prepared to leave in three weeks for the greatest adventure of his life traveling across the continent to Russia. However, at the rail terminal, the ticket agent informed him that a Frenchman traveling across Germany and Austria could pose a possible risk. Than the agent advised André to purchase a ticket to La Harve and book passage on a ship bound for Odessa, Constantinople or even Athens. When he arrived in Constantinople or Athens, his chances of traveling to Odessa would be much less dangerous. The ticket agent advised,

"You should leave soon to book your passage because the ocean voyage will take much longer than the trip by train."

He purchased a train ticket to La Harve. André did not know what the cost of passage would be on a ship but if need be he would work as a crew member to travel to the Orient. He knew that his parents would be disappointed to have him leave his homeland. They were also nervous about his immediate departure and the danger of traveling with Europe in turmoil. André had never been on a ship or even seen the ocean but his mind was made up to go to Odessa for a new life and maybe in the years to come he would return to his native France as a famous ballet dancer on the stage with the 'Ballet Russe'. His mother would be so proud of him.

Three days later he said his goodbyes with many tears and good wishes and boarded the train for La Harve at Gare Saint Lazare station. When he reached La Harve later that day he proceeded to the docks and found the shipping office. The kindly ticket agent in Paris had given him directions to where it was located. At the shipping terminal office he enquired about ships that were leaving for Constantinople, Athens or anywhere in the Mediterranean. The clerk was a heavy set man with a large nose and a hair lip who had a body odor that permeated the room.

"You are in luck my friend," the clerk said as he looked over the large board on the wall that listed the arrivals and departures of all ships that were scheduled in the port.

"The Thasos will be leaving on the morning tide the day after tomorrow. Ah, but they don't take passengers. If I recall, they were looking for a few crew members though."

"Do you think they would hire me?" asked André.

"Well you do look fit enough. A husky boy like you would probably make a decent seaman. But, oh, look at those hands 'Mother of God'; they are not calloused or dirty enough for life aboard a ship, my boy."

"My hands may not be calloused, but I am very capable of doing hard work. I have a strong back and strong legs."

He did not want to tell the clerk that he was a dancer for fear that the clerk would think he was frail and incapable of shipboard work.

"Well, the Thasos is a Greek ship with a crew of fifteen or twenty sailors. She is tied up on pier number two. You can't miss her. She is painted light blue like the colors of the ensign she is flying. And, Greek ships usually have very good food, not like the English vessels, phooey! The name of the captain is Constantine, but you better call him 'Captain Constantine' if you want to get hired on for the voyage. You can tell him that I sent you to him. My name is Armond. He'll know who I am. Now on your way, so Captain Constantine can size you up in the daylight and hire you on. Better to hide those hands when you talk to the captain. Good luck mon ami."

Pier number two was quite a walk from the shipping terminal, but the Thasos was easy enough to find. It was just as Armond had said; very light blue in color but it was not a very large ship as he had imagined it to be. André approached the gang plank and looked up. Well, the Thasos was not quite as small as it looked from a distance. He still could not imagine this small ship out in the middle of that big ocean but right now it was his only hope of getting to his destination Odessa. When he climbed the gang plank he was greeted by a crew member who addressed him in a language he did not understand. The sailor must have been Greek.

"I am looking for Captain Constantine," André said.

The sailor nodded and beckoned for him to follow. They entered through a strange metal door to a passage way that led to a ladder that went up through a hole in the overhead and it also went down through a hole in the deck. They climbed up.

Captain Constantine was on the bridge looking over his charts. He was a tall thin man with white hair and a white beard that adorned his weathered, suntanned face. With a peaked cap emblazoned with a gold anchor one could not mistake him for anything other than a sea captain. The sailor said something to the Captain in Greek and Constantine spoke to André in French.

"What can I do for you?"

"I am looking for transportation to Odessa or somewhere near there. I am a good worker and would appreciate a job working in your crew."

"Have you ever sailed before?"

"No, I have never even seen the ocean before!"

Constantine laughed. "Well, at least you are honest. I do admire that in a man. You look strong enough and the Thasos is in need of one more crew member for our voyage. What is your name?"

"André Basic, and I am from Paris. My father is a factory worker there."

"Why would you want to leave a city as beautiful as Paris and go to Odessa?"

"I was offered a good paying job in the theatre there."

The Captain hesitated a moment, then cautioned, "I think you had better tell the crew that you are an engineer going to Odessa to work for some French construction company. This crew is a tough bunch of men, but they are all good people. If you tell them that little lie, then they will not bother you about your theatre. It will be our secret."

"Captain Constantine, may I ask how long it will take for us to arrive in Athens?"

"The voyage will take about six weeks, providing that we have good weather all the way. The Thasos is making stops at Lisbon, Malaga, Spain, Palermo and Naples before we reach our home port of Athens. Welcome aboard André Basic. We will discuss your pay tomorrow when I will give you your assignment. Now pick up your bag and find the mate who brought you up to the wheelhouse and he will take you to the crew's quarters. We leave on an early morning tide the day after tomorrow but there will be plenty of work to be done before we sail."

Crew's quarters were two decks below the main deck. André was surprised to find that sailor's slept in hammocks. The mate directed him to an upper hammock as was appropriate for the newest member of the crew. The upper birth was less desirable because it was not as accessible as the lower one and it was warmer up there. A locker was provided for each crew member to keep their belongings. The crew was comprised of several nationalities. Most were Greek but there were two Spaniards, an Italian, a Russian and a Turk. The Turk was always getting in fights with one of the Greek sailors. They tell me that Turks and Greeks usually do not get along well. 'Si la vie'. Several of the crew spoke French which was very helpful to André. He was beginning to feel that this was going to be a great opportunity for him.

They arrived in Lisbon on the afternoon of the third day at sea. André was glad to have his feet on firm ground again even though the voyage was on calm seas with good weather. He began to make friends with several of the Greek sailors in spite of the language barrier. They were eager to learn French as much as he was eager to learn Greek. There were many laughs as each tried to master the others language. He had the privilege of tasting some Portuguese food for the first time in his life and saw some of the sights, especially the night life. His Greek friends were eager to show him that part of the city where the red light district was. After three days in port, they sailed for the Straight of Gibraltar and into the Mediterranean Sea. The palm tree lined quay at Malaga was so shallow that Captain Constantine had to wait several hours for the high tide to enter the port. Some of the cargo was unloaded and replaced by other cargo bound for the next port of call. The Thasos listed almost ten degrees to the port side at low tide making the process of unloading and loading a little more difficult. By this time, André's hands were blistered and as grimy as his shipmates. The work was hard but the adventure was worth it.

With calm seas and sunny days the Thasos arrived in Palermo, Sicily on the thirtieth day of July, 1914. While in port the news was that Germany had declared war on Russia and had invaded Belgium. World War I had indeed begun. André in his prayers thanked God that he did not try to go to Russia by train. Five days later, they learned that the Kaiser had invaded his homeland, France. This was a sad day for André. He would not be there to fight for his country. This fact had never dawned on him when he was making plans to leave. Now he feared for the safety of his mother and father back in Paris.

Naples was the next port of call and the last before the voyage ended in Athens. André's first look at Italy was the saddle shaped peak of Mount Vesuvius rising above the horizon. It seems to take hours to arrive at a port from when you first sight land out in the endless sea. The Thasos passed a strange looking castle perched on the rocks at the end of an island. It looked like a broken egg shell waiting to be washed away by the tides.

"What do they call that?" he asked one of his shipmates.

"Castle dell Ovo," was the reply of the Italian sailor.

Naples was a busy port. There were several ships tied up to the piers and many small fishing boats cruising through the expansive harbor. They had arrived early due to the good weather and had to wait several days for their cargo of steel to arrive from the local mill.

André was grateful for the extra time they had to wait in port. He knew that there was an Opera House in Naples but could not remember the name. It would be fun to visit there and maybe he could talk to some of the dancers. With that thought on his mind, he was summoned by the Captain. Captain Constantine asked,

"André, would you run an errand for me? I need you to go to the telegraph office and send this wire to our shipping office in Athens."

"Certainly Sir, but where will I find the telegraph office?"

"It is several blocks up the main street. I do not know the name of the street, but ask someone for directions. I have confidence you will find it."

"Thank you, Sir."

He took the envelope with the written message in it, and went ashore, with no idea of the adventure that awaited him in Naples.

At the Ufficio Telegramme, he met a beautiful Neopolitan girl named Antoinette. She knew that he had come from the ship and believed that he was a sailor. André spent that day and the next convincing her and her parents that he was a ballet dancer and not a sailor.

Three days later, the Thasos sailed for its home port of Athens with the cargo of steel on board from the mill in Naples. A very disappointed sailor stood on the deck and watched Naples disappear in the morning mist. He wished he could have spent more time in Naples with Antoinette. On the first day of August, they arrived in Athens. André was able to slip a letter destined for Naples into the outgoing mail bag. The next day he left the Thasos with his pay and an invitation to sail any time with Captain Constantine.

"King Neptune smiles down upon you, André Basic. You brought us luck when you came aboard the Thasos. We had perfect sailing weather all the way from La Harve to Athens. That is very unusual. Now, to get to Odessa, find the office of the Bek Shipping Company. They sail the Black Sea and operate out of Odessa. They do take passengers, so your lucky charm is still with you. I wish you smooth sailing on the remainder of your journey."

André booked passage on a Bek ship the 'Grand Duchesses Anastasia' bound for Odessa. They sailed past many beautiful islands in the Aegean Sea. He wished Antoinette were here to enjoy this beautiful scenery with him. As a passenger on this voyage, he was able to take in all of the sights in this fascinating part of world. They passed through the Dardanelles, a strip of water approximately 50 kilometers long and fifteen kilometers wide. There were many Turkish forts on the cliffs overlooking the Asian side. After some open water, they passed through the Bosporus, an even narrower strip of water, guarded by the fabulous Constantinople on the European shore with its Minaret's rising high above the city.

After two days of sailing the choppy waters of the Black Sea, André arrived at his destination, Odessa. Upon his arrival he found the Odessa Opera Theatre and was impressed by one of the most beautiful opera theatres in all of Europe. And also, by the warm welcome he received. The Ballet Company had arranged for a place for him to live, and he settled in but he could not forget the girl he met in Naples. He wrote several letters about his adventures and how he missed her. It was several weeks before her replies began to arrive. Antoinette sent him another picture of herself in her first letter so that he would not forget her. How could he. She is all he could think about, although he did enjoy the distraction of his new dance career.

CHAPTER SEVEN

At the Wheat Exchange in Lausanne, a telegram arrived saying that Emile and Yuri had arrived safely at the Beks home in Odessa. Jacques immediately rushed home with the good news. Everyone was relieved to know that they were safe. Maman went upstairs to tell Papa the good news. He was resting in his room. Papa had not been down for dinner in some time. It was shortly after he had returned from Bern that the coughing had gotten worse. Now he was expectorating blood with his coughing, and Jacques was very worried about his father's condition.

Jacques had received a reply from Lloyds of London and they refused to pay the claim on the shipment of wheat that was confiscated by the German Navy in the Black Sea. The refusal stated that the confiscation was an 'act of war', and that 'acts of war' were never covered, as stated in their policies. Papa did not have to know about this new development because it would only upset him and make his condition even worse.

The following week, the worst possible news came from The Repubique Francaise. The telegram was delivered to the door by two young officers of the Swiss Army. It read: The Republique Francaise regrets to inform you that your Son, Captain Michael Vesery has been killed in action at the Battle of Neuve Chapelle on 28th of March, 1915 while serving with valor as Liaison Officer to the Second Battalion of the British Expeditionary Forces.

It was signed, General Munoury, Commander 6th Army Republique Francaise.

The Vesery family was devastated. Friends and family gathered at their home to mourn the loss of the eldest son Michael. Monsignore Deruaz spent many hours consoling members of the family as a group and individually.

"The greatest sorrow is to lose a child, no matter what age the child is. Children are protected by the parents up to the time that they begin to make their own decisions. Michael made the decision to go to war. There was nothing his parents could do to stop that. He was a man and he made a man's decision, God rest his soul."

It was decided that they would hold off telling Emile the bad news for now. She had enough to deal with being so far away from home in her new life with Yuri.

When the house was quiet again and all of the mourners had left, a package arrived. The return address read: Sgt. Francis A. Galvin, 2nd Battalion, BEF. Maman waited to open the package until Jacques and the girls were there. Papa would not be included because that would upset him and bring on one of those terrible coughing spells and he did not need that. She also felt that she could not open the package when she was alone. It would be best if Jacques opened it, he would be the strongest. That evening when Jacques arrived home from the Wheat Exchange, there were four women gathered in the library, Maman, Olga, Lilly, and Margarette. Olga said, "Jacques, we agreed to have you open this package."

Jacques proceeded to open the package. It contained Michael's personal effects, a billfold containing two hundred and seven French francs, pictures of each member of the family and one of a pretty girl who no one in the family recognized. On the back was written 'I love you, Larisa'. That was a surprise! They looked at each other not knowing what to say. No one suspected that Michael had a girlfriend. There was a well worn Swiss Army knife, a bundle of letters from home and several from Larisa, with her return address from Cholet, France, a neighboring town of Chemille, where their grandparents lived. It also contained his BEF field cap and a letter in a sealed envelope addressed to Michaels mother and father. Maman opened the letter and read it out loud because it was written in English. It read as follows:

Dear Mr. and Mrs. Vesery:

May I start by saying that I am very sorry for the loss of your son Captain Michael Vesery. This may not be of much consolation, but I would like to tell you about how he fought and how he died. Captain Mike, as we called him in our unit, died in an artillery attack in the fighting at Neuve Chapelle in a nighttime barrage on the 28th of March. Shells were exploding all around us. He did not die alone. Many brave men were called that night. But my greatest memory of your son Michael was on Christmas Eve when the gunfire diminished. Captain Mike fashioned a white flag and walked out into 'No Mans Land' and appealed for a cease fire in the enemy's language. We all watched in amazement as he secured a cease fire for Christmas and returned as if he just gone for a walk. That was the bravest thing that I had ever seen in this war. I was Captain Mikes Adjutant and I am writing this letter to you from a field hospital. Again, My condolences to you and all of Michael's family.

Sincerely,

Sgt. Francis Aloysius Galvin.

They tearfully replaced the contents in the box, with the exception of the picture and address of Larisa. Maman placed the cover on the box and put it high on a book shelf, there in the library. Olga said she would write to Michael's girlfriend in Cholet.

Michael's death devastated Papa. He was ravaged by fever and was wasting away. The doctor told the family that the consumption was affecting his kidneys and bladder. Eventually Papa lapsed into pneumonia and passed away a month after word came about Michael's death. Again the Vesery home was filled with mourners and again Monsignore Deruaz came to console the family in their time of need. These were grim days for the family, with Michael and Papa gone and Emile so far away and the family business in trouble. They all agreed that Emile was not to be notified of Papas death either. Jacques came to a decision. He must go to Odessa to tell Emile of these tragedies personally. Papa would have expected him to go. Maman and Cousin Marie would have to handle the dwindling business here while he would try to get the shipments to the Wheat Exchange back on track. He sent a wire announcing his intensions to travel there. In return, he received a letter from Emile and Yuri explaining the route they had taken and the dangers involved. She told of the attack by Turkish torpedo boats at the Odessa harbor and the sinking of the Russian gunboat and other ships. One of the Bek ships was badly damaged and a sugar factory was destroyed by cannon fire. Many people were killed. It is dangerous to travel here, Emile warned. But, the future of the family business depended on Jacques going. Emile included the names, and addresses of the two Greek sailors that were their guide through Turkey and Bulgaria, Stamos and Yanni.

CHAPTER EIGHT

Preparations for his trip had to be made, and monetary funds were not as easily transferred now as they were in peacetime. Jacques needed a way to carry a large sum of money to Kiev for payment of the lost shipment of wheat. He went to the jeweler that the family had dealt with for years on the Avenue du Theatre, a few doors down the block from the Photography Studio and explained his problem to the proprietor. The proprietor said,

"Give me the amount of money you need to carry and I will select a number of stones to equal that amount. I will have them ready for you in two days."

Jacques agreed and returned two days later to pick up his purchase of assorted diamonds to cover what he thought they owed to the Ukrainian Wheat Co-operative. The diamonds would travel easier than that large of a sum in gold, although both are acceptable currency in any country. He also exchanged a small amount of his Swiss Francs for Italian lira, Greek drachma, and gold coinage. Now he felt prepared for any situation that might arise. And to protect his large investment, he purchased a small caliber revolver.

This summer of 1915, there were no ships bringing wheat from the Ukraine, and none were expected, so Jacques boarded the train to Rome in the middle of July. Maman asked him to stop in Milan to visit with her side of the family, but he had no time. The trip would take long enough without dallying in Milan. There were rumors that German submarines had sunk several merchant ships in the Mediterranean Sea so he decided to look for smaller vessels to take him to Athens. When he arrived in Rome, he immediately purchased a ticket to Bari, on the east coast of Italy, and caught the next train out. In Bari, he inquired about the ferry to Athens, and found that there were no ferries that went that far, but there was one that made a weekly trip to Patra on the western coast of Greece. It departed every Monday morning from this pier. That was very disappointing because today was Thursday, and that meant that he would have to spend the next few days in Bari. He decided to make good use of this time, knowing that some of the territory that he would travel through might be unfriendly

He booked a room in a small hotel near the Sainta Nicola di Bari Cathedral which was within walking distance of the ferry docks. There were ferry routes to various cities on the east coast of the Adriatic Sea, but only one went as far as Patra. Certainly there must be small boats that travel the Corinth Canal from Patra to Athens. The next morning after Jacques had breakfast he went shopping. He tried to purchase a leather belt that was two sided, two strips of leather stitched together, but he could not find one. He found a cobbler shop and ordered a belt to his specifications along with some heavy duty black thread, a package of heavy duty sewing needles and a thimble. The belt would be ready on Saturday. He inquired of the cobbler where he could find the nearest haberdashers shop. The cobbler directed him to a shop a few blocks away on Via Pasquale Villari. At the haberdashers, Jacques purchased a durable wool jacket with a lining. He spent the remainder of the day wandering the streets of Bari, making note of the restaurants, their menus, and questioning the local patrons about the food. Having located a place to have his evening meal Jacques returned to the hotel with his purchases.

Later that evening, Jacques returned to the Castellinaria restaurant for his dinner. The recommendation came from the elderly gentleman that he had spoken to on the street earlier in the day. It was the way he described the food with a gleam in his eye that convinced Jacques that this was the place to eat. That gentleman said that the 'Vegetables kissed by the Pugliese sun with orecchiette pasta' was an excellent choice and he recommended the 'sweet olives fried in a pan' for an appetizer. 'Magnifico!' Jacques enjoyed a leisurely meal washed down with a few glasses of a local red wine, and then coffee the way he liked it, strong and black. It was dark when he left the restaurant. On the way back to his hotel, he decided to take a shortcut through a back street that was very dimly lit. It was half way down the alley where he was accosted by a young man with a knife. Jacques said to the bandit, "Be calm, and I will give you what I have, but I must reach into my pocket."

The man nodded. Jack slowly reached his right hand into his breast pocket of his jacket, and then slipped his left hand unseen by the tough in the darkness of the alley into his pants pocket where he had his Swiss army knife. Jacques withdrew the billfold slowly and held it out to the thief with his right hand. When the thief reached for the billfold, Jacques punched him in the right shoulder with the point of the awl protruding from his left fist. The man screamed, dropped the knife and disappeared into the darkness. Jacques picked up the knife and returned to his hotel where he reported the incident to the desk clerk, who warned him not to use the back streets after dark. Jacques thanked the clerk and went to his room.

On Saturday after breakfast, Jacques picked up his new belt at the cobblers shop and returned to his room in the hotel. He slit some of the stitching on the top side of the belt and lined it with some small gold Swiss coins, and then he re-stitched the belt by hand. Next, he partially removed the lining of his new jacket and sewed some larger gold coins and the package of diamonds into the lining. This was accomplished by making a small hole in each coin. Jacques knew that gold coins have value no matter what country's name is stamped on them. On Sunday, he went to church at Saint Nicola Cathedral. He said prayers for Michael, and Papa, who had passed away, and for Maman, and the three girls, that they may be protected from harm. Monday morning he left the hotel, went to the dock with his bags and boarded the ferry bound for Patra. It was a good day; the sky was a beautiful azure blue.

The trip from Bari to Patra in Greece took a whole day, plus few hours. Just past noon on Tuesday they disembarked. Early Wednesday morning Jacques was aboard an intimate sized vessel with twenty-six Greek passengers and crew, entering the Gulf of Corinth. By late afternoon the boat entered the Corinth Canal.

The Canal cut straight through the Isthmus of Corinth for about six and one-half kilometers. It was carved through the sedimentary rock, and at the half way point, the ground rose eighty meters above the water line, almost obscuring the light from above. The canal was completed in 1893 and took twelve years to build, but was much too narrow for large ships, although it did serve its purpose, because the ocean route around the peninsular was more than four hundred kilometers. Jacques was aw-struck at the accomplishment he had just witnessed.

In Athens, Jacques found the address of Stamos, the man who was to be his guide. He was not at home, but his landlady said,

"I will tell him that you came by. He will be home tomorrow".

Jacques thanked the lady and returned to his hotel. The next morning after breakfast, Jacques went to the address and found Stamos at home. He was informed that Stamos would be his only guide. They took the train to Dedeagatch, bought two horses, and some supplies, and were on their way. When they crossed the bridge to the Turkish side of the border, they were not greeted as warmly as Stamos had been on previous trips. The two new guards were not as friendly. When Stamos inquired about the two guards that he knew, he was told that they had been found drunk on the job, disciplined and fired. Drinking alcohol is not permitted in the Muslim faith. However, the bribe was taken by the two new guards and they passed through into Turkey.

The journey went much faster with only two riders. They contacted the same fishing boat in Burgas, and Jacques was on his way to Odessa, by sea. The trip from Lausanne only took twenty-five days. Jacques was weary from the journey. When they arrived at the docks in Odessa, the captain sent a sailor to find Yuri who was working on his ship nearby.

Yuri greeted him by the fishing boat and brought him to their new home. The house on Stroganovskaya Street near Predtchenskaya Square was a wedding present from Vladimir and Angelena Bek. It was cozy and comfortable. Emile was overjoyed to see her brother when he arrived at their house. She had not been notified about the deaths of Papa or Michael. So the next day after he had settled in, he felt the time was right to tell

Emile. They were alone in the house. Yuri had gone off to work. Sitting at the kitchen table Jacques reached over and took both of his sisters` hands and told her that he had some bad news. Emile was devastated. She cried for sometime as Jacques tried to comfort his younger sister. When she regained her composure, he told her of the letters from Michaels` adjutant and from the girl Michael met in Cholet, and apparently fell in love with. It made Emile feel better that her oldest brother had someone to love him before he was killed.

In the ensuing days, Yuri brought Jacques up to date on the situation. The war was destroying both of their businesses. The Bek Shipping Company had two ships operating successfully from the Athens office, under Swiss flags in the Mediterranean. That seemed to be the only good news. The 'Alexander Pushkin' had been taken by the Germans and was being held at Constantinople, minus the cargo of wheat that they confiscated. Fortunately, the crew had been released into Greece. The Bek's ship, the 'Duke de Richeleu', lay badly damaged in Odessa harbor from the surprise attack by the Turkish patrol boats. The 'Grand Duchesses Anastasia' was tied up beside the 'Duke de Richeleu' while both crews were working on repairs. Unfortunately, both ships crews have been greatly reduced because most of the Russian members had been conscripted into the Army, leaving both ships with skeleton crews. Port Odessa was now being protected by a more alert Russian Navy. All ships in the Black Sea were completely cut off from the rest of the world due to the blockade of the Dardanelles by Germany and Turkey. It was of no use though, for Jacques to worry about all of this because he was told that all of the Ukrainian wheat was being taken by the Russian Army to feed the troops at the front lines, and the workers at the ammunition factories.

Jacques felt that he had an obligation to complete the transfer of the two ships by delivering his paperwork to the Russian Maritime Office in Kiev for legal documentation. He also needed to broker a deal with Boris Zaitzev at the Ukranian Wheat Co-operative in Kiev. If the war ended soon Jacques did not want to be on bad terms with Zaitzev. Jacques knew that Boris was a reasonable man, and would be willing to settle the matter.

The success of the Wheat Exchange and Bek Shipping depended on a speedy conclusion of the war. That did not look like it was going to happen. News of the war was not good. Jacques had two options. The first option was to travel the 450 kilometers to Kiev before the winter set in. The second was to stay in Odessa with his sister and brother-in-law and help restore the damaged ship to working order while the weather was still mild. The ships were vital for moving the wheat if the war ended soon. But if the war lingered much longer, it would all be in vain. He decided that the right thing to do was to stay and help with the work on the damaged ship to make it sea worthy.

When he told Emile and Yuri about his decision to stay, they were both very happy. Emile enjoyed having her big brother there, and Yuri said, "We can use all of the help we can get to repair the 'Duke de Richeleu'. Along with our meager crew my father and I have been working on it since before you arrived. Another pair of hands in always appreciated."

"Good, then I will start working tomorrow."

Work on the ship continued into the winter. Parts were salvaged from some of the other ships that were lying unclaimed in the harbor. Even the abandoned Russian Navy gunboat was fair game. Sections of deck were taken from other ships and welded in place while engine parts were also recycled. As winter approached, the work became more difficult because of the chilling cold. By the Christmas holidays, it was too cold to accomplish any work on the outside of the ship. Vladimir, Yuri`s father, announced that all remaining repair work would have to wait until after their Orthodox Christmas on January seventh. The crew was delighted, and so was Jacques.

On Christmas Day after the service at the Orthodox Church, they celebrated the holiday at Yuri's mother and father's house on the corner of Hersonskaya and Peter Velikiy Streets. It was a large stone house with a fireplace in every room. Later in day the house was filled with guests. Most of the guests were members of their crew; mostly Greek sailors who had no friends or relatives in Odessa to celebrate with. The meal was sumptuous. It started with the traditional red Borsch, Vareniki (dumplings),

Golubtsy (cabbage rolls). It ended with suckling pig, and the vodka flowed freely. Jacques complimented the host and hostess. "This was a wonderful party."

"Did you enjoy the food, Jacques?" Angelena asked.

"Yes, I enjoyed it immensely. I love Ukranian food, and the company was good also."

Angelena laughed. "We love Emile and we know that it has made her so happy to have you here to celebrate these holidays with our family."

"I am glad to be here too," Jacques replied.

It was a very cold winter for Jacques. He was not used to the cold temperatures at sea level where the air was full of moisture from the ocean. He was accustomed to the cold dry mountain air of Switzerland. This was bone chilling cold, and spring was three months away. He would survive! At least his sister's house was nice and warm. To fortify the body in the morning, a Russian breakfast consisted of hot black coffee, black bread with butter and a short glass of vodka in or out of the coffee. The vodka was definitely necessary to brave the cold outside.

Jacques was glad to be a help to the Bek family, and he reaped some benefits also. The heavy work was physically good for him. It also kept him warm on these bitter cold days. He worked side by side with his brother-in-law and the other crew members. When Yuri finished work at the end of each day, Jacques would stay and work a few more hours. He felt that it was only fair to give the newlyweds some time to be alone together. Work on the ship continued into April, 1916 when the 'Duke' was ready to sail. The shakedown cruise was scheduled for the end of the month. It was going up the Deniper River to Dnipropetrovsk where they would take on a cargo of wood from up river, bound for Odessa. The timing was perfect for Jacques. Dnipropetrovsk was almost half way to Kiev, and there were river barges that would make their way through the ice-strewn Deniper River to his destination, Kiev.

CHAPTER NINE

It was late on Monday morning of April 18, 1916, when Jacques finished packing his bag for the trip to Kiev. They were to leave on the evening tide for its first voyage since the 'Duke' had been damaged from the attack by the Turkish patrol boats. Yuri was sailing on the ship to inspect its sea-worthiness on its first cruise. They would part ways at Dnipropetrovsk where the ship would take on its cargo of lumber, and return with Yuri to Odessa. Emile was sad to see her brother leave. He would probably be away for several weeks while trying to persuade the Maritime Office in Kiev to process his paperwork in a timely manner. The Tsars government doesn't usually work fast, especially during a war.

Emile waved good-by from the pier and when she could no longer see the people on the ship, she walked to the top of the Potemkinski Steps that overlooked the harbor and waited until she could no longer see the ship as it disappeared over the horizon. On the long walk home, she felt the loneliness creeping in, and wished that they had not gone. Even though Yuri would return in a few days, her house would be quiet. She enjoyed the companionship of the two men. Jacques and Yuri were always telling stories that brought laughter to their home, and she too had many antic dotes to add. Like when Papa would tell the story about flying the kite with Jacques in it, and how Maman would get so upset when they laughed, and made jokes about it. Now she realized how much she missed her family, Maman and her sisters. Angelina Bek was a wonderful woman, and a great mother-in-law, and Yuri's sisters were very nice too, but they were not her sisters or her Maman. She thought about Lausanne and then about Michael, and Papa, and tears began streaming down her face by the time she reached her front door. Embarrassed and thankful that she was home, Emile pulled herself together, sat at the piano, and played her favorite music. That always cheered her up, or at least took her mind off her sadness.

The 'Duke de Richeleu' reached the mouth of the Dnieper River long before dawn and dropped anchor to wait for daylight. They would sail up 'the Cossacks route to the Black Sea.' But it was much safer to navigate this winding river in the daylight. The Dnieper is a wide, fast flowing river especially now when the melting snow and ice causes flooding in low lying areas. There are several routes through the estuary, some of which are not passable by a ship of this size. Shifting sand bars from the winter melt-off meant that proceeding with caution was necessary. Once they passed through the marshland of the estuary, the Dnieper became deeper and easier to navigate. After traveling slowly up-river for ten hours the captain ordered the ship to stop and drop anchor for the night. It took two days of intense navigating to reach Dnipropetrovsk.

In port, Jacques remained on board until the cargo was in the hold, and Yuri was free to make arrangements for Jacques' remaining journey to Kiev. Yuri had many friends along this river. Nikita Dobryakov was the owner of a river barge that plied the upper Dnieper River, bringing lumber down from the Carpathian tributaries. Nikita`s barge was the last of several to load its cargo into the waiting ship. Yuri called down from the ships deck in a loud voice, "Molodoi chelovek". He knew that would get Nikitas attention over the noise of the operation. Nikita looked up smiling,

"Yuri my friend, so you think I am a 'young man'? I should be so fortunate."

"Can you come up here?' Yuri replied, "I have a small favor to ask of you."

Nikita turned and grabbed hold of the rigging behind him and signaled for the boom operator to hoist him up to the deck above. Nikita was a small, wiry man with thick black hair and a beard. He appeared to be in his late thirties, and he wore the pleasant smile of a happy man. Yuri grabbed Nikita from the rigging and embraced him. "It is so good to see you, Nikita Andreyevich."

"I don't know about that," said Nikita. "What is this small favor you are about to ask?"

"Come up to the bridge and share some vodka with me. I have someone I want you to meet." Nikita followed Yuri up the ladder to the ships bridge where Jacques was leaning on the railing, waiting and observing the loading process. Yuri introduced them "Nikita Dobryakov, this is my brother-in-law, Jacques Vesery. Jacques, meet my friend Nikita Andreyevich." They shook hands.

"My pleasure," Jacques said.

"A pleasure?" "I don't know; in-laws are not always a pleasure," Nikita laughed with a wink. Then with a shocked look he exclaimed,

"IN-LAW!!!" "Yuri, you got married, and you did not invite me to the wedding?"

"Yes," Yuri exclaimed as the smaller man squeezed the breath out of him with a congratulatory hug. Over glasses of vodka, Yuri told of how he and Emile were married in Switzerland and of their arduous trip back to Odessa. He explained to Nikita what was going on with their shipping business and of the attack by the Turkish patrol boats.

"How are Regina and your four girls?" Yuri inquired.

"Five" Nikita said proudly, "but the last one is a son!"

They congratulated him, and poured another round. They celebrated with several more rounds until the bottle was emptied. Then they all turned in for the night.

Early the next morning, Nikita's river barge steamed north with Jacques aboard while the 'Duke de Richeleu' headed down river toward the Black Sea and Odessa with Yuri aboard. As they left the port, Nikita explained to Jacques that they were approaching a sixty kilometer section of the Dnieper River that was all rapids.

"Fortunately," Nikita said, "several years earlier, Tsar Alexander the 2nd had built a series of canals and locks to get around these rapids that would accommodate steam powered river barges. Unfortunately, this sixty kilometer journey will take all day because of the locks. But, what else do we have to do on this beautiful spring day?"

Surprisingly, the day went by quickly. Jacques found it very interesting to watch the operation of the locks. The barge would move slowly into the lock, then the gates would close behind them, and the water level would slowly rise until the barge was at the next level. Then the gates ahead would open and they would proceed. The gate would remain open to accept another barge waiting to go in the opposite direction. At Kremenchug, they took on coal for the remainder of the trip. The next two days on the river were not as pleasant due to the chilling rain that fell. Jacques helped wherever he could. The crew on the barge consisted of Nikita, who was the captain, and three crew members. The three crew members were older men in their fifties because all of the young men were taken into the Tsars Army. Nikita was worried that he too would be called to fight, but his occupation was vital to the war effort so he was not called. He spoke of his family, his beautiful wife Regina, their four daughters, and of course the newest arrival of their son. He was so proud to finally have a son.

"Jacques," Nikita questioned, "how did you learn to speak our language so well?"

"I learned it when I spent several summers in Odessa in my youth. One summer my father brought me to Kiev for a few days when I was fourteen. The only thing I remember about Kiev was that it was a quaint city with decorative churches and many statues everywhere we went. I am fortunate that I was born in a country that speaks three languages. My father was born in France and my mother is Italian, from Milan. My Maman insisted that we speak four languages in our home. Maman spoke to us in Italian and we children had to answer her in English, while Papa used his native French and we had to reply in German. At times it was very funny when we would all be talking in a different language at one time. Needless to say, the system did not always work well, but Maman was adamant that we learn as many languages as possible. I can also get by with a little Greek, Arabic, and Spanish thanks to my mothers insistence. Our wheat business demands that we can converse in various languages as well."

They talked about the war. Jacques told Nikita that his brother Michael was killed in the war fighting for France. Nikita said,

"My cousin was taken into the army in July of 1914 and we haven't heard from him since. We pray every day that he will wander home when the war is over. My Uncle Jozsef, his father, owns a tobacco shop on Khreshchatyk Street in Kiev. You should visit him. Tell him his favorite nephew sent you. He will give you some tobacco."

They passed farms and pine forests along the route which were often obscured by the high banks of the river. As they approached the green hills of Kiev, there were several small factories along the river banks. When they were slightly up river from the docks of the city, Nikita ordered the crew to stop the barge mid-stream, and drop the anchor. He lowered the small row boat that was suspended from the stern of the barge and had the deck hands drop it into the river, and then he rowed Jacques to the dock. Nikita said,

"Good-bye and God speed my friend. I am going to miss your good company. Stop in on my Uncle Jozsef and let him know where you are staying. I pass by here almost every week. We can get together for a drink. Sometimes I even bring the family down to visit my uncle. He and my aunt enjoy the children."

Jacques thanked Nikita, they embraced, and he headed up hill into the city to find a hotel.

CHAPTER TEN

It had been more than ten years since Jacques had been to Kiev, but he seemed to remember that he and Papa stayed in a small hotel a few blocks from the Dnieper River terminal. Up the hill, he found Sahaydachnoho Street, and turned right. It looked familiar. Three blocks on the left side of the street he recognized the hotel. It had not changed. The freshly painted white building stood out from the rest of the stone faced shops on the block. He entered the hotel and bargained with the clerk for the price of a room. He would be staying for a week or possibly more. Now that it was late in the afternoon, he did not want to search for a good restaurant so he asked the clerk for his recommendation.

"Turn left out our front door and follow Sahaydachonoho Street, a half of a block to the plaza. On the far side of the plaza, there is a very good restaurant. You cannot miss it."

Jacques thanked the clerk, picked up the key to his room, number twenty-two, went up to the second floor with his bags and settled into the room. Number 22, that was a good omen, it was the same number as his birthday in October.

The room was comfortable. He lay down on the bed to see if it was also comfortable. Two hours later he awoke, freshened up, dressed and went out to eat. The restaurant was just as the room clerk had said it would be. Jacques ordered the house specialty, 'Golubtsy', cabbage leaves stuffed with rice, meat, carrots, and fried onions and served with sour-cream. It was delicious; almost as good as the 'Golubtsy' that Angelena Bek served last Christmas. For desert he had peach cobbler, made of preserved peaches from the nearby farms. It was an excellent choice. Strong black coffee with a touch of vodka was the perfect conclusion to his meal. He would have to compliment the desk clerk for recommending this place to eat.

The next morning, Jacques rose early. Dressed in his business suit, he had breakfast in a small cafe on the way to the office of Boris Zaitzev. With directions from the desk clerk, he found Volodymyrska Street and the office of the Ukraine Wheat Co-operative. Boris Zaitzev was expecting Jacques, but he did not know what time or for that matter what day he would arrive. They had met ten years ago when Jacques was fourteen, and Papa had taken Jacques to Kiev on one of his many business trips. Jacques entered the office building on Volodymyrska Street, checked the directory and went to the third floor, found the door marked Ukraine Wheat Co-operative in gold lettering, and entered. The receptionist, a pretty blond Ukrainian girl, wearing a green dress with a décolleté neckline, sat behind her desk between two closed office doors. The door to the left was marked, also in gold lettering, 'Staff', while the one on the right in larger gold lettering said 'Boris Zaitzev, President'. The young lady inquired what his business was and asked Jacques to wait one minute. She knocked on the door of the president, poked her head in to his office, and then closed the door. Before she was seated again, Boris burst through the office door leaving it ajar.

"Ah", he exclaimed "a man where a boy once stood!"

They laughed and shook hands.

"Come into my office and make yourself comfortable."

When they were seated, Boris retrieved a bottle and two glasses from his desk draw and filled the glasses with vodka.

"I am so sorry to hear of the loss of your father and brother in such a short time. I will miss your father Michael Mihaylovick greatly. He was a wonderful man. We had some good times when he came here on business, and his business was appreciated too. How are your mother and sisters doing in your absence?"

"They are doing as well as can be expected. The war has slowed our business operation considerably. Did you know that my sister Emile married Yuri Bek?"

"I did hear a rumor to that effect but I was not invited to the wedding."

"I am sorry that you were not invited but they were married in Lausanne, and the Bek family did not even attend because of the war. Only Yuri came for the ceremony. He was lucky to get through just before the Germans shut down the Dardanelles. They are now living in Odessa, but it was not an easy trip for them to return to Yuri's home. I can vouch for that because I traveled to Odessa by a similar route."

"Yuri is certainly a gentleman for not disappointing your sister and the both of you are brave to travel here with wars and revolutions going on all over Europe."

"Thank you. Now, let's get down to business."

"Your father trained you well," Boris complimented.

They discussed the situation. They agreed that neither one could withstand the loss of the entire shipment of wheat, but Jacques wanted to be fair. The farmers needed to be paid for their crops. Lloyds of London, the insurer, would not be responsible for 'an act of war'. The Bek Shipping Company would not be able to claim possession of their ship until the war ends, and maybe not at all. They both did the calculations, and figures were exchanged on the value of the wheat that was lost. A compromise was reached after much discussion.

"Now, how are you going to pay for this?"

"I did not want to carry cash or gold, so I settled on diamonds. They are less bulky for their value and much easier hidden. To be fair, we can each invite some local jewelers and let then bid on the stones. That way we will get a fair price. Then we can settle the matter in rubles, if that is acceptable to you?"

"Excellent and you know how much you paid for the diamonds!"

They decided that Friday would be a good day to auction the diamonds and complete their transaction. Today was Tuesday and that would give the parties involved time to prepare. Now Jacques told Zaitzev that he needed to go to the Maritime Office to transfer two ships of Bek Shipping to Swiss registry. Boris did not think that plan would work but it was worth the try.

"I do not imagine that the Germans will let a ship go through their blockade no matter what flag she is flying." He also mentioned that all of the wheat was being purchased by the Tsars Government for the Army.

"I understand your concerns, but I want the transfer of the ships to be legal. It will eliminate any problems from your Maritime Office in the future, and protect the Bek`s interests. The Beks and the Veserys are all family now."

Boris gave Jacques the address of the Maritime Office on Bankova Street, and the name of his friend in that office, Ivan Glenko.

Later that afternoon, Jacques went to the Maritime Office with his paperwork in order. He met with Ivan Glenko, who assured him that his request would be taken care of, but that it would take time because of the priority of the war.

"Our office staff has been diminished because all younger men have been called into the Tsars Army. We must focus on getting war supplies into our country, and we are overwhelmed with the paper work. So you must be patient."

This news was very disappointing to Jacques. He may be detained here for many weeks.

Friday morning came and the diamond auction went well. The war created a shortage of diamonds in Russia. There was only a limited amount of stones being brought into Russia from South Africa. Industrial diamonds were scarce due to the manufacturing of war materials. Diamonds are also a good investment in war time for anyone with the rubles to buy them. They also travel well if one has to escape from a war zone. So Jacques' diamonds sold for well over what he paid for them in Switzerland. The jewelry dealers were happy, Boris was happy, and the wheat farmers would be happy also. Jacques was amazed at the profit he made, and he still had several stones to keep for insurance along with the gold sewed into his belt and jacket.

"That worked out very well," Boris exclaimed when the jewelers had left his office.

"Now you can treat me to dinner tonight. I know a very expensive restaurant that you will enjoy." Boris laughed a hardy laugh and said, "We will celebrate our good fortune together, my friend."

Jacques knew that Boris Zaitzev was several years younger than his Papa. He knew that Boris was married and had two children. They agreed to meet that night in front of the Co-op office at six PM. That meant that Jacques had the afternoon to spend as he liked. He decided that it was the right time to visit Nikita's uncle Jozsef. He needed some cigarettes, and he was only a few blocks from Khreshchatyk Street. When he reached Khreshchatyk Street, he turned left and found the shop conveniently located in the middle of the block.

He found Jozsef busy with a customer so he motioned that he was not in a hurry. The sale was made and the customer departed the store. There was no mistaking that Jozsef was Nikita's uncle. He was small and wiry with thick black hair and beard that was touched with gray. They had the same facial features, and the same pleasant smile

"Dobryi dyen," (good day) Jacques said, "Your nephew Nikita told me to stop by and say hello to his favorite Uncle."

"Ha! I am his only uncle. He has not been here to visit in weeks. When you see him, tell him that he is no longer my favorite nephew. But, his wife and children will always be my favorites. My wife and I enjoy his children so much. We have no grandchildren of our own, you see. We love when they come to visit us, but it has been a while since we have seen them. You know, with a new baby and all, it has become difficult for them to travel, but that will change."

"I am sure it will. I am Jacques Vesery, and your nephew Nikita graciously gave me a ride here on his barge form Dnipropetrovsk. He told me to let you know the place where I am staying so we can get together for a drink when he stops to see you."

"Well then, stay a while, keep an old man company and tell me about your trip. Have a cup of coffee with me."

Jacques accepted the offer.

They talked about Jacques' trip, the war, the wheat business, the tobacco business, the loss of Jacques brother and father, and the marriage of his sister Emile to Yuri Bek. Jozsef talked about his son who was at war and how they feared that he would not come back. Their conversations were interrupted several times when customers were in the shop, but the afternoon passed swiftly, and soon it was approaching the time Jacques was to meet Boris for dinner. Jozsef invited him to come back and visit any time. He enjoyed the company.

Jacques learned punctuality from his Maman. It was exactly six o'clock when he arrived at the front door of the Co-op building. He was expecting to meet Boris` wife and children, but to his surprise Boris came out of the building escorting two lovely young ladies. Jacques immediately recognized the voluptuous blond girl who was Boris` receptionist. The other young lady was a pretty petite girl with long black hair and an olive complexion. Boris introduced them.

"This is my receptionist, Dina, who I believe you have already met, and this is Irena, my bookkeeper. Meet Jacques Vesery from the Lausanne Wheat Exchange."

Jacques, being the gentleman he was, kissed the hand of each young lady. Dina smiled in acknowledgement, and Irena said,

"It is so nice to meet you. Rarely do we have the opportunity to meet the people that we send our wheat to."

Jacques noticed that he was still holding the hand that he had just kissed; they were so soft. Irena had a beautiful smile, the whitest teeth and gorgeous blue eyes, which is very unusual for a woman of her complexion. Boris broke in,

"Jacques, I did not think you would object to my inviting these beautiful young ladies to accompany us to dinner."

"It is my pleasure," Jacques said with a smile.

"Then let us be off," Boris suggested, guiding Dina and heading in the direction of Khreshchatyk Street.

"We will dine tonight at 'The Song of Tbilisi', a Georgian restaurant, and the food is excellent, as Irena will tell you."

Irena had a very cosmopolitan look about her. She was wearing a pale lavender suit with a long sleeve jacket that sported a beautiful wide white collar and matching cuffs on the sleeves. She had on a lace camisole blouse that peeked through under the jacket. The skirt was a very fashionable mid-calf length and she wore comfortable shoes that were of the latest Paris style. There was a small matching hat perched on her head that accentuated her beautiful blue eyes. Jacques assumed that she came from a well-to-do family, and that she spent most of her wages on her wardrobe. Irena also had an air of confidence about her that Jacques found very attractive.

Boris led the way with Dina on his arm while Jacques and Irena followed. The 'Song of Tbilisi' was on the next block past Jozsef's tobacco shop. Irena said to Jacques quietly,

"He only invited me along to make suggestions on the selection of food and wine."

"I am sure that is not true, but why would you say that?" Jacques asked. "Are you Georgian?" Yes," she said, "and my father is in the wine business."

When they entered the restaurant, the maître-de guided them to their table, paying special attention to Irena. The maître-de, a man in his fifties, seemed to know Boris and Dina as well. He inquired,

"May I ask who your friend is, Irena?"

"Oleg, may I introduce Jacques Vesery, a business associate. Jacques, meet Oleg. He is the owner of this fine restaurant, and a good friend of my father."

The two men shook hands. Oleg made a slight bow and said,

"My pleasure, enjoy your meal."

Then the waiter came to their table with menus. While Boris and Dina were looking at their menus, Irena leaned over to Jacques and whispered,

"I am sure that Oleg is looking out for my best interests when he inquired as to who you were. Please do not take offence to his question."

"No offence taken," Jacques said with a smile.

The two gentlemen deferred to Irena to order the wine. She suggested, Mukuzani, Tamada, a dry red wine for their dinner. When it arrived, she asked Jacques to do the tasting. He sniffed, swirled, and sipped, and gave his approval.

"An excellent choice," Jacques admitted.

Irena suggested an assortment of Georgian ethnic appetizers. They had soup, and the main course of four intriguing dishes; Khinkali (meat dumplings), Mtsvadi (pork barbecue), Lamb shish ke·bab and a stuffed fish dish. When the meal was finished, and the waiter removed the plates and the two empty wine bottles, Irena suggested they order a bottle of Khvanchkara, a semi-sweet red wine for desert, and all agreed. When they finished the last of the wine, Boris asked Irena if she would mind if Jacques escorted her home because they were going in the same direction. He and Dina were going in the opposite direction and that would save him time because he had to get home to his family. Irena agreed. Jacques did not appear to be a hatchet murderer. In fact she thought that he was rather nice.

CHAPTER ELEVEN

Outside the restaurant, Boris hailed a taxi, thanked Jacques for the dinner and left with Dina. Jacques was about to hail the next taxi when Irena suggested that it was such a pleasant evening, it might be nice to walk home.

"Isn't it a rather long walk," Jacques asked.

"The walk will help us to digest our food."

Jacques laughed, "That sounds like something my Maman would say."

Irena laughed too. As they started off down the street lined with chestnut trees just beginning their spring bloom, there were a few moments of awkward silence. Then Jacques said,

"Tell me about yourself?"

"I am the bookkeeper at the Wheat Co-op and have worked for Mr. Zaitzev for over a year.

I live with my parents, Inessa and Denys, on Voloska Street, about four blocks past your hotel. My father brings wine from our native Georgia to the markets of the Ukraine."

"And, what is your family name?" Jacques inquired.

"Our family name is Batatashvili"

"That is the name of my favorite poet," Jacques said, and he began to recite from memory.

The azure blue, the heavenly hue,
The first created realm of blue;
And o`re its radiance divine

My soul does pour its love sublime.
My heart that once with laughter glowed
Of grief, now bears a heavy load.
But yet it thrills and loves anew
To view again the sapphire blue.
I love to gaze on lovely eyes
That swim in azure from the skies;
The heavens lend this colour fair,
And leave a dream of gladness there.
Enamored of the limpid sky,
My thoughts take wing to regions high,
And in that blue of liquid fire
In rapture ecstasy expire.
When I am dead no tears will flow
Upon my lonely grave below,
But from above the aerial blue
Will scatter o`er me tears of dew.

The mist about my tomb will wind
A veil of pearl with shadows twined,
But lured by sunbeams from on high
Twill melt into the azure sky.

"Sky-Blue" Irena said, smiling.

"My Grandpa Nikoloz wrote that poem and many others."

"I am impressed," Jacques said, "and how could I not notice that your eyes are azure blue. Do blue eyes run in your family?"

"Only my grandmother had blue eyes, and she passed them on to me. None of the other members of our family have blue eyes, and I have no brothers or sisters. Do you have brothers and sisters?"   "Yes," Jacques said, "I have three younger sisters. Emile, the oldest was recently married to Yuri Bek and now lives in Odessa.   Olga and Lilly are still at home in Lausanne, Switzerland with my Mamam. My older brother Michael was killed in the war on March 28th of last year, fighting for France. Then my father passed away a month later; he was very ill."

"I am so sorry for your loss. That must be terribly hard for your mother. How is she able to cope with the loss of her husband and a son in that short period of time?"

"My mother is a very strong woman."

They walked in silence for a few minutes. Then Irena asked,

"Why was your brother Michael killed fighting for France when you are Swiss?"

"My father came from France, and his family is still there so Michel volunteered, and was made a captain because of his Swiss Army training."

"My fiancée Pavlo was also killed in the war.   He was with General Samsonov's Second Army

at the battle of Tannenberg.   News came that there were no survivors. That was in August of 1914."

"My sympathy is with you.   My brother Michael was twenty-six when he was killed. How old

was your Pavlo?"

"Twenty-six also.   I do not understand why nations have to

kill each other to settle their differences."

They walked a little further, in their own quiet world, when Jacques asked, "When is your birthday?"

"October 10th.   When is yours?"

"October 22nd, Jacques replied.

"And, how old are you?"

"Twenty-four, and you?"

"Twenty-two."

"Then we are both born under the same sign, Libra."

They both laughed. He had wanted to ask her that question but she had beaten him to it. Jacques thought to himself that Irena was a very clever girl, and he liked that.

Irena showed a confidence that Jacques found very attractive, along with her pretty face. She said, "Tell me about Switzerland and your city of Lausanne."

"There is so much to tell, that I do not know where to begin. Well, we have many high mountains, and most of them are snow capped all year long. Our most well known mountain is the Matterhorn, because it is shaped like a pyramid. Lausanne is on a big lake, Lake Leman. Across the lake to the south is Evian, France. When you ride the ferry from Evian you see a beautiful mirror image of the city, because it rises sharply above the lake like a crown. The point of the crown on the top of the hill in Upper Lausanne is our Notre-dame Cathedral where the Town Crier calls out the time every hour. It is a centuries old tradition."

"Like the Muslim's do from their minarets?"

"Yes," he laughed. "I never thought of it that way. Perhaps the idea for a town crier came from the Arabs.

After a thoughtful pause, Jacques said jokingly,

"If you will let me continue?" She laughed and nudged him with her shoulder.

"As I was saying, there is Upper Lausanne and Lower Lausanne; the fishing village of Vidy is in the lower part. Half way between the upper and the lower you will find our new train station, which was not quite finished when I left. There you can take a train to anywhere in Western Europe. In Vidy, my favorite place in the whole world, there are steam ferry boats with paddle wheels on the sides that go east to Montreux or west to Geneva. The lake there is lined with sycamores and tall pines. It is so beautiful. In the winter the wind blows across the lake and decorates the trees with icicles, and in early summer swans nest along the shore line to raise their young. Did you know that those beautiful birds mate for life?"

"No, I did not know that," she said. "You are so smart."

They both laughed again. She liked his sense of humor.

Jacques took back control of the conversation by asking,

"Were you born in Georgia?"

"Yes, I was born in Tbilisi, and when I was eight years old, my family moved here to Kiev because of my father's business. We go back every summer to visit. It is a long trip. My father's five brothers own a winery in Georgia, and he came to Kiev to increase sales. It has worked out well. I learned to be a bookkeeper in the family wine business. When I lost my Pavlo, I became very depressed, and at that time my father's friend, Boris Zaitzev was in need of a bookkeeper. Papa suggested that a change of scenery might be good for me. So I went to work at the Wheat Co-op. Now, here I am sharing my life story with a total stranger, a foreigner, who I met only a few hours ago."

Jacques broke in,

"A very charming Swiss gentleman, may I add, who is no longer a stranger, as you say, and who knows a great deal about you in these precious few hours that we have spent together. I owe a great deal of gratitude to Boris for inviting you to dine with us this evening."

"I am sorry. I did not mean it to be derogatory. I guess that I was just trying to be sarcastic."

She took his hand and looked up to him for forgiveness. Jacques held on to her hand as they walked on. He smiled and said,

"I forgive you, as long as you allow me the privilege of holding your hand."

She did not answer, but she did not let go.

They walked past the hotel where Jacques was staying. He had thoughts of inviting her up to his room. But he knew that such a bold suggestion would be insulting to her. Irena was definitely not that kind of a girl. They crossed the plaza and turned up

Skovorody Street, and then turned left. Irena stopped in front of the third house with sandstone steps that led up to the second floor.

"This is where I live," she said, still holding his hand. "Thank you for dinner. Did you enjoy the Georgian food?"

"Yes, very much and I enjoyed the company even more. Will I see you again?" Jacques inquired. "I would like that. Tomorrow is Saturday and I do not have to work. Would you like me to give you a tour of our beautiful city?"

"I would love that. After all, I am a stranger in a foreign place."

Irena laughed, and said, "Come by tomorrow morning at eleven o'clock to meet my parents, and then I will show you my town."

Jacques agreed. He kissed her hand. Irena turned, went up the steps and disappeared behind the large oak door.

The next morning, Jacques arose early, had breakfast and went to a haberdasher shop to purchase some new clothes. He wanted to impress her parents. He climbed the stone steps and knocked on the door at precisely eleven o'clock. The door was opened by her father, who invited Jacques in. Jacques introduced himself.

"I am Jacques Vesery. I do a great deal of business with your friend Boris Zaitzev, who so graciously introduced me to your charming daughter, Irena."

"I am pleased to meet you. I am Denys Baratashvili, Irena's father. Come into the parlor, Jacques, and make yourself comfortable."

"I am an admirer of your father's poetry."

"Why, thank you. I did not realize that his poetry was so well known in other parts of the world." At that moment, Irena's mother came into the parlor.

"My dear," Denys said, "I would like you to meet Irena's` new friend, Jacques Vesery."

"How nice to meet you, I am Inessa, Irena's mother. Irena has told us so much about you. I understand you are Swiss and do business with our friend Boris Zaitzev."

"Yes," Jacques replied.

"And, my dear, Jacques is familiar with my father's poetry," interrupted Denys.

"That's wonderful," said Inessa.

With that, Irena came flying down the stairs, out of breath,

"I am sorry that I am late, Jacques. Did you meet my mother and father?"

"Yes, we introduced ourselves and were carrying on a very nice conversation," Denys said.

"You two had better get going if you want to see all the sights of Kiev today."

"Before you leave, Jacques, would you like to have dinner with us tomorrow evening," Inessa inquired? We will have dinner at five."

Jacques graciously accepted the invitation.

When the young people had left, Inessa said,

"This young man seems to be very nice, and Irena seems to like him. She told me they have a lot in common, and he is such a gentleman. I am so happy for her. She has finally met someone to take her mind off Pavlo. We must thank Boris for introducing them."

Denys agreed and said he would stop by the Co-op office on Monday and thank him.

"I will bring him a bottle of our best wine."

CHAPTER TWELVE

It was a sunny day in May with blue skies and a fresh scent in the air. They walked one block to the Kontraktova Plaza, where Jacques hailed a taxi to take them across town to Besarabska Plaza. The taxi took the same route that they had walked the previous evening. It seemed to Jacques that the ride was much longer by taxi than when he had walked it with Irena. Across Besarabska Plaza was the newly built covered market. Irena suggested that they stroll through it. Jacques found it to be interesting, although like most men, he was not much of a shopper. There was a wide variety of goods; souvenirs, confectionery, handcrafts, wines, textiles, chocolates, jewelry, drinks, and food of every description. Like all women, Irena was a born shopper and her attention was on some silk scarves that she was rummaging through. Meanwhile, Jacques bought her a pair of gold earrings with little angels on them, because he remembered she had mentioned that she liked angels. She immediately put them on.

"How did you know that I liked angels?" Irena asked.

"You mentioned that you liked angels at dinner last night."

"That was sweet of you to remember. Thank you."

By now it was lunch time, and Irena suggested they have something to eat.

"Would you mind sharing a 'Vareniki' with me? There are several booths that sell them. They smell so delicious, and each of the vendors specializes in different fillings. I would like to try several of them, but I could not eat more than one or two whole ones."

"I don't mind at all. I come from a big family so there were many times when food was sampled or shared. In fact I was the family food tester. Our cook, Margarette always tried out her new recipe's on me. My sisters always teased me about being responsible for what Margarette prepared in the kitchen."

They purchased one Vareniki, and found a bench where they could sit to eat. Irena unwrapped it and held it up for him to take a bite. He did, and then she took a bite.

"Umm," she said, and her big blue eyes lit up like a little girls at a picnic. Jacques was enjoying watching her eat. They tried several more Vareniki, had some cold tea to drink then left the market.

"That was fun," Jacques commented. Irena agreed.

She took hold of his arm and they strolled down Taras Shevchenka Boulevard, under the tall chestnut trees. They walked to the Taras Shevchenka Opera House on Volodymyrska Street. Stopping to enjoy the beautiful façade of the building, Irena shared some historical facts about the Opera House.

"Taras Shevchenko was a famous Ukrainian poet and artist. The building was completed around 1901. I have seen several ballets, and two operas here. I love the ballets, but the operas are my mother's favorite. This Opera House is noted for its excellent acoustics."

These facts were of little importance to Jacques. He just enjoyed being with her, the sound of her voice, and the enchanting way she expressed herself. As they moved on, Irena talked about some of the ballets that she had seen and the ones that were her favorites like 'The Nutcracker', 'Coppélia', and 'Swan Lake'. She asked Jacques if he enjoyed the ballet. He admitted to having seen a few, and offered to take her when there was one in town.

That statement brought on another question that Irena was reluctant to approach, because she was beginning to have feelings for Jacques. But, it was something that she had to ask. "How long are you staying in Kiev?"

There was a long pause. She stopped walking, turned to him, and held his hand. It was a question that he did not want to face either, because now he did not want to leave. He was unsure how to answer the question.

Finally he answered, "I do not want to leave, because of you. I came to Kiev to fulfill some business obligations. Now those obligations seem so unimportant to me."

He told her of the business he had to take care of in Kiev, the money that he felt he owed Boris, and the papers he was waiting for from the Maritime Office.

"My plan was to satisfy Boris and his wheat suppliers. Then wait for the Maritime Office to process my papers. I thought that in a week or two, I would be on my way back to Odessa. Now I realize that your grandfather sent me a message in his poem years ago, that I should look for a girl with azure blue eyes. He even gave me your name, and now that I have found you, how can I think of leaving!"

She looked up at him with a tear glistening in her beautiful blue eyes, and said,

"Please stay."

"Yes, I believe I will stay," he said with a far away look in his eyes, and she kissed him on the cheek.

They proceeded down the avenue in silence, realizing what was happening to them. Irena broke the silence.

"We are passing one of the places of interest on our tour. This is the entrance to the ancient walled city of Kiev, 'The Golden Gate'. It was built by 'Yaroslav the Wise' in the eleventh century."

"If we tarry here, will we become as wise as Yaroslav?"

They both laughed, temporarily putting aside the more serious implications of their last conversation. Holding hands now, they continued. Ahead, Jacques saw the golden domes of a church that he remembered from when he came here with his Papa.

"I remember this church," said Jacques."

"Ahead is the Cathedral of Saint Sofia. It has thirteen golden domes, and was built by our wise Prince Yaroslav in the year 1037. We should go inside and see the beautiful paintings on the walls." They spent a few hours viewing the frescos and discussing them.

"Tomorrow is Sunday. I will be coming here to church with my mother and father. Would you

like to join us?"

"I would not be intruding, would I?"

"Not at all, then it is settled, you can be at our house at 8:30 AM tomorrow morning, and we will all go together."

The afternoon passed quickly. When they left the Cathedral, Jacques hailed a taxi to take them to the restaurant on Kontraktova Plaza. They sat at a table in the corner, discussing their past, their families, and the future. They talked quietly over dinner. He told her that on Monday, he would go to the Maritime office to see if the papers were ready. If they were, he would ask for copies to be sent to the Bek shipping Company in Odessa. He would retain the originals in the event that the copies were lost, which was always a possibility in times of war.

"I will write to my sister and explain that my return to Odessa has been delayed. Then I will look for a small apartment to rent for a few months."

This news made Irena very happy. He told her that now that he had found her, he was not about to let her go.

It was a short walk to Irena's home. They talked for a few minutes on the front steps. Then with a finger under her chin, he lifted her beautiful face and kissed her gently on the lips. She threw her arms around his neck and kissed him back.

"I am so glad that you are staying. I will expect to see you at eight-thirty tomorrow morning!"

She turned, ran up the steps, and once again, disappeared into the house.

Eight-thirty Sunday morning, Jacques was knocking on the oak front door of Irena's house. He was welcomed into the house by

Irena, who announced that they would be leaving as soon as mother and father came down.

"We always walk to Saint Sophia's Cathedral. It is on the bluff at the top of Andriyivsky Descent. Mother always says that way we get to do our penance before we go to church. It is a very steep climb."

Jacques laughed.

"Your mother is a very wise woman, but it can not be any worse than the hills of Lausanne.

You see, we have an 'Upper Kiev' and a 'Lower Kiev', called Podil, and in between it is the 'Andriyivsky Decent'.

"Touch!"

They both burst out laughing.

At mass, he prayed for each member of his family, and he thanked God for bringing him here to meet Irena. He then asked God for guidance in his life. After mass, the walk back to the house was a lot easier going down the 'Andriyivsky Decent'. By this time, the artists were out displaying their paintings, jewelry, sculptures, and 'Pysanky''; the beautifully painted Easter eggs that the Ukrainian's are famous for. She held on to his arm as they strolled down the hill, a slight distance behind her mother and father, stopping to enjoy a particular painting or Pysanky.

"It is nice that you came to church with us this morning. Now I will have your company all day long instead of just this evening."

"You are so smart. Who do you get your intelligence from, your mother or your father?"

"Both," she said with an impish grin.

They spent the day together, sitting in the small garden behind the house in the afternoon sun. When it began to get cool, they moved into the parlor, where they joined Inessa and Denys. They asked what Switzerland was like? Jacques explained the whole story to them and why he was here in Kiev. He talked about his family; his three sisters, his older brother Michael who was killed in the war fighting for France, his mother and the death of his father. Irena and her parents listened intensely as Jacques told his story, and how he spent several summers in Odessa with his Papa.

At dinner, Jacques opened the conversation by asking Denys and Inessa how they liked living in Kiev. They both admitted that they missed their native land of Georgia.

"Although after fourteen years, we are used to living here. Kiev is a comfortable place to live. We have good restaurants, the Opera and the Ballet. It is a beautiful city with much history, and we are able to make a good living here. Georgia is a beautiful country also, much like your Switzerland with high snow capped mountains. You have your Alps, and we have our Caucasus. The climate in Georgia is a little milder than here, where we are able to grow our grapes, of course, and citrus, tea and hazelnuts in our fertile soil," Denys said.

Denys was a husky man, about four inches shorter than Jacques' six foot frame. He had thick black hair, a full mustache, dark eyes and a slightly hooked nose. Irena inherited her good looks from her mother, Inessa. She was a beautiful woman with dark brown eyes, and a wonderful smile.

"Denys and I both come from large families. Denys has five brothers, and I have four sisters and a brother. All of my family lives in Tblisi. We have many relatives to visit each summer."

Irena chimed in. "I have so many cousins that it is hard to remember all of their names. I love to go there every summer."

When dinner was finished and the table was cleared, Inessa suggested that the young couple take advantage of the pleasant evening, and stroll down to the waterfront a few blocks away. Irena was thrilled at her mother's suggestion.

"Now I do not have to wash the dishes," she whispered to Jacques.

"Is that your regular contribution to the function of the house?"

"Yes. Let's leave before mother changes her mind."

She then motioned him toward the front door. They walked down to the Dnieper River while there was still a glow of daylight in the sky. Because it was Sunday evening, and there was no traffic on the river, it was mirror calm. The lights from the other side of the river were already reflecting on the water. They shared the beauty of the night with other lovers walking hand in hand along the quay. They talked and kissed, and after an hour or so returned to Irena's home.

After Jacques had said good night and thanked them for their hospitality, Irena's parents began to question her about her feelings for her new friend. She told them that she liked him very much, and reiterated that they had a lot in common. They confirmed that they thought he was very nice also. As the protective parents of their only child, they told her that they approved of her seeing him as long as he was not going to leave Kiev, and break her heart. She told them that tomorow, Jacques was going to make arrangements to stay in Kiev. Inessa and Denys embraced their daughter and told her how happy they were for her.

CHAPTER THIRTEEN

Monday morning, Jacques rose early. He went for a quick breakfast and then went straight to the Maritime Office. He did not have an appointment to see Ivan Glenko, so he had to wait. When he finally was admitted to Mr. Glenko's office, he was told that the approval had not come down from the Commissioner's Office as yet. Jacques then inquired how long that would take and then asked if he could pick up the originals and have copies to send to Bek Shipping in Odessa. Glenko agreed to make a second set of papers to be sent to Odessa, but he could not put a time on when the Commissioner would sign the papers.

"The war, you know!"

It was a short walk from Bankova Street to the tobacco shop of Jozsef Dobryakov, Nikita's uncle. He was greeted warmly when he entered the shop.

"Where have you been? Nikita stopped in and was looking for you. He was on his way down river with a barge full of lumber. He wanted me to tell you that he would be back here in Kiev in five days, but that was two days ago."

Jacques explained that he had met a young lady that he found quite attractive, and now he was going to look for a small apartment to stay for a while.

"Ah! My friend, you are in luck. I have just the place for you. There are two small furnished rooms with a bathroom behind the shop that Nikita uses when he is delayed here in Kiev. Come! I will show you. And, as I mentioned before, he has not stayed with us in some time. If he does come by, he can stay with me and my wife upstairs in our apartment. We have extra rooms; my son's empty room and another. I know that Nikita won't mind that I am renting it to his friend and I can use the extra income."

This was perfect for Jacques because it was located only a few blocks from the Ukraine Wheat Co-operative where Irena worked.

They agreed that the situation was amicable for both of them.

"I will ask my wife Elena to straighten up the rooms while you gather your things from the hotel where you are staying."

Jacques left the tobacco shop and three hours later, he returned by taxi with his bags. He found the rooms to be small but adequate. The bedroom had a bed, an armoire, a dresser and a window that looked out onto a fenced in yard that seemed to be slightly larger than the room. The sitting room had two comfortable chairs, a counter with a hot plate and a cabinet that contained dinnerware for two that was graciously placed in the cabinet by Elena, Jozsef's wife. There was also a small table to eat at and a small icebox. The icebox was void of ice because it had not been used in months. Jozsef told Jacques that he expected a delivery of ice in the morning and that he would leave a note for the iceman to leave an extra block of ice for him. He would have to wash his dishes in the bathroom sink but, that small inconvenience could not outweigh the many good aspects of the apartment. Jacques was very happy with these arrangements.

Jacques thanked Jozsef and Elena for all they had done to accommodate him. Then he took a few hours to settle into his new home. When he had arranged everything to his liking, he looked at his pocket watch. It was 5:43 PM. Just time enough to freshen up and meet Irena when she left the Wheat Co-op at 6:00 PM. With this new location, her work was only a few blocks away. Irena was surprised and delighted to find Jacques waiting for her on the street by the front door of the building. He could not wait to tell her about the events of his day and she was anxious to hear all about it.

"I found an apartment. It's small but comfortable and convenient. "

"Where is it?"

"You know the tobacco shop that my friend Nikita's uncle owns by the 'Song of Tbilisi' restaurant where we had dinner. Jozsef, the uncle, had two rooms on the ground floor behind the shop that was vacant, and I rented them. Uncle Jozsef kept the rooms vacant for Nikita and his family to stay in when they came to visit."

"That is wonderful, and so close to where I work."

"Elena and Jozsef invited us both over for dinner tomorrow evening, if you are able to come. Then you can see my apartment."

"How nice of them to invite me for dinner, and they do not even know me. I will bring a bottle of my father's best wine and I will let my parents know that I will be home a little later tomorrow. They worry about me, you know."

"Parents are that way," Jacques replied.

Then he hailed her a cab, kissed her good night and went for a bite to eat before retiring to his new living quarters.

The next morning, he penned a note to Irena, delivered it to the Co-op, and asked Dina, the receptionist in the office to please give it to her. As soon as Jacques left the office, Dina brought the letter back to Irena's office. She giggled, and whispered,

"A love note from your Frenchman."

Irena opened the letter immediately and read it.

Ma bien Chere,

I know that it has been but a few hours since I saw you last night but I miss you already. I will meet you in front of the Co-op building at six o'clock this evening. It will be a long day for me until we are together again. Until tonight!

All my love, Jacques

Dina waited anxiously while she read her letter, then Irena burst out laughing.

"He is so sweet," she exclaimed, "the letter is written half in French and half in 'pigeon Ukranian'."

They laughed again.

"I think he likes you."

Then Dina raised her eyes as she closed the door and returned to her desk in the reception room.

Jacques came back to the tobacco shop after delivering the letter. Being a businessman and a salesman, he found it very interesting to mingle with the customers and talk to Jozsef when the shop was empty. Jacques was a smoker, so he held a common bond with all of the clientele. That evening while Jacques went to meet Irena at her work, Nikita arrived at Uncle Jozsef's shop. He was pleasantly surprised to find that Jacques had rented the rooms behind the shop.

"By the way, Aunt Elena invited Jacques and his new girlfriend to join us for dinner this evening. He will be surprised to find you here when they arrive."

"This day is full of surprises. This Frenchman doesn't let

any grass grow under his feet, does he?" and they both laughed.

The Dobryakovs welcomed the young couple into their home. Dinner was excellent. Jacques was happy to see his friend even though he was the brunt of much teasing by Nikita. It was all in fun and the quick-witted Irena held her own in the teasing department. The evening was a light-hearted and cheery one. Aunt Elena and Uncle Jozsef enjoyed their company. Irena thought that Nikita was very funny. She said that she never laughed so hard in all of her life when Jacques was escorting her home that night.

Upon his return, Jacques found Jozsef and Nikita working on a bottle of vodka in the tobacco shop. After Jacques arrived, Jozsef bid them both goodnight and went upstairs to bed. Nikita gave Jacques the news about how poorly the war was going, and about the labor unrest all over Russia. Then the conversation turned to Uncle Jozsef and how he was doing with the tobacco business. Nikita said that his uncle was a poor business man and that his records were poorly kept. He could not understand how Uncle Jozsef was still in business.

"I am a bookkeeper." Jacques responded. "If your uncle doesn't object to me helping, I can set up a simple set of books so he will be able to see where his money is going. Give me a week or so of hanging around the shop, and I will be able to straighten things out."

"That would be wonderful. I will talk to Uncle Jozsef in the morning. I am sure he will listen to my advice. He usually does."

The next morning Jacques wrote two letters dated the twenty-first of June 1916. The first one was to Maman, and the girls in Switzerland. He told them that he would be staying longer than he expected in Kiev and that he met someone who was very special.

"Her name is Irena. I have rented a small apartment and am waiting for the papers to be approved by the Maritime Commissioner."

The second letter went to Emile in Odessa explaining the situation as he did with Maman and the girls.

CHAPTER FOURTEEN

In the next few weeks, Jacques helped out in the tobacco shop with the purpose of learning how the business worked. Along with cigarette tobacco, and rolling papers, they sold chewing tobacco, creamy snuff, dipping tobacco, gutka (a paste), fine ground snuff, snus, topical tobacco paste and tobacco water as an insecticide. They also sold pipes and hookahs. Now he was able to make up a set of books that reflected the operation of the business. He kept the system simple so Jozsef would be able to handle doing the books on his own. Uncle Jozsef was thrilled that he would be able to keep track of every ruble that came and went in his business. He was forever grateful that Jacques helped him with this aspect of the business, and offered to pay him for his time. Jacques would not accept any payment. He said it was his gift to his friend. A few days later, Jozsef gave him a present of a solid silver cigarette case. Jozsef knew that he could not refuse his gift because it had initials, J.V. engraved on the cover.

Jacques and Irena met every Wednesday evening for dinner. It was a standing date, and they spent the weekends together, mostly at her parent's home. On weekdays, he would write a little love note to 'Ma bien Cherie' or 'The pixie that stole my heart' and deliver it to Dina at the office or meet Irena as she arrived at work in the morning. If two days would pass without a note, Dina would inquire of Irena, if everything was alright or, if they had had a fight?

One Wednesday evening, at dinner they were discussing the books of the tobacco shop when Irena started to laugh. Jacques inquired about why she was laughing. She told him the story about when Boris had fired her.

"Several months ago, Boris decided that he could keep the books himself, so he gave me a weeks notice and said that he would no longer need my services. During that week I changed some of the title headings on the ledger pages. For two weeks, he tried to figure out what was wrong but could not, and asked me to come back to work the next week. He told me that he thought he would have time to do the books, but he really did not have the time for it in his busy schedule. I agreed to return, but at a higher wage."

Jacques thought that this story was very amusing. This girl was really clever. More than he could have imagined. While they were on the subject of Boris, Jacques inquired if he was still married?

"Oh yes. Dina is his mistress. He pays the rent on her apartment from the Co-op."

Jacques was not surprised.

In July, Jacques went to the jeweler that purchased most of his diamonds and picked out a setting for one of the remaining stones in his possession. His intension was to ask Irena to marry him. A few days later, he picked up the ring. It was a plain setting but it showed off the stone beautifully. He intended to ask for her hand this coming Saturday.

They spent the day on Saturday with her parents. In the evening, when they walked down along the Dneiper River after the evening meal, he began casually by saying, "I noticed you are wearing the gold angel earrings that I gave you when we went to the market on our first date. When I was in Odessa, my sisters husband Yuri took Emile and me to eat at a cafe near the Potemkin Steps. There was a Gypsy trio playing while we ate. They played one song several times. Apparently it was a crowd favorite, and I could not forget the lyrics or the tune."

He sang:

"There is a story the Gypsies know is true.

That when your love wears golden earrings

She belongs to you.

An old love story that's known to very few,

But if you wear those golden earrings,

Love will come to you.

By the burning fire, they will glow with ev'ry coal.

You will hear desire whisper low inside your soul.

So be my Gypsy;

Make love your guiding light.

And let this pair of golden earrings

Cast their spell tonight."

"That's beautiful," Irena said as she squeezed his hand. "You are such a romantic."

"Now I have a question," Jacques said.

They stopped walking and she turned to face him in the fading evening light.

"Have your golden earrings cast their spell tonight?" (A long pause) "Will you be my wife?"

She looked into his eyes.

"Oh yes, I will. I love you and I know that you love me but do you want me to be the mother of your children?"

"Yes. How many children do you want?"

"Oh,I would like to have at least a half dozen children. I always feel cheated by being an only child."

They kissed. Then Jacques reached into his pocket and held out the little velvet box containing an engagement ring. She opened the box with tears streaming down her beautiful face. As Jacques kissed away the tears, he took the ring and slipped it on her ring finger.

"The ring is beautiful. I will keep it on, but you will have to ask my father for permission to marry me. I can't wait to show it to Mother and Father, but only after you talk to him. How could you wait all day to surprise me like this?"

"It was not easy!"

As they started home with their arms around each other, they passed an older couple holding hands who smiled at the young lovers. When they entered the house, Irena went directly into the kitchen where her mother was finishing up after dinner and asked her mother if she could do anything to help. Inessa immediately noticed the glow on her daughters face, and the redness of her eyes and knew that she had been crying but they seemed to be tears of happiness. She gave her daughter an inquisitive look. And Irena blurted out,

"Jacques just asked me to marry him and I said yes. Now he is talking to Papa to get his permission. Look, I have a ring."

Inessa hugged her daughter and suggested that they wait until Jacques and Papa were finished talking and Papa called them into the sitting room.

When Denys, Irena's father, called his wife and daughter into the sitting room, he and Jacques were standing in the middle of the room.

"Come here, Irena," Denys said with his arms open. "I have only one question. Do you want to spend the rest of your life with Jacques?"

"Yes!"

"Then I give my permission for the two of you to marry. We have only one daughter, so it is very important to us that she be happy." They celebrated the occasion with embraces and a few glasses of their best wine.

Then Inessa said, "We will plan the wedding for next May. I am sure that many of our relatives will want to come here from Georgia for the occasion. That will also give Jacques' family members time to make plans to come here from Odessa and Switzerland." It was agreeable to all.

After Jacques left for the evening, Irena suggested that Jacques accompany them on their annual trip to Tbilisi in hopes that her mother and father would agree. Inessa and Denys thought that it was a good idea that he go along with them so he could meet their families.

"We will invite Jacques tomorrow when he comes for dinner."

Irena was thrilled. She was sure that Jacques would be happy to meet their relatives in the Republic of Georgia.

August of 1916 came quickly. On Monday, the 1st, day of the month, the four travelers boarded the train at the railroad station in Kiev on Kominternu Street bound for Rostov. That would take them to the half way point of their journey on the 1700 kilometer trip to Tbilisi. From Rostov, they would board another train bound for Groznyy, and there they were being met by Inessa's brother who would drive them over the mountain pass into Georgia. In all, the trip took three and a half days. They spent the first week with Inessa's family in Tbilisi visiting with her brother, four sisters and many of Irena's cousins. Irena was happy to show off her engagement ring and her fiancée. On the second week, they took a train west to the wine country of Kutaisi where the Baratashvili family greeted them warmly, and escorted them to their nearby vineyards outside of the town. Irena and Jacques enjoyed the peacefulness of the Baratashvili's expansive vineyards. Their wine production supported six families and many field workers. It was very good quality wine.

Jacques was impressed by the hospitality of these fun loving relatives of Irena. He enjoyed their wine, spicy food and songs. In the evenings, they would gather in the garden with their guitars and mandolins, and sing and tell stories until the wee-hours of the morning. On one occasion, when Irena and Jacques were alone walking through the vineyards, under the blue skies and the warm afternoon sun, they stopped to make love in the fresh green grass. After a week in the wine country, they returned to Tbilisi to see the few relatives that they missed on their first week there. Then it was back over the Caucus Mountains to Groznyy and on the long train ride west to Kiev.

Upon their return to Kiev, Jacques found the tobacco shop closed. He thought it rather strange that the shop was closed on a Wednesday. He used his key to enter and knocked on the upstairs door. Elena, Jozsef's wife, answered and told him that Jozsef was in the hospital with a heart attack, and that there will be an extended recuperation period but that Jozsef was feeling better. It was good news that Jozsef would live and bad news was that the shop would not bring in any income. So Jacques visited the hospital and told Jozsef that he would tend to the shop in his absence.

"Relax and get well. I will take care of your shop until you are fully recovered."

Jacques spent every day in the shop tending to customers. In the slack periods, he had time to write long letters to his Maman, Olga and Lilly and also to Emile and Yuri. He told them of his engagement to Irena and explained that he was staying in Kiev for the winter. By spring, he would return to Odessa with the maritime papers on the transferred ships. The paperwork should be ready by then.

It was several weeks before Jozsef felt well enough to venture downstairs to see how things were going in the tobacco business. He sat in a chair behind the counter asking numerous questions and was pleasantly surprised to find that Jacques was handling things very well. Each day he would spend longer periods of time visiting the shop as he recovered.

One morning in the beginning of October, a Major in the Russian army came into the shop to buy tobacco. He noticed that Jacques had a French accent and started to converse in French. Jacques was delighted to speak to someone in his native language. The Major inquired where Jacques was from and why he was here working in the tobacco shop. Jacques gave a brief synopsis of his situation.

"Please excuse my rudeness. I am Major Dmitry Moskaleff and I did not mean to pry into your private business, Jacques, but it was so nice to speak French with someone that I forgot my manners."

"No offence taken. May I call you Dmitry, Major?"

"By all means. I am only a Major when I am among members of the military. I am a Cossack from a small town here in the Ukraine. I work for General Tatischev in St. Petersburg."

"So, you are a long way from your post."

And they both laughed.

"They sent me here because I am familiar with the territory. I will only be here for a few weeks, than I will be moving on."

Dmitry brought Jacques up to date on the war and the unrest in all of Russia. Jacques told of his brother being killed at the battle of Neuve Chapell in France, of his intended trip to Odessa, and his relationship to the Bek Shipping Co. Dmitry was familiar with the Bek Shipping Co. They spoke of their girlfriends and exchanged photos. Dmitry withdrew his girl friends picture from his breast pocket, as did Jacques. They both laughed. Dmitry commented,

"We both keep our loved ones close to our heart."

They made arrangements to get together for dinner one evening. Then the Major left the shop just before noon.

Several evenings later, they met for dinner at a café on the outskirts of the city. They talked of their adventures. Dmitry was curious about Switzerland and the Swiss Army. He told Jacques what it was like living in St. Petersburg, and of the riches of the Tsar and his family, and all of the aristocrats in Russia.

"I am lucky to be in the Army with the rank that I have because my family is not rich, but we are Cossacks. I have work to do here for several weeks, and then I will visit my parents on my way to Odessa. God only knows how long they will keep me there before I return to St. Petersburg."

They shared several drinks of vodka. Then Dmitry left to return to his billet and Jacques was left to find his way back to the shop under the influence of quite a few glasses of vodka.

Jacques slept well that night. He found it difficult to get up the next morning, but his usual breakfast of black coffee and black bread stopped his head from spinning and allowed him to function for the rest of the day. On the weekend, at Irena's home, he told them of meeting Dmitry, a major in the Army. He happened to mention that Dmitry worked for a General Tatischev. Denys, who was up on his politics, said,

"Oh my! Do you know who General Tatischev is? He is the Tsars Aid-de-Camp. Your new friend Dmitry is an important person, and he must be here on important business. Why don't you invite Dmitry to our home next Sunday evening for dinner, Jacques? It will be interesting to get caught up on all that is going on in the seat of authority."

"If it is your pleasure, I will invite Dmitry to come for dinner next Sunday. I am sure he will enjoy having a home cooked meal. He is a pleasant, well mannered fellow and I think you will enjoy his company as much as I did."

At this point in the relationship of Irena and Jacques, he was considered a member of the Baratashvili family. He spent weekends at their home and was a regular occupant of one of their guest rooms. Dmitry graciously accepted the invitation. He had dinner with them on that following Sunday. It was an enjoyable evening. Dmitry talked of his Cossack traditions and his girlfriend in St. Petersburg, while Denys and Inessa told of their relatives in Georgia, and Jacques told stories of his family and his homeland. When the evening ended, Jacques and Dmitry took a cab to the other side of town and went their separate ways. Before they parted, Dmitry thanked Jacques for inviting him to his fiancée's home for dinner.

"I am glad that Denys suggested that I invite you to dinner."

"Well then, I will see you at the tobacco shop the next time I am free, my friend. God speed," Dmitry said. And they parted.

CHAPTER FIFTEEN

It was almost two weeks before Dmitry returned to the tobacco shop. He had been very busy with meetings at the military installation outside of Kiev. He had run out of the mild Turkish tobacco that was sold in Jozsef's shop, and was forced to use the much stronger Ukrainian variety which he was not happy with. This was his first day off so he took a few hours to relax and spend time with his new found friend who spoke French. In St. Petersburg, it was popular to speak French among the aristocrats and upper echelon of military officers, but here in the Ukraine, it was not spoken at all. They talked when Jacques was not waiting on customers in the shop. In the conversation, Dmitry inquired how things were going with the transfer of the ships papers. Jacques told him that he was very disturbed by the fact that there had been no word from Ivan Glenko or the Director of the Maritime Office. They seemed to be ignoring him.

That afternoon, Dmitry took it upon himself to visit the Maritime Office in his Army uniform. Ivan Glenko was very apologetic and escorted Dmitry immediately to the Directors office. The Director also apologized for the delay of the paper work on the Bek's ships, and told Major Dmitry Moskaleff that the documents he was interested in would be ready by noon of the next day, and available for pickup at Mr. Glenkos office. Dmitry thanked the Director and returned to the tobacco shop with the good news. Jacques was amazed that his new friend took the time and had the influence to facilitate such immediate results. Jacques thanked Dmitry over and over. The next day, Jacques retrieved the documents from Ivan Glenko's office and thanked him. They were the original copies, and were all in order.

By the beginning of November, Dmitry had concluded his business in Kiev and was anxious to see his family in the small village 84 kilometers north east of Dnipropetrovsk. He announced that he would be leaving at the end of the week. Jacques inquired about his travel plans and mentioned that Nikita was due to stop here on his way down the Dnieper River with his last shipment of lumber for the winter.

"Nikita is Jozsef's nephew and a friend of my brother-in-law, Yuri Bek. I am sure that he will have room for you on his trip down to Dnipropetrovsk."

So when Nikita arrived, arrangements were made for Dmitry to travel downriver the next day. Before they parted, Dmitry told Jacques to look him up in Odessa at the Military Attaché's Office in Odessa.

"Your brother-in-law will know how to find me. I am sure that my business will keep me there for several months."

Jozsef's recovery was slow but by Christmas, he was back in the shop on a fulltime basis. His doctor told him that he should not smoke any more. That news was hard to take for a man who owned a tobacco shop, but his wife and Jacques saw to it that he did not imbibe or overwork himself. Now, Jacques had a little more time to spend with Irena for the holidays.

It was a rather quiet Christmas even though the winter season was much more socially active. There were concerts to attend, the opera, and ballets. Tchiakovsky's "The Nutcracker" was always a favorite prior to Christmas, and Irena and Jacques enjoyed seeing it at the Taras Shevchenko Opera Theatre accompanied by Irenas parents. Irena's family was small here in Kiev. There were only three in her family and Jacques had no relatives here in Kiev. There were get-togethers with friends, the Zaitzevs and others. Irena and Jacques were invited several times to Elena and Jozsef's because Nikita had come down to visit with his wife and family. Children always make the holidays more enjoyable. The winter was unusually cold and there was a lot of snow. The Dneiper River was frozen solid which gave them the opportunity to ice-skate on the weekends.

As the winter passed, Jacques became anxious to deliver the transfer papers of the two ships to his brother-in-law in Odessa and see his sister Emile. Irena was not happy with him leaving, but he promised to be back in three weeks or less. While Jacques was preparing to leave, the news came that the revolution had begun up north and within a few days, Tsar Nicholas II had abdicated leaving much of the country in chaos, but here in Kiev things seemed to be normal. On Monday, March 20th, 1917 Jacques bid a tearful goodbye to Irena as he boarded Nikita's steam barge on the first trip of the new year downriver to Dnipropetrovsk. There was still some ice remaining in the river. It was passable for the barge, but when they approached the Dnieper River Rapids, there were other barges waiting to enter the locks to go downstream. Word was being passed along that the locks were closed because the workers were on strike in sympathy with the revolution that had begun in St. Petersburg. After several days of workers demonstrations, the Army was ordered to fire on the demonstrators. The next day, the Army mutinied and that led to the Tsar's abdication.

After some time, the barge operators decided that they would operate the abandoned locks themselves. They did not need to use the pumps to progress downgrade. All they had to do was open valves to let the water out of each lock to flow downstream, then open the gates and proceed to the next lock. There was no thought of a return trip. After all, how long could this worker's strike last? Each lock held four barges at one time so the process took longer than usual, but the decent was accomplished. There was some worry that they would not be able to return upriver after they unloaded at Dnipropetrovsk. The barge operators agreed that this interruption could not last long enough to prohibit their return upstream. After all, this was a major shipping lane.

At the Dnipropetrovsk docks, Nikita talked to the merchant ships captain to arrange passage for Jacques to go to Odessa. He explained that Jacques was related to the Beks and he knew that the captain would oblige. It took six days to arrive in Odessa; longer than Jacques had expected. He found his way to Emile and Yuri`s house on Stroganovkskaya Street. He knocked on the door and was greeted by a very surprised and very pregnant Emile. She leaped out the door into his arms to hug him, almost knocking him off of the front steps.

"Easy!" Jacques said. "I see a lot of things have changed since I left for Kiev."

"Yes. You have been away for almost a year."

"You look well. When is your child due to arrive?"

"In two months. Don't just stand there, come in. Tell me about Irena."

Emile went into the kitchen and served tea and black bread with orange marmalade while Jacques was taking off his coat and settling in a chair at the kitchen table. She knew that that was his favorite.

"Now, tell me about Irena. I have never seen you so excited about a girl before. It must be love." He told her about how they met, where Irena came from and his trip to Georgia with her parents. He went on about the tobacco shop and Yuri's friend Nikita and this trip back to Odessa.

"I have talked enough. Tell me about yourself and Yuri. Have you heard from Maman and the girls back home?"

"Yuri is fine. He will be home shortly. The last letter that I received from home was written by Olga. Maman is sick with consumption, just like Papa had. There is very little happening at the Wheat Exchange. Olga and Marie seem to be handling things. They had a shipment of wheat come in from Egypt and another from Spain last fall. And the banks would not lend any more money for future shipments.

When Yuri came in, he was surprised to find Jacques sitting at the kitchen table.

"What did we do to deserve a visit from my favorite brother-in-law?"

"I finally brought the transfer papers on the two ships from the Ukrainian Maritime Office. That is probably a bigger surprise then my arrival. How are you Yuri? Congratulations on making me a future Uncle."

He offered Yuri a smoke from his silver cigarette case. Yuri looked at the case with Jacques initials engraved on the cover and commented,

"Nice case. Where did you get it?"

"It was a gift from Nikita's Uncle Jozsef for working in his tobacco shop when he was sick," "Very nice."

When he lit up the cigarette, he told Jacques that his whole family had decided to go to their summer house in Kerch while the revolution is going on.

"We are taking only our clothes and valuables, and will be leaving within the week on one of our ships. It will be safer there. Emile and I don't want our son to be born in the midst of hostilities."

"Or a daughter?" Emile added.

The next day, while the Bek clan was packing to leave for Kerch in the Crimean Peninsula, Jacques took that time to look up his friend Major Dmitry Moskaleff at the Military Attache`s Office. Dmitry was glad to see him, but was surprised to find out how he got there.

"I have had word that the barge canal has been closed down and there is a log jam of barges waiting in vain to bring their cargo down to Dnipropetrovsk. There are no ships going upriver because they are afraid that there will be no cargo to bring back. I have finished my work here and will be leaving in the next few days to return to Kiev and then on to St. Petersburg. Traveling will be dangerous. Many of the Army units have mutinied and are roaming the country side," Dmitry said.

"That is why my sister and brother-in-law and his family, the Beks, are going to Kerch for the duration of the hostilities. They felt it would be safer there than here in Odessa. They are sailing on one of their own ships in a few days and I am sure that you and I would be welcome to go with them." Dmitry liked the idea.

"It would not shorten the kilometers, but we would be traveling in territory more familiar to me, and I would be able to visit home again."

Back at Emily's house, Yuri was preparing a hiding place for some important papers and some silverware that they did not want to carry along. He had removed some stones inside the fireplace and with all of the items wrapped securely he placed them in the cavity. He replaced the stone in the opening and mixed up a small bucket of cement with a touch of carbon in it to match the burnt inside of the fire box. Jacques suggested that they write down exactly where things were hidden so as not to forget their location. Yuri thought that it was a good suggestion, and gave Emile that job. Then Jacques asked Yuri if he and Dmitry could travel along with the family, because they had agreed to travel to Kiev together on horseback.

"By all means, Jacques, we would enjoy having two more hands on the ship, but you will have to sleep in the crews quarters below if you do not mind. The crew is short handed. We are leaving on the afternoon tide tomorrow."

So Jacques got in touch with Dmitry about the plans. Dmitry arrived at the docks before the Bek clan and was settled in long before they sailed around 3:00 PM. When they arrived in Kerch they had to hire two horse carriages to deliver the large group with all of their belongings to the house on Tomogennaya Street. The so called summer house was large enough to accommodate the entire Bek family including Angelena's mother and several guests. The house had been closed up for the winter so the shutters were opened along with the windows. The breeze blowing in from the Sea of Azov had the house smelling sweet and fresh in no time at all.

The next morning Jacques and Dmitry set out to buy horses and supplies for their trek to Kiev, and the following morning they left on their journey. Jacques was anxious to be with the love of his life, Irena, back in Kiev. He knew that she would be worried about him. It took them four days to reach the Isthmus of Perekop that connects the Crimea and the Ukraine. They did not want to push the horses, not knowing if fresh mounts would be available along their route. Dmitry concluded that it would take them about two weeks to get back to Kiev at the rate they were traveling. This was troublesome to Jacques, but what choice did he have? They agreed that it was wiser to travel along farm roads and avoid the larger towns along the way, where larger groups of rebellious people may be gathered. Now they were traveling north across the Steppes where wheat fields were all they could see for miles in every direction with the exception of small groups of farm houses as they traveled along.

Four days later, they arrived at Dmitry's family home near the town of Yurivka. The last two days, they had pushed the horses knowing that fresh horses would be available at his parent's farm. Their arrival sparked a joyous reaction from his family. Cossacks had a tradition of military service. At least one boy from each family attended military school to become an officer. Dmitry, being the oldest, was given that opportunity and he made his family proud. His two younger brothers chose to remain home and work the fields with their father.

The news that Dmitry had arrived home, brought aunts, uncles, cousins and neighbors to their farm to see him. His brothers brought out their bandores and the party started. They danced the 'Hopak', their national dance, and the celebration of this surprise visit lasted late into the night.

The next morning, they were outfitted with two beautiful, strong, fresh horses. These were not draft horses; they were Akhal-Teke horses and were one of the oldest breeds of saddle horses. They were developed in Turkmenistan for their ability to withstand drought, heat, and cold. These sleek animals are a beautiful honey-gold color, and known for their endurance. Jacques' first thought was that Dmitry's family may never see these prized horses again. Dmitry's answer was,

"Not to worry, Jacques. If I let these fine horses go in Kiev with a slap on the rump and tell them to go home, they will return to this farm. I am confident of that."

Before they were on their way, Dmitry's brothers warned them of the peasant unrest in the area, and that there were rumors of army deserters roaming the Ukraine.

CHAPTER SIXTEEN

On their third day of travel, late in the afternoon, while riding through a thickly wooded area, they were stopped just past a bend in the road by a band of deserters from the Army. These men were on foot and they had some guns. There were about thirty of them in this shabby band. They were gathered around a large farm wagon hitched to four horses. Dmitry ordered them to stand down and let them pass.

"I am on the Tsars business and order you to let us pass."

They laughed at him and said

"The Tsar is gone, and now the people have the power, Comrade."

When Dmitry tried to turn around, he found that several men emerged from the woods, blocking their retreat, and these men also had guns. It was apparent that they had just stolen the wagon and horses from a nearby farmer. They told Jacques and Dmitry to dismount, and they did. They had no choice. They were outnumbered by several guns even though most of the deserters were unarmed.

A brutal looking man who was apparently the leader stepped forward and asked Dmitry who he was.

"I am Major Moskaleff Adjutant to General Tatischev, and I order you to let us pass."

The leader slapped Dmitry across the face which infuriated him. As he reached for his cavalry sword, several guns came up pointing at the two of them.

"You are nothing!" screamed the leader.

"The Tsar is gone, the Army is gone, and so is your General Tatischev, probably!"

The gang of deserters all laughed and hollered in agreement. The leader commanded Dmitry to take off his uniform jacket, which he did reluctantly.

"Now, very carefully hand me your pistol." He did.

"Now loosen the belt that holds your sword scabbard and let it fall to the ground." He did.

"Now we can talk," said the leader.

"Who is your friend, he doesn't look like a soldier." Dmitry shrugged and said,

"I do not even know his name. We met on the road several hours ago and he told me he was going to Kiev, and asked if he could travel along with me. I told him that I would not mind the company, so here we are," Dmitry lied.

"Oui," Jacques confirmed, then added "Da."

"Then you are a bourgeoisie foreigner." said the leader, looking at Jacques. "And where are you from?"

"I am Swiss," in as much of a French accent as he could muster.

"I thought that Swiss citizens used the German tongue."

"In my country, we use three languages."

"Then say something in German."

"Dubar es Fericht" (you are crazy) while looking into the leaders eyes.

The leader laughed, not realizing what Jacques had said, looked at his men and said,

"It sounds like German to me."

The gang all nodded or shrugged in agreement.

"These are nice horses," one of the deserters said.

"Yes, they are very nice horses, and we all know that the Tsar's Army travels on foot like we had to do. So we will take the horses. I need a good horse," said the leader. "Search these two and see what else we may find that is useful."

They took the Majors money and his hat, and then turned to Jacques. They found his small pistol, his watch and the billfold with his money and his passport. The watch was a gift from Papa on his fifteenth birthday. It was an 'Omega Grand Prex Paris 1900'. His stomach churned when they took it from him. He thanked God that they did not take his belt with the gold coins in it, or found the diamonds sewn into his jacket. Neither, did they find the photograph of Irena that he kept in his shirt pocket next to his heart, or the letter that he had written to Irena the last night that they were in Kerch. The silver cigarette case would have been gone too, if he had it in his pocket rather than tucked in his sock. That made his cigarettes more accessible while riding on a horse. The leader took everything; the money, the watch, the two pistols, Dmitry's sword, the Majors cap and jacket, and put them on. Then he mounted the Majors Akhal-Teke horse and threw his old tattered corporals jacket on the ground in front of Dmitry.

"I will leave him my old jacket, so he will not freeze to death tonight" the leader shouted out loud and his men laughed and cajoled again.

"Look at me! I have been promoted; a corporal one minute and a major the next. Comrade Major Yurovski."

And he snapped a salute to his men who all returned the salute sloppily.

"Shall we kill them now?" one of the men shouted.

Comrad Yurovski said,"Nyet! We will eat now and leave them a present later when we go on our way. They tied their hands behind their backs and made them sit on the ground back to back tied together while they took food from the wagon that they had stolen. Then they built fires and cooked some chickens that were acquired from the unfortunate farmer or farmers whose horses and wagon they had appropriated. There were loaves of bread being passed among them, but no food was offered to Jacques or Dmitry.

Whispering to each other, they decided that they were going to be killed when the gang was ready to leave. They worked on their bindings, first on the rope that held then together. When that was accomplished, they started to work on each others bindings. Jacques thanked Dmitry for the lie he told about not knowing him.

"That story may have saved our lives if we are lucky. These deserters are too stupid to realize that these two fine horses came from the same stable." Then Dmitry asked,

"What did you say to Yurovski in German?"

"He had no idea what I said, 'I called him crazy,' and they both chuckled quietly.

By the time the gang finished eating and was ready to leave Jacques' ropes were untied and he was working on Dmitry`s. At this point, their captors seemed to be ignoring them. Some of the group had already started walking in the direction of Kiev. Others who were handling the horses and wagon were taking up the rear of this disorganized column. As the deserters started up the dirt road with the supply wagon rumbling behind them, Jacques and Dmitry began to feel relieved, but they did not move until it would be safe to do so. Then, when the wagon was almost a half kilometer away, Yurovski turned on his horse and came galloping back. He stopped a short distance away and said,

"I almost forgot to give you aristocrats your present. I hope you have pleasant dreams."

With that he pulled the pin from a hand grenade and tossed it in their direction. Then he turned and galloped toward the disappearing column of deserters.

In the fading light, the grenade flew through the air, hit the road and bounced toward the two men sitting on the dirt with their backs to each other. They were not tethered any longer, but were unable to move out of the way fast enough from a sitting position.

"Down," Dmitry yelled, as the grenade zigzagged end over end at times bouncing a few feet in the air and finally coming to rest a few feet on Dmitry`s side of the two prone men. It all

happened in a split second. There was a loud roar and, BOOM!!!
Then all went blank.

CHAPTER SEVENTEEN

On the road that Jacques and Dmitry had traveled earlier that afternoon, was a cluster of eight farm houses that seemed to be deserted when they had passed through. But it was planting time and the farmers were probably out plowing the fields, they thought. It was the European style to have the farm houses together and up close to the road. There were many good reasons for this style of farming. Being close to the road was a must in the winter time when the drifting snow made travel and communication very difficult. The system usually worked well for this small group of Cossack farms. But earlier on this day, a band of Army deserters had stopped by to re-supply their motley band. Their leader, Yurovski, ordered his men to go into each house and take all of the available food. It was easy picking, because all of the men and most of the women were out in the fields planting or plowing. There were only a few children and one frightened woman left in the community. It was Zona, the children's school teacher who had the good sense to hide with the children in their cold cellar which was in the barn behind the house. She was warned of the band approaching on foot by Ivan, the oldest student who heard the noisy group and looked out the window to see what was going on. Because they were on foot and not in much of a hurry, Zona had time to safely get all seven children hidden and quiet before the deserters reached the community.

Some of the deserters entered each house snatching up loaves of bread, cans of loose tea leaves, bottles of vodka, utensils and anything else that they fancied. Others went through the barns taking the horses and as many chickens as they could catch and kill. Yurovski had two of the men hitch four horses to the very large wagon that stood in front of one of the houses. They loaded their booty on the wagon and left. As they were leaving one of the men asked if they should set the houses on fire. Yurovski said,

"No, don't burn the houses; we may have to come back this way someday for more food."

Then they all laughed.

Zona waited until all was quiet, then had Ivan sneak out of the cold cellar to look around. The band of brigands had gone. Ivan reported that he only saw dust rising from the road a good distance away. Leaving the other six children in the cold cellar, she told Ivan to go quickly into the fields where the group was plowing and planting, and tell them what happened. He left, running as fast as his legs would carry him. Then she looked around her house to take stock of what was taken. There were a dozen heads of the chickens that the band had taken for their dinner lying in the barnyard. All of the food in the house was gone. The wagon that was in front of her house and the horses from the barn were gone. That was at a quick glance. She fell to her knees and thanked God that they had left without finding the children or her. Then she retrieved the other children from the cold cellar.

The men and women of the small community were far out in the fields, almost three kilometers away. The rolling hills of the Steppes completely blocked them from hearing or seeing their homes. The eight men were busy plowing with four teams of oxen and the seven women and two older girls were sowing the seeds. They were all busy with their work, when young Ivan came running over the last hill, screaming and out of breath. The women responded first as he collapsed in his mothers arms. One of the women called to the men, while the others tried to question young Ivan. When he told them what had happened, they tethered the oxen and rushed back to the village, each to their own home. After they surveyed the damages, they all met in the barn of Zona and Grygory, Zona's husband. Grygory was the elder of the community. His first wife passed away several years before and the marriage between he and Zona was an arranged one. She was twenty years younger than Grygory.

When the meeting started, the men agreed that they would have to go after the thieves. The problem would be that they were outnumbered by at least two to one and what few weapons they had were gone. All they had left were knives and axes or shovels. It was decided that they would come upon the bandits while they were sleeping and butcher the bastards. That plan was dashed when one of the women suggested that the horses that they had taken would give them away. Then the rest of the wives chimed in, and said that they did not need dead husbands. It was finally decided that after dark, four of the youngest men would go to the woods to investigate the situation. If the bandits were still in the area, they would most likely spend the night in the woods. Then they barricaded the doors and windows of the house that they were all staying together in, and prepared for another attack. They did not think that these men were savages or they would have gone into the fields to find them and kill them. At dusk, they heard the sound of an explosion coming from the far side of the wooed area adjacent to their fields.

The four chosen men, led by Maksym, the father of young Ivan, waited until the moon was on the rise. Then they stole out through the barn, leaving the rest of the village residents barricaded in Grygory`s house. After their eyes adjusted to the moonlight, they proceeded up the road. Before entering the wooded area that the road ran through, they paused to listen for any signs of life. All was quiet. They assumed that the Army deserters had moved on, but they still proceeded cautiously. Walking single file with ten meters between each man, they approached the bend in the road. At about fifty meters past the bend, Maksym could see the hole that the blast created. Maksym approached the hole with great caution. Then, in the darkness, he saw a body in the tall grass at the side of the road. It was covered with blood and dirt from the explosion. The second man said,

"Over here is another body. He seems to be dead."

"So is this one," said Maksym.

Checking the area further, he found evidence that the band of robbers was larger than they had thought. There were chicken bones and other litter that would suggest that there were about thirty in the band. He sent two of the men ahead on the road to see if any of the deserters were still there or if they had left the area. When they returned, they reported that they had followed the wagon tracks out of the woods and over the next incline. The bandits were nowhere in sight.

Meanwhile, Maksym and the other farmer went about fashioning two stretchers out of saplings. They used the dead men's jackets and their own while slipping the poles through the armholes to make two complete stretchers. They laid one body on each pallet and when the other two men returned, they carried the bodies back to the farm houses for a proper burial.

Upon their return, it was decided that the men would take turns standing watch during the night, in the event that the band of deserters decided to return. When the women were cleaning up the bodies for their interment, Lidiya, Maksym`s wife, cried out,

"Oh! This one is not dead! He has a badly broken leg and is unconscious but alive!"

They took off all of his tattered clothing and wrapped him in blankets while one of the women went to fetch Grygory to fix the broken leg. Grygory was not a doctor, but he was the most experienced when it came to wounds.

When Grygory arrived, he examined Jacques' entire body. First he addressed all of the small fragments that were embedded in Jacques' legs, thigh and buttocks and some cuts on his head. He removed the fragments, cleaned and dressed the wounds.

"None of these wounds could be fatal, but we don't want him to get infections. We need boiling water to sterilize my tools and a bottle of vodka in case he wakes up. Thank God that those thieves knew nothing about cold cellars. They must have all been city boys."

That aroused a chuckle from the group.

Young Ivan asked, "What are you going to do about his broken leg?"

118

So Grygory explained that Jacques had a compound fracture of the tibia and that he would cut the leg open and put the bone back in place to repair it.

"Just like a broken piece of wood! Then we will pray that no infection will set in and that our patient will live. His body has had a terrible shock."

"What is our patient's name," Ivan asked?

"Well, we will not know that until he wakes up and tells us." Grygory laughed.

"Then wake him up and ask him what his name is," Ivan insisted.

"My boy, I do not think that it will be possible to wake him up because he is unconscious. Now enough of the questions and let me get to work."

The women had the water boiling and clean linens available to dress the wounds and bind the leg. Grygory washed his hands and arms with brown soap and boiled water. Then he had one of the women pour vodka from the cold cellar over his hands and arms and let them dry. He tied a tourniquet around the leg just above the knee. Next, he told his assistant to put an oak fid in the patient's mouth so he would not bite his tongue off during the operation. Now he took his straight razor which was sharpened and sterilized and cut away the flesh to expose most of the bone. The fracture was long and ugly. When he attempted to reset the bone, Jacques screamed, his eyes fluttered open and then he passed out again. Now the bone was in place, and Grygory drilled a hole with a sterilized straight shank bit in the hard surface of the bone with a hand drill and screwed in a sterilized brass wood screw. Before he drilled another hole, the tourniquet was released allowing blood to flow into the leg so as not to loose the leg. The tourniquet was replaced and the operation proceeded. Down about four or five centimeters, he drilled another hole and repeated the process. During the process, the patient moaned and his body twitched several times, but he was being held down by two strong men. Another hole was drilled about another four centimeters down the leg and another screw was inserted. The wound was stitched up, allowing for drainage. The leg was bandaged and a splint was applied to both sides of the leg. Now the operation was complete. It would be up to the women of the village to change the dressings and care for the patient. Lidiya volunteered to have the patient stay at her house.

"I have the two boys to help me keep an eye on him."

It was determined that the dead man was an Army Officer from the quality of his pants and boots. This was belied by the corporal chevrons on the jacket they found near his corpse. They buried him in their village cemetery with a semi-military ceremony. Ivan and his brother Lev did a rifle salute over the grave with their wooden guns. Bang, bang, bang! Then Dmitry was laid to rest.

They transferred the patient Jacques to the house of Maksym and Lidiya, being assured that he would receive the best of care. The two boys were thrilled to take part in watching over the wounded man, and they knew that their mother would be a good nurse.

CHAPTER EIGHTEEN

It was three days before Jacques' eyes fluttered open. He was in great pain.

"Where am I," he asked in his native tongue, French.

The boy at his bedside could not understand him so he called his mother. Lidiya came to the bed and introduced herself.

"I am Lidiya and I am taking care of you. You are at our farm house and have been wounded by a bomb blast."

Now Jacques began to realize that he was in the Ukraine and began speaking in Ukrainian. "Where is Dmitry," Jacques asked in a whisper?

At first, she did not comprehend but when she realized what he was asking, she told him. "Your friend was killed by the bomb blast. He probably saved your life because he took the full impact of the explosion. The fragments that broke your leg almost tore his body apart."

She propped him up and made him drink some water. The pain was so bad that he asked to lie back down again.

"Before you lie back down, do you want some vodka for the pain?"

He nodded. She handed him the bottle half filled and he took several gulps. He coughed and shivered, then lay back down. Lidiya placed the bottle by his bedside and told him that one of the boys would be here at all times.

"If you need anything, they will summon me."

Jacques nodded and closed his eyes.

When the pain woke him, he reached for the bottle and took two more swigs. It was then that he realized that the boy was watching him.

"What is your name," the boy immediately inquired?

It took a moment to focus before he answered.

"I am Jacques. What is your name?"

The boy was thrilled that the patient could talk.

"I am Ivan. My brother Lev and I are taking turns watching you."

"How old are you Ivan?"

"I am eleven and my brother Lev is nine. My father found you past the bend in the road in the woods. We buried your friend in our cemetery over the hill. He was all bloody and some of his guts were hanging out. Was he a soldier?"

"Yes, he was a very brave soldier and a very important one."

At that moment, Lidiya came back in the room and scolded Ivan for bothering the wounded man. Jacques waved his hand in a motion that let her know that he was all right with answering the boy's questions.

"Momma, his name is Jacques," Ivan said proudly. "He said that the soldier that we buried was very brave and very important."

"That's good, now you let Jacques rest." And she left the room.

Ivan couldn't wait to tell his brother what he found out about Jacques and the soldier. It was not long before Jacques opened his eyes again and found Ivan still watching him. Immediately, the inquisitive boy started asking questions again, as boys often do. Ivan asked, "Are you a soldier too?"

"No!"

"Then why were you riding with a soldier and where were you going?

"My friend, Major Dmitry Moskaleff and I came from Kerch in the Crimea and were traveling together to Kiev when we ran into some Army deserters. They tied us up and then they tossed a hand grenade at us when they left."

"They must have been the same bad men that robbed our house and our neighbor's houses the day that Papa found you. They took our horses, and the wagon, and chickens, and all the food they could find. They didn't find us because we hid in the cold cellar at Zona's house. I saw them coming through the window and told Zona. She is our teacher. Mamma and Papa and the rest of the people were way, way, out in the fields when that happened. I ran out to tell them about it," rambled Ivan.

"Then you are a very alert and a very brave young man," Jacques complimented.

Ivan smiled proudly with a very toothy grin. He was tall for his age and his smile showed wonderful dimples. The conversation with Ivan helped to take his mind off the pain. Later that day, when Lev arrived home from school, Ivan brought him up to date on the patient and the soldier.

The next day, Lidiya noticed that Jacques had become restless and confused. He also had a fever. So, she notified Grygory as she had been instructed to do. This evening when he and his wife Zona visited the patient to change the dressings, he brought his razor and ordered some boiled water. By the time the water was ready, Jacques had consumed enough vodka to make the next procedure painless. He had an infection and the wound had to be opened and cleaned out. It was easy enough to find because that part of the leg was all red and swollen. Grygory sterilized the wound with pure alcohol, and a compound of moist tea leaves wrapped in a sterile cloth was placed on the infected area. Thankfully, the infection had not gone into the bone. Then Zona applied fresh bandages. Grygory instructed Lidiya to call him, should the patient become delirious and burning up with fever. Then we may have to remove his leg.

It took several days before the fever subsided. But it was a setback in his recovery. Now it was time for Jacques to ask questions. He wondered where his clothing was or if it had all been destroyed. He decided to question the boy rather than alert Lidiya to the fact that there may be something of value in his clothing.

"What happened to the clothes I was wearing?" he asked Ivan.

Ivan pointed to a shelf above the bed.

"They are up there on the shelf."

"Could you get them for me?"

"Why do you need your clothes? You can't even get out of bed. You have a broken leg," the boy said. Jacques thought quickly.

"I have a picture of my fiancée in one of the pockets and I would like to have it so I can look at her beautiful face."

"What is a fiancée?"

"It is a girl to which one is engaged to!"

Ivan still looked puzzled! So Jacques added,

"The girl in the picture is my girlfriend, Irena and we are 'engaged' to be married."

"Where does she live?"

"Irena lives in Kiev."

"That is a long way from here," Ivan said. "I have never been to Kiev. What is it like?"

"I will tell you all about Kiev if you get me my clothes."

The boy stepped up on the bed and reached for the neatly folded pile of clothes on the shelf, retrieved them, and handed then to Jacques. On the bottom of the pile was his tattered jacket. Next was his shirt, then the underwear and sox. On top was his cap and under the cap was his silver cigarette case with seven cigarettes and several stick matches His clothes had been washed with the exception of the jacket and cap. Neatly tucked in the shirt pocket was the picture of Irena and the letter he had written to her a few nights ago. It was a short note saying that he was on his way and that he was doing well. Things had changed considerably since he had written it. He kissed the picture and kept it out along with the cigarette case and the letter. Then he tucked them all under his pillow. Jacques casually felt the lining of the jacket. What remained of his diamonds were still there.

"Do you have my shoes?" He inquired of Ivan.

Ivan pointed to under the bed near the head. He reached under the bed, and found the shoes with the belt neatly curled up in one shoe. These were simple honest people. How could he have not trusted them? He felt embarrassed.

A little while later, Lidiya came into the room.

"I hear that you were looking for your clothes. The pants are gone. We had to cut what was left of them off of you, but we will find you another pair of pants when you are able to get up. I imagine that the rest of your possessions are gone along with your horse."

She asked if he needed anything and Jacques thanked her. Before she left the room to continue with her chores, she said, "The picture; is that your wife? She is very pretty."

"Thank you. She is my fiancée," Jacques added as Lidiya nodded and left the room.

The two boys were glad to see Jacques' health returning, even though he would be bedridden for some weeks. They spent long hours listening to the stories of his travels, and of Kiev. They had many questions. Jacques even started to teach them to speak a little French. Lev was very observant and had a good memory. His dark hair was a contrast to his brothers blond locks, but there was no doubt that they were brothers.

When he was feeling better, he explained to Lidiya and Maksym about his situation. He told them about his family's involvement in the wheat business and about the ship's papers that needed to be delivered to Odessa. He then went on to tell them that Irena was the reason for his returning to Kiev. He asked Maksym if it would be possible to post the letter in the near future that he had previously written to Irena. Now he would have to add a long post script to the letter telling her of his broken leg and that it would take him a few months to recover before he could return to Kiev.

A few days later, Maksym had to go to the market several kilometers away. He posted the letter to Irena. He was told that the letter may take a long time to arrive because of the present political situation in Russia and the Ukraine. He confirmed that the Tsar had indeed abdicated and that there was a Provisional Government in place, but it was on shaky ground. The Bolsheviks were causing trouble and unrest among the workers. They had tried to take over the government once, but had failed.

"It is very dangerous to travel these days, as you and I well know," Maksym explained. "You are welcome to stay here as long as you wish."

In the fourth week, he was allowed to hobble around the house on a pair of crutches fashioned by another member of the little community. They helped him with everything. He was grateful, but did not like being a burden.

In the middle of July, the splints came off of his leg. He was still very weak and shaky. And now he walked with a slight limp. You could see the dark spots in his shinbone where Grygory had inserted the brass screws to hold the bone together. A scab remained on one of the places where the skin had not quite covered the screw. Jacques was anxious to return to Kiev but Maksym said that he should stay and rebuild his strength before he attempted to travel that far. After all, Kiev was over four hundred kilometers away, and he was probably going to have to walk most of the way. Jacques agreed, but only if he could do his share on the farm. By the end of September, he was able to keep up with the other men in the village. He told them that he would like to stay to help them bring in the harvest as repayment for all that they had done for him. They saved his life, and he wanted to show his gratitude for that. He told them,

"My family has been in the wheat business for many generations in France, but I have only been in the sales aspect and now when I return to Switzerland, 'I can say that I know the wheat business from start to finish'."

The wheat harvest was going to be a problem. It would have to be accomplished with borrowed horses and a borrowed wagon. That may mean the loss of a portion of their crops due to a late harvest. Jacques listened to their discussions of the problem and he felt guilty. After all, these people saved his life and he was capable of paying his debt to them by using some of his hidden gold pieces or diamonds. That evening, he asked Maksym what the price of four new horses would be. And then, what it would cost to replace the farm wagon. The answer surprised him. These days a person could live comfortably on one hundred rubles a month in Kiev. Before he went to bed, he cut some of the stitches in his belt and removed five one-hundred ruble gold coins and placed them in his shirt pocket.

The next morning after breakfast, he offered the five-hundred rubles to Maksym to buy four horses and a wagon. Maksym was shocked by the offer.

"Where did you get that kind of money?" he blurted out.

In confidence, Jacques explained that he had sewed the coins into the belt in case of an emergency. Jacques said,

"And this is an emergency!"

"How can we accept this money from you and how can we pay you back?' Maksym asked.

"You have saved my life. That is repayment enough and besides, I have been making a living selling your wheat in Switzerland for many years and at a good profit, may I add.

"Well then, I accept your gift when you put it that way. We will go to the market today and look for horses and a wagon." Maksym said, emphatically. "But do not tell anyone why we are going. We will surprise them."

Maksym suggested that they ride to the market with an oxcart, but Jacques insisted that they could walk there faster. They had an early start, so they agreed to walk the fifteen or so kilometers. After arriving at the market place around two o'clock in the afternoon, they took another two hours to pick out four sturdy draft horses, and a used wagon. There were some rubles left over from the purchase, so Jacques told Maksym to buy a present for his wife and something for the boys, which he did. Jacques would have bought the gifts himself but under the circumstances, he felt it was not proper to buy gifts for another man's wife and children Then they hitched the horses to their new wagon and headed back to the farms.

It was dark by the time they arrived home. The racket that Maksym made, by running the horses at full tilt over the last hill, caused a panic at the village. The neighbors thought at first that they were being attacked by the group of Army deserters that had stolen their horses a few months ago, until Maksym reined up the horses in a cloud of dust in front of his house.

"You scared us to death!" Lidiya came out complaining. "And where did you steal these horses?" Now all of the neighbors were gathered around when Maksym announced that the horses and wagon were theirs. There was a cacophony of questions coming from everyone in the group, all at one time, until Maksym held up his hand for silence. He was still sitting in the driver's seat of the wagon, while Jacques had dismounted and disappeared into the darkness as soon as they arrived. These horses and wagon are a gift from Jacques to our community for saving his life. There was another round of questions but Jacques was nowhere to be found.

After they all inspected their new gift, the group crowded into Lidiya`s house to celebrate. The men rounded up Jacques and a few bottles of vodka, and the party began. Several of the men brought their bandores. They began playing and singing while the others danced the hopak around the potbellied stove in the middle of the room. There were salutes to Jacques and to the horses and for the success of the harvest and so on, and so on, and so on, as they celebrated into the night.

The next day, preparations were under way to bring in the harvest. They all worked hard, including the children. The horse drawn reaper and the thrasher were brought out of their respective barns. The women prepared the bags to transport the grain to the market and the harvest began. They spent long days in the fields. It was hot dirty work, but eventually the harvest was gathered and the grain delivered to the market. A pig was roasted to celebrate the conclusion of the harvest. Then the small village echoed with the sounds of singing and dancing long into the night as only Cossacks could do. During the festivities, Jacques announced that he would be leaving in two days. It would not be easy for him to leave. These people had become like family to him. He had only one request before he left. That was to make a proper grave marker to honor his friend Dmitry.

When that task was accomplished, the villagers gathered to send him off on his journey. The two boys were sad to see Jacques go but they held back their tears like strong boys were expected to do. Jacques told the boys that he would come back to visit them some day. Then he mounted the horse that he had picked up at the market when they brought in the harvest and rode off down the dusty road in the direction of Kiev.

CHAPTER NINETEEN

The first day on the road was uneventful. Jacques stopped in another farm village for the night. One of the farmers was good enough to let him water his horse. He paid for feed and asked to sleep in the barn for a few more rubles. The farmer agreed. The next morning, Jacques was up with the rooster crowing and out on the road. He thought that if he could cover about 20 kilometers a day, he would reach Kiev by mid November. There were several nights that he slept in the fields along the road. This was farm country and there were no hotels or places to eat. The next few days were also uneventful, but after a week, the weather turned colder and his traveling plans were slightly curtailed. On the tenth day of his journey, the sky became cloudy and the wind began blowing down from the north. There was an early winter storm brewing and Jacques knew he had to find shelter sooner than he usually did. By the time he reached the next small farm village, snow was falling, covering the ground. He managed to persuade a farmer to let him take refuge in his barn for a few rubles. By that evening, the wind was howling outside and the snow was drifting. The farmer took pity on Jacques and invited him into the house to sleep on the floor by the potbellied stove. In the morning, the snow was drifted up against the barn door. It was still snowing hard and the wind was still blowing furiously outside with this early winter storm. Jacques was invited to stay and for a few extra rubles, they fed him. He appreciated having cooked meals.

Three days later, Jacques said farewell to the farmer and his wife, who graciously let him stay while the storm lasted. He settled up after they had dug themselves out of the snow drifts and he was on his way. Traveling was difficult. The roads were mostly blown clear on the high ground, but these Steppes are rolling hills and there was also low ground where the snow was somewhat deeper. The horse struggled in the deeper drifts, so Jacques tried to go around the deep snow by leaving the road and riding out on the harvested fields. That did not always work out well. There were times that he had difficulty finding the road again in this wonderland of white. He thought that he was traveling in the right direction. The sky was still thick with grey cloud cover, so it was hard to tell where the sun was. By midday, Jacques found himself crossing the tracks that his horse had left some time ago. Now this was very depressing. In his effort to see Irena again, he was going nowhere. He must find the road that headed northwest to Kiev, and he must find shelter for tonight. Sleeping out under these conditions was not an option. Even the horse that was a breed developed by the Turkmen for their endurance and the ability to withstand heat or cold would not survive a night out in these elements.

Jacques was determined to move forward, but which direction was forward? If he could not determine the way to Kiev, he still had time to return to the farm, where he spent the last few days, before it would become dark. He must take time to think about his situation. He was on high ground with nothing but white rolling land all around him as far as he could see. He gathered as much chaff that remained from the wheat harvest from a wind blown section on top of a hill and piled it up while his horse rested. Then he lit the pile of dried straw-like material on fire. The heat felt good, but the pile burned off rapidly leaving a distinctive black area on the landscape. He would ride in ever widening circles around the burned spot until he found the road. On the third trip around, he found the road that did not have his saddle horses hoof prints. Satisfied that it was the right direction, he set off again. After riding for more than an hour, he came upon a fairly large group of farm houses to seek refuge in.

The next day dawned with clear azure blue skies and bright sunshine. The snow was melting so the road became muddy, but that was more acceptable to Jacques and the horse. At least it was a slight bit warmer. He inquired about how far it was to Kiev and was told that he had a little less than 150 kilometers to travel.

That meant that he had approximately one week to go. After a few days, the landscape began to change. He passed through several small towns, and then he came across a railroad track. Following the tracks in the direction of Kiev, they entered a town that had a railroad station. He inquired if there was a passenger train that went to Kiev. The conductor told him that there were trains that went into Kiev, but that they were infrequent these days.

"Why?" Jacques asked.

The conductor told him that there were only a handful of the older railroad workers, like himself, that were still operating trains because they had not been paid in two months.

"If you stay here in the station, a train may come along. Some people in the waiting room have been here for days but I have a feeling a train will be coming soon," added the conductor.

"Wonderful!" Jacques said sarcastically. "Then, where can I sell a horse?" he asked.

The conductor gave directions and Jacques thanked him and left the station. After he sold the horse, he returned to the station waiting room and joined the group of waiting travelers.

Jacques slept that night on the hard wooden bench near a potbellied stove that kept him nice and warm through the night. The next morning, he was awakened by, of all things, a train whistle! Luckily, the train was going to Kiev. He bought his ticket and boarded the crowded train. Unfortunately, this train did not travel much faster than the horse that he sold. It stopped several times before they reached the station on Kominternu Street. Jacques was excited to be back in Kiev. He could not wait to see Irena. It was the middle of the afternoon and a weekday so Irena would be working. He briskly walked the several blocks to the Ukraine Wheat Co-operative. When he went up to the third floor, he found the office closed with a padlock on the door. This was awfully strange. He had a sinking feeling in the pit of his stomach. Something was definitely wrong.

Next, he walked the two and one-half blocks to the tobacco shop. Jozsef was shocked to see him.

"Where have you been? We thought that either you were dead or that you went back to Switzerland. You left here in March and said you would return in two weeks," Jozsef scolded. "Here it is the end of November and much has happened here in Kiev. The Ukrainians have formed the White Army to fight the Marxist Reds that have taken over the government. The Tsar and his family are being held prisoner. Your girlfriend has stopped coming by and asking for you. She was very upset the last time she stopped by and that was two months ago. You are alive and I am happy for that, but now you walk with a limp. What happened?"

Jacques then related the whole story of his trip to Odessa and then to Kirch, the broken leg, and the death of Dmitry. Jozsef listened to his story in awe. Then he told Jacques to stay. His room had not been touched.

"Your belongings are as you had left them," Jozsef said.

Jacques then excused himself, saying that he would be back, but first he must go to see Irena and he left the shop. There were no taxies available; in fact, he did not see any on the street at all. It was a long walk but he set off in the direction of her house. It was dark when he reached the Baratashvili residence on Voloska Street. The house was dark. He knocked on the large oak front door, but there was no answer. Then he pounded on the door and still no answer. He walked through the ally to the rear of the house and pounded on the rear door. The next door neighbor was aroused by the noise that he was making and came to her back door.

"Who is there?" she asked.

"Can you help me," Jacques pleaded. "I am looking for Irena Baratashvili; she is my fiancée. "They are not here," the woman answered.

"Where did they go?"

"They packed up in a hurry and left for Georgia two months ago," the woman said.

He was shocked. He thanked the woman and began the long walk back to the tobacco shop. What should he do now? Where should he go? How can he get to Georgia? How long will that take with the trains running the way they are and everyone on strike. No transportation, no communication. Is Irena all right? Did they make it back to Georgia and their family? These thoughts ran through his head all the way back to the tobacco shop.

When he arrived at the shop, he realized that he did not have a key to get in. He knocked on the door and waited. He knocked again and Jozsef unlocked the door.

"I heard you the first time you knocked, but I am an old man and do not move so fast any more. I was expecting that you lost your key with all that you have gone through. How is Irena," Jozsef asked?

"She is gone," Jacques said forlornly. "She went with her parents back to Georgia."

"I feel so bad for you. What are you going to do now?"

"I don't know. I guess that I will go to Georgia to find her. I know where her family is and I will find her."

Jozsef thought for a minute then said,

"It is a long and dangerous trip to take these days. Don't be foolish, Jacques."

Jacques asked how his nephew Nikita was doing, and Jozsef told him that Nikita had taken his family up in the Carpathian Mountains and into Romania back in May and he had not heard from him since.

"Nikita begged us to go with them. He feared that it would be dangerous for us to stay here, but Elena and I are getting too old to move that far away. They took only what they could carry on their backs when they left. Nikita was worried about what was happening in our country and did not think it was wise to stay," Jozsef told Jacques.

Jacques was surprised that his friend Nikita had made a life changing move of this magnitude with such a very young family.

"Do you know what is going on?" Jozsef asked. "Did you know that America joined in the war against Germany in April and just a few weeks ago the Bolsheviks took over the Russian Government?"

"No! But I did notice that everyone seems to have stopped working. There is no postal service, the trains are almost all standing abandoned, and there are no taxis on the streets. It looks like most of the businesses are closed."

"That is because the Red Army has been formed and they are taking over the country. It is the beginning of a civil war. But I am too old and tired to do anything about it. So I will stay here until they come and close my shop and put me out. Then I will stand on the bread lines with everyone else.

Jacques replied,"Our thanks to Vladimir Lenin and his Bolshevik friends."

"I know of that Marxist Lenin. He lived in Geneva for a while, espousing his revolutionary propaganda to anyone who would listen. Then he left and came back to neutral Switzerland when the war started. It is my guess that he did not want to get into a real fight for his country. He settled in Zurich, so the newspapers said. So now he is back in Saint Petersburg with his Marxist ideology. I truly feel sorry for this country. I remember that my father went to Geneva University to hear him speak. He was invited to go hear Lenin by a good friend, who was a socialist. My father, as I remember, was not impressed."

"Enough of the political situation in Russia," Jozsef said. "What are you going to do about your situation?"

"I would like to leave tomorrow, but that would be reckless of me. So I will take your advice and wait until the weather starts to warm up a bit before I go," Jacques admitted.

"Good, now we can both sleep easy tonight," added Jozsef.

CHAPTER TWENTY

By December of 1917, it was evident that the Bolshevik Government that had taken over was not going to tolerate any resistance to their 'Communist Manifesto'. Leon Trotsky had taken charge of the Red Army as Commissar of War. However, forces loyal to the Tsar were forming in the Ukraine, known as the White Army. They were joined by the Czech Legion. Both of these armies sorely needed arms and ammunitions to bring the battle to there enemy, 'The Red Army'. Eli Marrazzo was a small arms dealer in Italian guns who operated in Odessa. He had never dealt in large quantities but he did have the contacts to do so. His dealings with Baretta and other gun and ammunition factories in his homeland placed him in a perfect position to supply arms to the White Army

It was just before Christmas, that he was summoned to the Military Attaché Office in Odessa. Eli was presented with a purchase order for a large quantity of small arms and ammunition signed by General Wrangle, commander of the White Army. After Eli read over the purchase order, the Officer questioned,

"Can you deliver this order?"

Eli answered, "Yes, but I will have to charge enough rubles to make a profit on the transaction of this size. I am sure you realize that these arms cannot be shipped here in the usual manner. The Germans have the Dardanelles blocked off to all shipping, and I know that you are aware that there is a war going on. It is winter, and I will have to bring the shipment by truck over the rugged mountains of the Balkan Peninsula, where the roads are extremely poor, until we can reach the Danube River Basin. It may take a few months to deliver the arms to Odessa."

The Officer replied, "We are aware of the difficulty you will have in supplying our arms. We are willing to pay the price in gold to defeat the Bolsheviks who threaten our beloved country 'the Russian Empire'."

The next day, Eli made arrangements to travel across the Balkan Peninsula, and to look for a passable route over the mountains. He placed his orders by wire to the Italian manufacturers for the goods he needed, and notified his cousins back home to purchase the trucks necessary to deliver the goods. This whole operation made Eli very nervous. There were so many unknown factors involved. Eli needed trustworthy people to carry out this mission. He knew he could trust his cousins and their friends. Several of the men had to be mechanics to maintain the trucks on this arduous journey, and some had experience in the area as smugglers. The best route was laid out. He prayed that they would not be hindered by the heavy snows that plagued these mountains every winter. By the time he reached Durazzo on the east coast of the Adriatic Sea, the ferry carrying eight trucks heavily laden with small arms and ammunition, had arrived from Italy and were being unloaded onto the dock..

In a matter of hours, the caravan set out on their journey with the four trucks loaded with small arms in the lead. The four trucks that were carrying the ammunition took up the rear of the convoy. Ammunition has a tendency to become volatile under certain circumstances. These trucks would travel with some distance between them and the rest of the convoy. The weather was cold and there was a considerable amount of snow to contend with, but these men could handle this kind of whether. It took almost three weeks to cross the mountains. The convoy arrived at the Danube River on the border of Romania with seven trucks and two horse drawn carts with all of their cargo intact. One of the lead trucks had broken its front axel going over a mountain pass. It was unloaded and pushed over the cliff to make way for the rest of the caravan to pass on the narrow road. Three men were left to guard the cargo while Eli purchased the two sturdy horse-drawn carts in the next small town, with eight strong draft horses to rescue the merchandise from high up in the mountains.

Traveling through the Danube River Valley was so much easier than the terrain that they had just covered. In comparatively no time at all, they were crossing the border into the Ukraine, and Odessa was only a few days travel away.

The men in the convoy were happy to reach their destination. It took the whole morning to unload the arms and ammunition into the large basement room of the Military Attaché Office. The White Army Officer who was in charge had the men stack the guns and ammunitions right up against the rear wall of the room to the height of the ceiling, then concealed them behind crates of other military equipment that was not quite so useful. The next morning, Eli`s men left to return to their home-land by the route they had come, with payment in gold for the Italian Arms manufacturers, and their pay in two of the trucks. Eli had prospects to purchase the remaining trucks from him before he went to meet them at the docks in Durazzo.

By the time the transaction had been completed, it was the beginning of February and Eli had been away from his family for a long time. He had missed the children's Christmas. So, before he returned, he went shopping for presents for all six of the children and his Ukrainian wife. He also profited enough rubles for his family to live on for at least a year. It was a joyous reunion.

CHAPTER TWENTY-ONE

A week after Jacques arrived in Kiev, he went shopping at the Covered Market across from Basarabska Plaza. He found that the Market looked quite different from the last time he was there with Irena. Then, it was filled with vendors hawking their goods and crowds of shoppers milling around but now it was almost empty. There were only a few vendors and they seemed very nervous about doing business here. Jacques was hoping to find some items that he needed for his journey. He was looking at a used army canteen when he looked up and saw Dina, Boris Zaitzev`s 'receptionist'. He called to her. She looked up.

"Jacques," she said with a shocked expression?

She did not look very happy to see him.

"You came back! Irena did not give up hope that you would come back for her. Her mother and father almost forcibly took her away with them when they left some months ago. There was a group of people from Georgia that decided to go back to their homeland. Do you remember Oleg, the owner of the 'Song of Tbilisi'? His family went also. Irena was very upset when they left. She wanted to stay with me to wait for you because she said that she knew that you would return. But that would have been impossible because when Boris left with his family, he stopped paying the rent on my apartment. The bastard left without even saying good-by."

Jacques asked politely, "Where did he go?"

"He probably went back to the family farm. He always talked about the farm where he grew up. It is somewhere east of here. He did not go to visit often because it was several hundred kilometers away. I hope he didn`t owe you money because he will be very difficult to find."

"No, he did not owe me anything," Jacques replied casually.

"Enough of Boris, how are you doing?" Jacques asked.

"I am living with a friend in her very small apartment. I have no job and nowhere else to go. I came to the market to see if I could sell a few pieces of jewelry; they are gold. They were gifts from Boris. He was very generous when he was with me. I miss him," Dina said forlornly. "Now I just have to move on."

"That is a good attitude to have," Jacques replied with a compassionate smile. "If I can do anything to help you I would be glad to, but my situation is not much better than yours. I am living back at the tobacco shop, thanks to Jozsef's generosity. I will be leaving in the early spring to find Irena."

He explained why he was away so long; the trip from Odessa to Kerch, the hand grenade explosion that broke his leg and the re-cooperation period, the farmers who helped him and his journey back to Kiev. Dina added that she was jealous of Irena for having a man that would go through so much trouble for her. Jacques blushed. Then she gave him the number of her friend's apartment on Pyrohova Street where she was staying and they parted.

Jozsef insisted on keeping his shop open every day, even though there were very few customers. It was the only tobacco shop still open in Kiev. Jacques kept him company during working hours. They were discussing Jacques journey when Jozsef suggested that he try to buy a gun for the trip. There had been a gunsmith in Kiev but he had closed his shop several months earlier. Jozsef knew someone who came into the store occasionally for tobacco who hinted that he had some guns to sell on the black market.

The very next day the man Jozsef had mentioned came into the shop. Jozsef did not know his name but he told the man that Jacques was in the market for a fire arm. Jacques introduced himself to Vladislav and told him that he was interested in a small pistol and some ammunition. Vladaslav said that he could supply such a pistol in good condition, and that it would cost two hundred rubles in gold. He would meet Jacques at the end of Voloska Street by the river in Podi tomorrow evening at five o'clock. Jacques agreed.

Jacques knew that it was a fairly long walk to Voloska Street. That was the neighborhood where Irena used to live. Jacques was familiar with the area because of the many evening walks that they had taken along the Dnieper River front. Jacques decided to take the shortest route which was down the Andriyivsky Decent. He stopped at the top to look down at the panoramic view of Podi. It was a depressing sight on that cold winter afternoon. The trees were bare and the monument standing tall before him of Volodymyr the Great, reminded him of his beautiful Irena standing there telling about the statue on their first real date. He could hear her saying that it was Volodymyr, 'The Duke of Kiev' that introduced Christianity to the Ukraine back in the year 1015. As he continued down the decent, he noticed that there were far fewer artists showing their works inside of the shops. In fact, most of the shops were closed. It was a sad comment about the political turmoil in the country.

On the way to his rendezvous with Vladislav, the black market gun dealer, he passed by Irena's house. It was evident that someone was living in the house. There was smoke coming from the chimney and there was a light on in one of the back rooms. Jacques heart leaped. He ran up the sandstone steps and knocked loudly on the oak door. There was no answer. He knocked again and still no answer. On the third try, he saw someone peek out the window and then a voice from behind the door said, "What do you want?"

"I am looking for Irena Baratashvili."

The old lady behind the door replied, "No one is here by that name. They left months ago. Go away."

And then there was silence. He knocked again but it was in vain. His heart sunk to a new low. He turned away from the familiar oak door and slowly descended the steps to the street, extremely disenchanted. Not looking back, he continued to his meeting with the gun dealer, walking slowly. The glimmer of hope when he saw the smoke rising from Irena's chimney, and the letdown feeling when he realized that she was not there, took the wind out of his sails, so to speak.

It was beginning to get dark, now the sun had just set in the west. Jack saw the outline of a man standing with his hands in his coat pockets, looking out over the Dnieper River. He called the man by name and Vladislav turned around and smiled.

"You are alone?"

"Yes."

"You have my rubles?"

"Yes," he answered again. "May I see the pistol?"

Vladislav handed the revolver to him wrapped in a cloth. Holding it close to his body with his jacket opened, Jacques inspected the weapon and found it satisfactory. He handed Vladislav the two-hundred rubles and put the wrapped pistol in his inside jacket pocket. Then the dealer gave Jacques a box of cartridges which he slipped into an outside coat pocket. Without another word they turned and went their separate ways.

On January seventh, the tobacco shop was closed for the holiday. It was Christmas Day in the Orthodox Church. Jacques was celebrating the day with Jozsef and Elena in their apartment above the shop. It was just the three of them. They were sitting in Elena`s kitchen talking when they heard a knock on the door of the shop downstairs.

"Now who could that be? I will go and see who it is."

He went down the stairs and a few minutes later, came back up talking to someone with a woman`s voice. It was Dina. She had stopped in the shop several times since Jacques had returned. This time Dina had a Christmas gift for Jacques. It was a wool watch cap that she had knitted herself and a very nice one at that. Jacques immediately tried it on and thanked her for such a thoughtful gift. When Elena found out that Dina was going to spend Christmas day alone, she insisted that she stay for dinner and spend the rest of the day with them, and Dina did.

Jacques spent the rest of the winter preparing for his trek to Georgia. One of the items he needed was an up to date map of the Ukraine. After several hours of inquiring around the city, he found a printer in Podi, the craftsman`s region of the city, that had just what he was looking for. They were military maps printed for the Tsar's Army. He spent long hours studying the maps and deciding on which route to take. He knew that the Dnieper River was not passable. Rumor had it that the river was cluttered with abandoned barges and of course frozen over for the winter. It seemed to him that his best option was to travel overland due south to Odessa. It was over four-hundred kilometers from Kiev and it would take him almost a month to get there. In Odessa, there was a chance that he could find a ship, maybe even a Bek ship, that was headed east on the Black Sea in the direction of Georgia. There was even a chance that the Bek family had returned to Odessa and he would get to see his sister Emile and his new nephew or niece. Emile`s baby was due to be born in the end of July, of the past year. The baby should be six or seven months old by now. These thoughts began to fill his mind with nostalgia for his days in Lausanne and his family and friends there. At last his thoughts turned to Irena. She was the driving force behind him now and he could not wait for this winter to be over.

One of the last items he needed was a warm jacket to replace the tattered one he had picked up in Bari, Italy, three years ago. He transferred the two diamonds that he had left into the lining of the new jacket. Thank God that his belt still contained several of the gold coins that he brought with him from their bank in Lausanne. He needed a warm wool blanket and a waterproof oil skin for bad weather, and a good pair of boots for the long journey. Jozsef recommended a cobbler that he knew that could make him a pair of boots that would compensate for the slight limp that Jacques had from the hand grenade explosion that had broken his leg. He was happy to find out that the new boots did compensate for his limp and made it more comfortable to walk. These items were obtained over the weeks before he left Kiev.

In March of 1918 the Bolshevik Government accepted the dictated peace treaty to end the war with Germany. It was time for Jacques to move on. It was time to leave Kiev and time to find Irena in Georgia. Jozsef and Elena were very sad to see him go. He was almost like the son that they assumed now was lost in the war. Elena gave him a Saint Christopher medal to protect him on his journey, and that brought back memories of his Papa and praying with Monsignore Deruaz in his church back in Lausanne. Jozsef supplied him with enough tobacco to last several weeks. They wished him a safe trip and God speed, knowing that he would most likely never return to Kiev.

CHAPTER TWENTY-TWO

Early one morning in the middle of March, Jacques left the tobacco shop with his backpack. He came across an old man on the outskirts of the city and asked him for directions. The old man gave him directions to go to the farmers market and there he may find a produce wagon going south. Luck was with him. At the produce market, he found a farmer who had just delivered a wagon load of potatoes to the market and was headed south in the direction of Bila Tserkva. Bila Tserkva was at least one-hundred kilometers to the south. The farmer dropped him off at a small town where he could buy a horse.

This horse was not the fastest animal in the world but her endurance was good. She kept up a steady pace. The weather was good, the sky was blue, and Jacques was happy because he was making good time. Many kilometers past Bila Tserkya, Jacques was halted at an Army checkpoint. The soldiers asked where he was going and what his business was. Unfortunately, he had no papers. He had lost his passport before the grenade attack. That lousy Yurovsky took it with his watch and the pistol he had at the time. He explained that he was a Swiss national, and that being, he had a neutral status traveling in the Ukraine. The corporal of the guard post was confused by his statement and did not know what to do with Jacques. He did not look like a spy, so he assigned two privates to escort Jacques to Regimental Headquarters. Before they entered the large military encampment, Jacques questioned his escorts as to what Army they belonged to. They told him that they were with the 3rd Rifle Regiment of the Czech Legion. Jacques was surprised at the great number of tents as far as the eye could see, that were set up in the camp. There must be thousands of soldiers here, he thought to himself.

At the Regimental Headquarters, the two soldiers conferred with a sergeant who in turn went inside the very large tent and re-appeared with a Lieutenant. The sergeant dismissed the two soldiers and the Lieutenant began to question Jacques. Where was he going? Where did he come from?

"Let me begin at the beginning. I came to Kiev to pay a business debt," he began.

Then he told the lieutenant how he went to Odessa and there met his friend Major Moskaleff. They traveled together to Kerch on a Bek ship. He and Dmitry had to return to Kiev but on the way they were detained by a band of Russian Army deserters who threw a hand-grenade at them when they left, killing the Major and badly wounding himself.

"And when was that," asked the Lieutenant?

"That was almost a year ago. And here I am trying to return to Odessa again."

"Wait here," the Lieutenant ordered.

He went inside the tent and returned with a Major. Major Bellinski introduced himself and shook Jacques hand. Then he said, "Please step inside. General Kaledin would like to speak with you."

Jacques did not expect to be interrogated by a General. He was, alas, only a foreign traveler.

Jacques was ushered into the large tent by Major Bellinski and asked to wait. Then the Major disappeared behind a tent flap door. He could hear a quiet conversation going on in the next room but could not make out what they were saying. Several minutes later the Major re-appeared and said, "General Kaledin will see you now."

He followed the Major into the room.

"Please sit," the General said.

It was more of an order than an invitation. The Major stood at attention behind Jacques.

"At ease Major," was the next words from the General.

Then he began to question Jacques.

"What is your name, where are you going and how did you know Major Moskaleff."

"Excuse me, General, may I start at the beginning," Jacques offered?

The General nodded. Jacques went through his story as briefly as he could until he came to the Army deserters and the grenade attack. It was then that General Kaledin became interested in all of the details. Jacques admitted that, had the grenade landed between him and Dmitry, they would both have been killed. He went on to describe the band of deserters and the man that was leading them.

"His name is Corporal Yurovski. He took our horses along with Dmitry`s cap, uniform jacket, pistol belt and sword. He also took our money. He took my watch, pistol, and my passport. That is why I carry no identification papers today."

General Kaledin began, "Thank you Jacques, for the report of Major Moskaleff's death. We had no idea what had happened to Dmitry. He just disappeared. He was a brave soldier. I knew him well. He worked for me in Odessa before he left for Kiev. I had no idea how he was going to get there, so there was no way of tracing his steps. Traveling alone these days is not very good for your health, if you know what I mean. The Russian Army will miss the Major. He was a promising leader. As for the so-called Major Yurovski, we have heard of him and his band of misfits. They have been causing trouble around the Ukraine. Yurovski is a Bolshevik and it is rumored that he commands a unit of the Red Army now. Major, would you escort Jacques to a visitor's tent for the night. Then show him to the Officers Mess for the evening meal. It is the least we can do for a friend of Major Moskaleff. "Dismissed!"

"Thank you General," Jacques said.

"It was my pleasure."

Major Bellinski gave a snappy salute and they left the Regimental Headquarters tent.

It was a short walk to the Officers Mess. Directly behind the large Mess tent, there were several tents for visiting officers. On the way, Jacques questioned Major Bellinski.

"Why are there so many troops here?"

Bellinski answered, "We are waiting for orders to go to the rail head in Smila. From there we go by train on the Trans-Siberian railroad to Vladivostok, then on to the western front to join the battle with the Allied forces in France. Several trainloads of men have been sent, but it is a long journey and there are not enough trains. At least one company has been shipped out, but there are many more to go. We have been waiting here for several weeks now and General Kaledin is very frustrated with these plans. We cannot fight the Germans here on the eastern front because the Bolshevik Government signed a peace treaty with our enemy. Our hands are tied."

"It is an awfully long way to go to get your men to the western front," Jacques commented. "They will have to travel around the world to get to a place two-thousand kilometers west of here. It will take months to move that many troops."

"I know it seems like a ridiculous way to go but it is our only option," Bellinski said with a shrug. "On a much more pleasant note, tomorrow is Sunday and there will be a Roman Catholic mass on the parade field at seven hundred hours, if you would like to attend."

The Major stopped in front of one of the tents, with the flaps tied back and motioned to Jacques that these were his quarters for the evening.

"Your horse is being taken care of and I will return to escort you to our evening meal, but for now, 'duty calls'". Then the Major returned to Headquarters.

The next morning Jacques was awakened by the camp bugle call. He dressed and followed the long lines of soldiers headed to the parade grounds for Mass. It had been a while since he had attended a Catholic Mass. He had been to the Orthodox service many times with Irena, but he had not been to a Catholic Mass since he left Bari, Italy on his way here two years ago. It felt good to hear the service in Latin. He was surprised to see that he was not the only person in civilian clothing. The mass took a long time because of the large number of soldiers receiving communion, it was more than the three priests could handle in a timely fashion. When Mass was over, Jacques found his way back to his tent where Major Bellinski was waiting for him. He gathered his things and followed the Major to where his horse was being kept. Jacques thanked the Major for being such a gracious host and asked him to thank General Kaledin. They wished each other well. Then he mounted up and rode out of the encampment. The sun was shining, the sky azure blue, and Jacques had a full stomach, compliments of the Czech Legion. There was still some snow in places the sun did not touch to melt it away, but the sky was a clear azure blue the color of Irena`s eyes. There were a few puffy white clouds with their little grey bellies aimlessly floating by. It was a beautiful day. There was a new determination in his and the horses stride. He missed the love of his life. But he felt good that he was on his way to see her again.

It was a long way between towns. The wheat fields of the Steppes went on endlessly. The warm sun was melting the winter's frost and it was almost time for the peasants to start plowing their fields. Jacques preferred to seek shelter for the night in a farmer's barn. For a few rubles, he might feed his horse or even get a hot meal. The peasant farms were also a good source of news of what was going on in the area. He did not want to run into the same kind of problem that happened when he was traveling with Dmitry. He may not be lucky enough to survive another incident like that. If a friendly barn was not available, he would seek a wooded area where there was some water and grass for his horse. The protection of the woods was also a better alternative than setting up camp in the open fields, so he plodded on.

CHAPTER TWENTY-THREE

Major Yurovski, as he now called himself, kept busy by recruiting deserters from the Tsar's Army or anyone else that had socialistic views from either side of the war. There were some from the Czeck Legion, Czecks, Slovaks and also a few German, and Austro-Hungarian prisoners of war that joined his ranks. Like Yurovski, most of them were poor peasants or students of Karl Marx. They joined with Yurovski one at a time, or sometimes in groups as large as fifty men. Nikolay Yurovski's numbers grew rapidly. Now that the Bolsheviks had taken over the government of Russia, he had gained the confidence of his men. He promoted most of the men in the small group that he initially started with to Lieutenants, as long as they agreed with him and followed his orders. Those that did not received a bullet in the head. Most followed orders. He needed their loyalty and insisted that they not tell anyone that he was merely a corporal. Actually, he had worked his way up through the ranks to master-sergeant but unfortunately, he had let a prisoner escape from the prison camp in Kazakhstan where he was stationed back in 1908, and he was demoted to private for that minor infraction. Then private Yurovski was immediately transferred from the Siberian Prison Camp to an infantry unit in Murmansk. The transfer and demotion was a blow to his ego as well as a great disappointment. He really enjoyed being a prison guard. It suited his sadistic nature.

Sometime after the escape and Yurovski's transfer, the Commandant of the Prison Camp became aware of the importance of the prisoner who escaped. The escape was a political prisoner. The Commandant paid dearly for his over-sight and the flight from confinement of Leon Trotsky. Yurovski was not alone when they snuck Leon into a garbage can destined for the dumps, but as the man in charge, he was held responsible for the prisoners escape. Before the escape, he had arranged special privileges for his fellow Marxist. He gave Trotsky the opportunity to write his revolutionary papers, and influence other prisoners and guards alike about Karl Marx's revolutionary theories. With the tutoring of Trotsky, he became a true believer in the 'Communist Manifesto', and of 'The Revolution'.

Nikolay Yurovski was born on a farm near the town of Cheboksary on the upper Volga River. His mother was a Mordvin and his father was a Tatar. Both were born into serfdom on a large Manor as was Nikolay and his siblings. As serfs, they were subject to the soil and the will of the Lord of the Manor. Nikolay was a rebellious youth and the object of many beatings by his drunken father or the Lord of the Manor. Whoever got to him first! When he was almost fifteen, he had figured out a plan to leave the Manor for good. If he worked hard and put himself on good behavior, he would gain their trust. Then when an opportunity came, he would steal away and be free. He would go to Moscow and make a life for himself. He was big for his age, and strong enough from the hard work on the farm.

So it happened that he was told to assist in bringing produce from the farm to the market. After several trips, he had familiarized himself with how the market was laid out and formulated a plan for his escape. At the market place, he unloaded the wagon of farm produce almost entirely by himself while the driver and his helper watched. The two men joked about how strong he was and what a stupid child he was. 'All brawn and no brains,' and he saw them laugh at him. They told him to water the horses and feed them while they went for a drink, which he did with full knowledge that his time had come. When the men returned, they told Nikolay to get in the back of the wagon for the ride home to the Manor, as he usually did. He laid down on the open tailgate and pretended to go to sleep. The driver and his helper were engaged in conversation when they approached the gates leading out of the market, and as they passed through the gates, Nikolay slipped off of the tailgate unnoticed and hid behind one of the stone pillars of the gate.

He waited for a fully loaded wagon to leave the market destined for one of the cities up river, knowing full well that it would be going in the opposite direction as the wagon he just got off. He ran behind it, grabbed the tailgate and hoisted himself up far enough as to not be seen by the driver. The teamster drove his truck directly to a dock on the Volga River where Nikolay slipped off and hid among some large crates. Before he left the truck, he grabbed a handful of carrots from one of the boxes he was sitting on. From his hiding place he watched the workers load the produce from several trucks and wagons onto a small barge. He ate a carrot while he watched. Now he had time to reflect on what he had just accomplished. He had just escaped a life of slavery and that bourgeois Nobleman that owned the Manor where he was born. There will be no more brutal beatings by his miserable father. He thought to himself, "I will miss my poor mother, but her life will be easier without me around." Next he thought about how badly the wagon driver and his helper had treated him and how they laughed at his stupidity. Now he realized that the joke was on them, and he almost burst out laughing. When the Lord of the Manor finds out that he is missing a young healthy worker, he will punish them in front everyone and they will be laughed at. This was a very satisfying thought.

It was almost dark when they fired up the steam engine on the barge and a sailor untied the ropes from their moorings. As the barge began gradually pulling away from the dock, Nikolay made a mad dash for the rear of the barge and he jumped. Landing solidly on the stern of the barge, he held on while they moved to the midstream of the river. Then he looked for a place to sleep until they docked. He found a place between the crates of vegetables that suited his purpose as long as it was dark. While lying there in the dark, he realized that his only worldly possessions were the clothes on his back and a handful of carrots.

When the sky began to lighten, he was awake and ready to move. They had been traveling all night to the steady throb of the steam engine. There were only two men on the barge; the helmsman and the sailor who stoked the firebox of the steam engine. Nikolay did not see either of them since he came on-board. The sun was high in the sky by the time they started to pass some houses and buildings along the shoreline. When there were more buildings in sight and a dock off in the distance, the engine began to slow down. Nikolay prepared to disembark. The sailor secured the bow line, and then he came to the stern to secure the barge to the dock. At that moment, Nikolay jumped past the sailor to the dock almost knocking the sailor into the river. The sailor yelled and cursed at him but he was fast enough to disappear before the sailor could recover from the surprise

"What city is this?" Nikolay inquired of the first person he passed on the street?

"Novgorod," was the passing answer he received.

He was hungry. He walked around the neighborhood to get a feel for the town. On one of the side streets there was a bakery with loaves of bread displayed on a board along the sidewalk. The third time he passed the bakery, he stole a loaf and ran. Later that day in another neighborhood when it was getting dark, he observed a wealthy looking old man walking along a main street. He followed the man and when the man neared an alleyway, he slipped his belt off and threw it around the man's neck from behind and dragged him into the alley. Then he punched the man in the side of the head knocking him unconscious. Taking the man's money, he hurriedly left through the alley to a back street. He was lucky. The old man's wallet contained one-hundred twenty-seven rubles. That was enough for him to live on for at least a month. Nikolay had not seen that many rubles in his whole life. That was so easy to do! He could do it again! His father and the Lord of the Manor had taught him well.

He felt conspicuous walking around in this city wearing the clothing of a serf. The next day, he bought some new clothes and a knife to protect him self, or threaten a victim with. He rented a room in a boarding house and made his living for the next few months robbing people, and items from stores, that he could sell. The last attempt at a robbery did not go so well. He almost got caught. Maybe it was time to change his profession. Winter was coming on and it was getting colder. A few days later, he ran into a group of soldiers who were looking for recruits for the Tsar's Army. It was an offer of a warm place to sleep this winter, warm clothes, free food, adventure and respect. They asked how old he was and he told them he was sixteen. Then they signed him up.

Private Yurovski liked the Army. He liked the fact that he was one of many equals. Yes, he had to answer to his superiors but he promised himself that some day he would be a superior. He was tough, and got into his share of fights, but he always seemed to come out of them a winner. That was not because he was the superior fighter, but because he was used to taking more punishment to his body than anyone else could take. He would just outlast his opponent. That came from his conditioning as a youth. He rose to the rank of Sergeant by the time he was twenty-two, but that was before he met comrade Trotsky who was a prisoner in the prison camp, and he was demoted to a private. That was all in the past. Now, he commanded a group of several hundred men who called themselves 'The Peoples Army'. They roamed the countryside burning the Manor Houses of the Nobility, and dividing the land among the serfs who tilled that land. It was the only fair thing to do. All of Russia was going to be a 'Workers Paradise'.

Yurovski and his personal 'Revolutionary Army' had traveled almost a thousand kilometers over the Steppes wreaking havoc among the wealthy land owners. There were many Manor Houses that went up in flames, lots of looting and even a few hangings. His army did not like to waste bullets if it was not necessary. Arms and ammunition were scarce in comparison to the number of men in his company. They traveled a rambling course westward to the Dnestr River in the foothills of the Carpathian Mountains, then went south through the agricultural land of the river basin. Odessa was his final objective.

The numbers of his peasant army grew by leaps and bounds. The group was composed of deserters from whichever army passed through last and serfs from the farms who heard the promise of free land for farmers. Nikolay was becoming charismatic in his espousing of Karl Marx theories, and 'The Revolution'.

"The proletariat will become the ruling class and Russia will become a 'Workers Paradise'. I escaped the slavery of serfdom to join the army where I learned to fight. Now I fight for the rights of the oppressed. Join me and we will fight together against the tyranny of the bourgeoisie," Yurovski would scream to his crowds of followers.

They would respond with loud cheering and chants of, 'Down with the Tsar', and 'On with the Revolution'.

When they advanced closer to Odessa, Major Yurovski decided that it would be wiser to see what the situation was like in the city, so he sent a few of his lieutenants to reconnoiter. They entered the city two at time so as not to be conspicuous, while the rest of the rag-tag Army camped in a wooded area some seventy kilometers to the north. The advanced team reported that the city was quiet but that there was British and French war ships anchored in the harbor with battle-ready troops on board. That put a damper on his grandiose idea of taking the city by storm. He would be a hero if he could take this strategic port for the Bolshevik cause. Now it was decision time and Nikolay knew that he was not experienced enough to make that decision. One piece of information he did not have was whether the telegraph office was open. He sent his closest aid Lieutenant Stepanovich back to find out the status of the telegraph office. Stepanovich returned with the good news that the telegraph office was operating.

Not knowing what to do, concerned him greatly. He could not let his men perceive that he was not the great leader that they were relying on. Nikolay had heard the news that his friend comrade Leon Trotsky had been appointed the People's Commissar of War, and in charge of the Red Army. So he formulated a plan. He would go to the telegraph office himself and boldly send a telegram to his friend Trotsky in Saint Petersburg. He arrived in Odessa with two body guards and Stepanovich, but went into the telegraph office alone. He retrieved a blank message sheet and took Stepanovich aside. He said,

"I have terrible handwriting. Would you write the message for me?" Stepanovich obliged. The message read:

To: Peoples Commissar of War, Leon Trotsky, Red Army Headquarters, Saint Petersburg, Russia.

Message: I am at the gates of Odessa, leading one thousand comrades. Await your instructions.

From: Your good friend, Sargent Nikolay Yurovski

He returned to the office and handed the clerk his message to be sent. The clerk read it and looked at him like he was crazy. Then the clerk asked,

"Do you really want to send this message?"

"Send it!" Nikolay growled with the voice of authority.

The clerk immediately went to the telegraph key and sent the message.

"How long for a reply," Nikolay asked?

"It could take a day or weeks," replied the clerk.

He left the office but stayed in the city to wait for a reply.

CHAPTER TWENTY-FOUR

In Saint Petersburg, now known as Petrograd, The Commissar of War was sitting at his desk in the office of the Red Army Headquarters. His assistant entered the room with a pile of memos and messages for the Commissar to look through.

"Comrade Trotsky, in the pile of messages is a telegram that I almost put in the trash basket, but then I thought better of it. Maybe you can make sense out of it. It came from a Sergeant Yurovski." Then he placed the pile on the desk, and waited. Comrade Trotsky shuffled through the papers until he came to the telegram. His eyes scanned down to the message. It read: *'I am at the gates of Odessa leading one thousand Comrades; await your instructions.' Signed, Sergeant Nikolay Yurovski* Leon thought for a minute, scratched his head and then said to his assistant,

"Yes, I do remember now. Sergeant Yurovski was the one who helped me to escape from the salt mines in Siberia. That was ten years ago. I wondered what had happened to him. Surely he was punished for letting me escape. They stuffed me into a garbage pail from the guard's barracks and sent me to the garbage dumps. Then I just walked away. Yurovski was a devout Marxist. He escaped from a bourgeoisie farm somewhere near the Volga River. He was fifteen when he joined the Army. I do not know how he became a sergeant because he could not read or write. He was a sadistic guard. The only thing that saved me from his wrath was my belief in the revolution, and the fact that I was a 'Political Prisoner'. I would consider Yurovski one of my most loyal and attentive students."

Comrade Trotsky weighed his thoughts. Then he said to his assistant,

"Odessa is a strategic seaport almost out of our reach. It is controlled by our enemy, the White Army. I am sure that they have no idea that Yurovski is within striking distance of their city, with a thousand men. We can take them by surprise. I will formulate a plan but that will take a little more time. Send a telegram off to that telegraph office in Odessa addressed *To: Comrade Yurovski: Message: Promote yourself; you are now the Commanding officer of the Red Army of the south.' Have someone check daily at the telegraph office for further instructions, otherwise stay invisible. Signed: Comrade Trotsky."*

His aid left the room immediately to send off the message.

Red Army Headquarters had a plan in the works for the following week that included several moves that the Bolsheviks had in mind to solidify their power. That plan included an attack in Moscow on the headquarters of the anarchists to relieve them of their power. Leon Trotsky knew the town of Odessa well. He went to school there. If he could arrange for an attack on the Military Attachés Office in Odessa, it would be an additional victory for the new Red Government. The day after the first telegram was sent, there was a second telegram with instructions for Yruovski to capture the Military Attachés Office in Odessa.

A reply came to Yurovski two days after he telegraphed Trotsky. Nikolay was overjoyed when he got the reply from his friend.

"We are now a unit of the Red Army," he told Stepanovich. "You wait here in the city for a telegram with further instructions. You may have to wait several days. Do not return to our camp until Comrade Trotsky sends us our orders."

"Yes major," Stepanovich said with a big smile on his ruddy face.

He was happy to be part of the Bolshevik Revolution and the new order in Russia. He felt that the future held promise for working class people in this great country where he was born. His father was the foreman in a factory outside of Moscow which afforded him a decent education, but he was still one of the working class. When he joined the Army, they sent him to Officers Training and he was a lieutenant when his unit was almost entirely wiped out by the Germans. He and seven other members of his unit retreated to a point where they had no contact with any other Army units. It was then that they stumbled into the camp of Corporal Yurovski and a dozen deserters. Yurovski put up a very convincing argument for deserting the Tsar's Army and becoming a Bolshevik and part of the revolution. So they joined him.

Stepanovich was surprised when he went to the telegraph office the next morning and found a message waiting for him. It read, *To: Yurovski, Message: Attack and hold Military Attachés Office on 12 April, notify when secured.' Signed. Comrade Leon.* The message was concise but he realized that he would save valuable time by reconnoitering before he returned to the camp. Today was the 9th of April. They would need time to plan and organize this operation. He found the location of the Attachés Office and took mental note of the surrounding area, the side streets and which would be the best approach. He stayed for several hours walking the neighborhood and making mental note of the people coming and going from the building. He waited until working hours were over and counted the number of people who exited the building. His officers training had served him well. Then he set out for the encampment. When he reached the place where they had left their horses outside of the city, he found a soldier and two horses waiting for him. They mounted up and rode through the night, arriving at the camp just as dawn was breaking.

The Major was awakened by the sound of horses arriving. He dressed quickly and was met by Lieutenant Stepanovich as he exited his tent. Stepanovich said in an excited voice,

"Major, we have our orders."

"Good," said Yurovski. "Tell me about them."

The Lieutenant read the telegram, knowing full well that his commanding officer could not read. Then he finished his report with all of the details that he gathered after he read the telegram.

"Excellent," said Yurovski. "Can you draw a map of the location?"

His Lieutenant nodded.

"Good then, we will have breakfast and work on a strategy when the light is better."

After they had eaten, Comrade Stepanovich drew a map on the tailgate of one of the wagons.

He said that he believed they could take the Office easily with two hundred men if they went in at the end of working hours.

"Good idea," added Yurovski. "We will have another two hundred men waiting outside the city if we need them. We will enter the city from different directions and in small groups. Make sure that the first strike force and the second strike force are both well armed. I know that we do not have enough arms and ammunition to go around for everyone. The rest of the encampment can break camp and follow us down to Odessa after the strike forces have deployed."

Lieutenant Stepanovich asked for volunteers to be in the two strike forces. There were many who stepped forward. He took only the soldiers who were armed. Then he assigned the other Lieutenants their jobs. Some were platoon leaders and other were assigned to transport the remainder of the forces south to Odessa. The strike force was given their instructions. There were four lieutenants, with 50 men each. Stepanovich, being the highest ranking among the lieutenants, was the leader of the two platoons that were to cover the rear of the building. Major Yurovski was the leader of the two platoons that would cover the front of the building. The primary force traveled south on horse drawn carts while the officers rode horses. The reserve group brought up the rear of the column with the only two machine guns that the company possessed. It was early morning on the eleventh of April when they began their march south.

When they reached a secluded place, where it was suitable for a large encampment, near the outskirts of Odessa, they made camp and reviewed the strategy for the following day. It was decided that the small groups would follow the railroad tracks into the city. They would not be that noticeable traveling along the tree-lined rail route. There were two rail lines entering Odessa. One came in from the north and ran along the coast to the port. The other came in from the west and went directly to the passenger terminal. The majority of the men went in by that route. They took their time as they filtered through the city to the Military Attaches` Office building. The men were all in position before the end of the work day.

There were a few people who left the building early. Comrade Yurovski ordered them followed and killed quietly. When the great majority of the workers began pouring out of the main entrance Yurovski ordered his men to 'Open Fire!' It was a slaughter. When they stopped coming out, he ordered his men to storm the building and kill everyone inside. Stepanovich and his men in the rear of the building became confused. They did not know what was going on until several people tried to escape through a rear exit. His men automatically shot them without his command to fire. By the time the Lieutenant realized what was happening, it was all over, and the building was secured.

In the next few minutes Comrade Yurovski gave orders for several of the men to return to the camp outside the city and return with enough wagons to cart off the dead bodies. He also gave orders to drag out all of the dead and kill the wounded before the wagons arrived. Lieutenant Stepanovich arrived in the front of the building just as his commander was entering the front door.

"You did not follow our plan!" He screamed.

"Calm down Lieutenant, your plan worked perfectly. I just altered a few minor details. These people deserved to die! They uphold the bourgeoisie Nobility that suppresses the workers of Russia. They are our enemy. They are friends of the ones who enslaved me and my family. They beat me unmercifully when I was a child. I have no compassion for them," Yurovski yelled. Your plan would have spared most of these antagonists to fight another day under more favorable conditions for them. Do you understand what I mean?"

The building that they had just taken was a greater victory than Yurovski could have imagined. They found some guns and ammunition stashed in the basement along with other military equipment that Yurovski found useless. There still was not enough guns to equip all of the men in his company. There were direct telegraph lines to Petrograd and to Moscow. After they had taken stock of the situation, Comrade Yurovski gathered his lieutenants for a meeting.

"Comrades, we have done well, but I cannot take the credit for the success of this mission. Comrade Stepanovich, please step forward. This mission was a success due to your careful reconnaissance and planning and I am promoting you to Captain Stepanovich," Yurovski announced. The group clapped loudly in recognition of his promotion.

While the building was being cleaned up from the bloodshed, Yurovski had a telegraph sent off to Commissar Trotsky in Petrograd notifying him of their Red Army's great success. The next job was to go through all of the paperwork that they had inherited and sort out what was important. Captain Stepanovich assembled a team of several of the better educated men to accomplish this task. This job helped him keep his mind off of the slaughter that he had caused by underestimating the brutality of his commander.

CHAPTER TWENTY-FIVE

Jacques knew he was nearing Odessa when he could smell the salt air from the ocean. He guided his horse to a southeasterly direction. When he was nearing the city, he came across a small tidal creek that ran down to the Black Sea. He followed it down to the coast. It was a bright clear day and there was a refreshing breeze blowing off of the water. The salt air felt invigorating although he was weary from his journey. Following the coast line, he looked up and saw the Voronteov Lighthouse in the distance. He entered the city from the north along the coast road. He arrived in Odessa on the afternoon of the 11th day of April, 1918.

It was a short distance from the water front to Stroganouskaya Street where his sister Emile and her husband Yuri`s house was located. Jacques did not expect to find them here. He stabled his horse in the small carriage house behind their house. There was enough hay in the barn to feed the horse, and he pumped fresh water from the well into the trough so the animal could get a drink. Then he found the hiding place in the yard where a key was placed, in case of an emergency. When he entered the house it was just as they had left it almost a year ago. The first thing that he did was prime the pump in the kitchen so he would have water in the house. There was a can of tea leaves and enough dry goods to sustain him for at least a few days. He made a pot of tea on the coal stove. Then he thanked God and Margarette Cogny for teaching him how to cook and bake bread. He mixed up a batch of dough, kneaded it, and set it out to rise, while he heated water for a bath.

He could not remember when he had taken a bath last. Now that he was inside the house, he realized how much he smelled like his horse. A bath would feel great. He placed the dough in the oven, then slipped into the warm bath water and almost fell asleep. It was good to be clean after so many days on the road. After the bath, he put on one of Yuri`s robes and checked the oven. The bread was ready and it smelled delicious. He found several bottles of wine in the cellar and decided that he would make a meal out of what dried meat he had left from his journey, the fresh bread and some wine. When he finished eating, he went right to bed and slept until the next morning. The birds singing outside his open window woke him early.

When he got up the first thing he did was shave off the beard he had cultivated on his month long journey. He left his usual mustache intact but trimmed it to a manageable size. There was a lot he wanted to accomplish today. He needed food. That was his first priority. Next he would check the harbor to see if there were any Bek ships moored in port. Technically, he owned two of them. He should also check on Yuri`s parents house, he thought, and then go to the Military Attachés Office and report the death of Major Moskaleff, in the event that they had not been informed.

After a breakfast of fresh bread and tea he went shopping. The market was crowded and there were long lines but he was patient. He noticed that the people leaving the market were carrying very little bundles. Now he began to appreciate that his sister had left a supply of dry goods in the house; flour, rice, dried beans, yeast, tea, and spices to sustain one person for a few weeks. He was disappointed that he could not get many of the things that he needed, but there was a food shortage and he considered himself lucky to obtain what he did. He returned to the house with his meager groceries, and put them away. Then he went off to check on the Bek`s house. It was on the way to the port. Walking several blocks down tree-lined streets to the Bek home, he noticed that there were several small groups of men carrying guns headed in the opposite direction. Upon inspecting the house, he did not notice any difference from when they left months ago. The windows were dirtier but that was to be expected. He did not have a key so he could not look inside but nothing seemed to be disturbed. Next he walked down the hill to the port. There were no Bek ships tied up to the docks or moored out in the bay. That was very disappointing. There were, however, several French and British war ships anchored further out in the Black Sea. Jacques wondered why they were lurking there.

It was the middle of the afternoon when Jacques headed for the last stop on his mental itinerary, the Military Attachés Office. Two blocks from his destination, Jacques rounded a corner onto the street where the Office was located. He stopped dead in his tracks. There was a man with a Majors jacket and a military hat on his head, and a sword in a scabbard attached to his belt standing with his back to Jacques. The Major was not more than five meters away, looking at a gold pocket watch in his hand that Jacques recognized. It was Yurovski. He was in the process of giving instructions to a group of armed men. Jacques quickly stepped back around the corner and flattened himself against the building. He did not know if the armed men noticed him. Apparently they did not. They were paying strict attention to their leader's instructions. After a few seconds, when no one came after him, he turned and walked quickly away from the scene. Then he ran around the next corner, only to see an unarmed man in a White Army uniform down the street being attacked by three men with guns. Yurovski`s men! He watched from a distance while the Bolshevik soldiers stabbed the man repeatedly and left him to die on the street. He ran away from that part of the city zigzagging through streets until he felt he was safely away from the area. Out of breath he stopped to rest in front of a house with limestone steps that protruded to the sidewalk, for protection. No one was following him.

At the next intersection, he recognized where he was. It was only a few blocks from his sister Emile`s house, where he was staying. Then he heard a volley of shots off in the direction of the Military Attaches Office where he saw Yurovski and his Red soldiers planning for an attack. The cacophony of shots lasted until he reached the house. When he was inside the house, he could no longer hear the gunfire. Did it stop or was it that he could not hear the gunfire from inside the house? He opened a window and listened. The shooting had stopped. Yurovski and his Bolshevik Army had completed their attack on the Attachés Office building. Reflecting on what Jacques had just witnessed, he realized that the Reds were taking over this city now, and he would have to be very careful. He knew what kind of a vicious man Yurovski was.

That night, Jacques shaved off his mustache. Yurovski, or one of his men might recognize him if he fell into the hands of the Bolsheviks. He needed a plan. He packed his saddle bags for a quick escape from the city if it became necessary. Tomorrow morning he would go down to the docks where the fishing boats were tied up and inquire if any of the boats were going east.

Jacques did not sleep well that night. He rose before dawn and left the house. The fisherman usually set out early on their quest for a good catch. There were several of the larger boats preparing to leave before dawn. They were fishermen and seemed to be oblivious to what was going on in the city. Jacques spoke to men on each of the boats only to find that they were all going south for the day and returning to port that night. One of the captains suggested that he go to Illichivsk.

"It is only twenty kilometers south of here. There is a larger boat there that goes out for several days at a time, the 'Viktoriya', and they fish along the Crimea coast."

Jacques thanked him and returned to the house. Before noon he was on his way to Illichivsk. The horse was well rested. But now it did need the exercise. He did not want to ride through the city. Odessa seemed to be filling up with members of the Red Army. He headed north-west through the streets lined with private houses, and away from the inner city. When he reached the outskirts of town, he made a wide circle around Odessa through the outlying farms. Then he turned south toward Illichivsk. As he was approaching a main road into the city from the west, he noticed some Army units marching eastward into town. They were poorly equipped and not very well organized. They must be Bolsheviks. There were two units with several hundred men in each. So, Jacques held his distance until they passed. When they had passed out of sight, he dashed across the road and continued on his way.

When he reached Illichivsk, it was late in the afternoon. He went straight to the docks, but there was no large fishing boat there. He inquired and found that the Viktoriya would be back at the end of this week, and that they did cast their nets off of the coast of Crimea.

"When they return, they stay in port for two days before they return to the sea," said the old man sitting on the docks.

Jacques thanked the old man. Then he looked for a place to spend the night before returning to Odessa.

The next day, he returned to Odessa by the same route he had taken to come to Illichivsk. When he approached the road that came in from the west, there was a variety of trucks going into the city carrying Red Army equipment. They had large red stars haphazardly painted on the sides of the trucks. He entered the city very cautiously and made his way back to the house on Stroganouskaya Street. Then he prepared to leave the next day, after he went to the market.

In the morning he went to the market very early to see if he could buy some dried meat that he needed for the journey. The market was jammed with people trying to buy food. It was not the same as it was two days ago. People were pushing and shoving. Fights were breaking out and the vendors feared for their lives because they were sold out of food as soon as the market opened, but they could not leave. In a few short minutes, Jacques found himself in the middle of the crowd being pushed along. There were shouts and screams coming from the outer perimeter of the market mingled with the noise inside. Then there were shots fired and the noise diminished somewhat. Jacques was tall enough to see above the crowd. There were Bolshevik soldiers, some with guns and some with batons, forcing the people into the crowded market from all sides. Then the soldiers roped off the people inside the market and pointed their guns at the crowd. There were over a thousand people trapped inside the ropes. The shouting and screaming subsided when several more shots were fired into the air. Then a loud voice announced that they would be allowed to leave one at a time and in an orderly manor. Anyone who protested would be shot on the spot. Then the crowd grew silent. Jacques thought that it would take forever for all of these people to leave one at a time. There were exits on three sides of the market and the process went rather quickly.

Jacques did not want to be the first to leave. He held back to observe what the soldiers were doing. They seemed to be checking identifications as the people were leaving. That was a large problem for Jacques because he had none. He also had a small pistol concealed in his belt behind his back, but the jacket covered it well and maybe they would not find it. Before the crowd thinned out too much, he decided to get rid of the pistol. He saw a space under one of the stalls in the market, slowly worked his way through the people around him, bent down to tie his shoe and slid the pistol under the stall. He did not want to be the last one out of the market either. He moved toward the exit, in the middle of a group. When he reached the exit, they asked for identification, which he did not have. Then they hustled him off to join a small group that they were holding for a second interrogation.

This group seemed to consist of merchants and business men. There were no women in the group. Jacques' French accent gave him away as a foreigner. There were two men speaking German. One young man had a French accent. Most of the others were silent and scared. Jacques worked his way through the small group toward the young fellow with the French accent. When he was next to the young man, he whispered in French,

"Why are they holding you?"

The young man was startled at first to hear someone speaking in his native tongue.

"I do not know why they are holding me. I have the proper papers," he replied softly.

"You are French?"

"Swiss," Jacques answered. "Lausanne."

"Paris," the young man said. "I am a dancer at the Odessa Opera Theatre."

Jacques nodded.

"I am here on business but it is a long story."

Their conversation was abruptly stopped by a soldier shouting at then to form a line by two's.

"Follow the Captain. Anyone who steps out of line or talks will be shot. Now march!"

They formed lines of two's quickly and followed Captain Stepanovich.

Jacques immediately recognized the Captain from a year ago. He was one of Yurovski's men when his leg was broken from the hand grenade blast. He also realized where they were going. They were headed to the Attachés Office which in all probability was now Red Army Headquarters. When they reached the building, they were ushered onto a large room in the basement.

There were twenty-seven of them in this basement room with one large steel door. There was a sink and a toilet in one corner of the room. A single electric bulb that dimly lit the room hung from the ceiling. The room had a high ceiling and three small openings up close to the ceiling for ventilation. The openings were too small for a man to get through. On closer inspection, there were iron bars imbedded in the concrete closer to the outside of the basement wall to discourage anyone from trying to get in or out. All of the men in the room were of a young age and it appeared from the way that they were dressed that most of them were upper class business men. In better times, Odessa welcomed foreign traders but with the revolution in progress many had gone back to their respective homelands. Some of the streets in the city were attributed to the city's openness; Italianskiy Street, Frantsuszkiy Street, Grecheskaya Street, Evreyskaya Avenue (Jewish), and Arnautskaya Street (Albanian)

After the door had slammed shut, the young Frenchman came over to Jacques. He had dark hair, high cheekbones and a muscular body. He introduced himself.

"I am André Basic."

"Jacques Vesery."

And they shook hands.

"Do you think they are going to kill us?" André asked?

"If they had intensions of killing us, we would be dead by now." Jacques confided.

"Then why do you think they are holding us here," André asked?

"I do not know, but if we ask these other men, we may come up with an answer," Jacques suggested.

"Good idea," André agreed.

CHAPTER TWENTY-SIX

In the dimly lit basement room, that seemed to be an empty magazine, Jacques held up his hand and called for the attention of the other men in the group. When he had the attention of the other men he asked,

"Does anyone know why they picked us out to be held for further questioning?"

Then he asked the same question in German, Italian, Greek, and Arabic. Now he looked at all the men and determined that he had the attention of everyone.

"Good. I have had some experience with the commander of this Red Army unit. A year ago, my friend and I were captured by Major Yurovski and his men on our way to Kiev. We had our hands tied behind our backs and were sitting on the ground. When he left, he threw a hand grenade at us and left us there in the road for dead. I was lucky. My friend Major Moskaleff took the brunt of the explosion, and was killed. A farmer found me and patched me up. Now I walk with a limp. Major Yurovski was a corporal who deserted from the Russian Army. He only became a major because he stole my friend's jacket and cap along with my watch. Yurovski is a ruthless man.

"I know how ruthless he is," a fellow captive said. "I saw it with my own eyes. I was looking out the window across the street from this building when they captured it. They shot the unarmed people coming out of the building in cold blood. When the shooting was over, they killed the wounded and piled the bodies on lories and took them out of the city to be buried,"

Several of the other men told stories of the attack by the Red Army. Some told of killings in the streets and others said they saw the lories leaving town piled high with bodies. Jacques thanked them for their comments. Then he said,

"I was born in Switzerland. My family has a wheat trading business and I came here on business. If we share our stories, we may come up with the reason we are all prisoners."

A Man who spoke with a different accent said he had been in the German Army.

"I am Polish but I was a conscript into the German Army. I became a prisoner of the Russians, but I escaped and found my way to Odessa."

André added,

"I am from Paris, but I could not return because of the war."

Then the others came forward one by one. Hraird was a young Armenian whose parents sent him to Odessa from Constantinople because they feared that it was not safe for Christians to remain in Turkey. There was a Romanian Jew who had a business in Odessa. There were several Greeks, Italians, and Germans in the group. They were all prisoners of the Bolsheviks.

Then Jacques took it upon himself to summarize the situation for the group.

"We are all of fighting age and it seems that we are all foreign born. Is that correct? There is no one here who seems to be an invalid. Is there anyone here who has broken the law?"

They all looked at each other and shrugged. One man said,

"It seems that we are all upstanding citizens."

That brought on a chuckle from some of the men.

"Then why are we here?" others asked.

"I don't know," Jacques said. "We will have to wait and ask our captors."

It had been dark outside for some time before they heard a noise at the entrance. The heavy metal door was opened. Two men with rifles came through the door first. The next person to enter the room was Captain Stepanovich.

"All prisoners against the wall" he shouted!

The prisoners moved quickly to the walls for fear of being shot by the two guards.

"You are all bourgeoisie foreigners," the Captain announced. "You are all enemies of our new revolutionary government. You will be held here as prisoners in this empty magazine until we receive further instructions on what to do with you."

Then another soldier came in with a sack with nine loaves of stale bread and threw them on the floor.

When the door slammed shut, there was a mad dash for the loaves of bread in the middle of the large room. These men had not had anything to eat since this morning before they went to the market. An Italian man was the first to reach the loaves. As he picked up the closest loaf from the floor, a burly Greek kicked him in the ribs sending him sprawling across the room. The Greek grabbed the loaf that the man dropped, and announced,

"This one is mine!"

Jacques yelled, "STOP! There is enough bread for everyone if we divide the loaves equally."

Jacques noticed that the Greek was very large and looked like a bull elephant.

"Who made you boss?" the burly Greek yelled.

"In all fairness, we should divide the bread equally. We are all hungry, and we are all in here together," Jacques replied in a subdued voice.

Then the Greek stepped up to Jacques, and yelled,

"I am the boss here. Not you."

He was a few centimeters shorter than Jacques, but outweighed Jacques by at least forty-five or fifty kilograms. His arms were thicker than Jacques legs. He looked like he might have been a weight lifter. With one hand, he shoved Jacques, knocking him down unexpectedly. When Jacques hit the floor, he quickly rolled to his right and sprung to his feet while the burly man charged like a bull. Jacques side stepped and hit him with a hard right to the head. This infuriated the Greek. In the exchange, he shot a hard right to Jacques ribs, and grabbing his left arm, the powerful man spun Jacques around and hit him in the face with a left hook. The blow stunned Jacques for a second. Groggy, he stumbled back as the group made room for the two men that were fighting. The big man charged again. There was another blow to the ribs and Jacques heard a crack. He knew that he could not let the Greek hit him in the ribs again. Jacques had one advantage on his opponent. His reach was almost ten centimeters longer than the husky Greek. His only chance of survival was to keep the Greek at a distance

Jacques backed away, then faked a left and landed a right square on the Greeks nose. Blood streamed down his face. He put his head down and charged again using his head like a battering ram. Jacques seized the opportunity, pushed the bulls head up with a straight right arm extended, and brought a left uppercut blow to the man's jaw. The Greek stood up straight with a dazed look in his eyes, dropped his arms to his sides and fell backward to the floor, as a cheer rose from the other prisoners. He was out cold. Jacques went over to the small sink in the corner of the room and washed the blood from his face and hands.

"Someone throw some water on his face and wake him up."

They were hesitant, but one of his compatriots filled the bucket and poured it on the prone mans face. He awoke dazed and beaten, but said nothing and went to the far corner of the room to sulk. André and the Polish soldier collected the loaves of bread and divided them equally among all of the other prisoners, including the Greek with the bloody nose.

Jacques looked to heaven and quietly thanked God for not letting him get killed and his father for giving him and his brother boxing lessons.

André said,

"That was some fight. I thought the Greek was going to kill you. You have a bad bruise on your right cheek."

"That's not the worst of it. He broke a couple of my ribs," Jacques announced.

"Maybe so, but he looks worse off than you do," André laughed.

The next morning, two more prisoners were brought to the room. Jacques determined that it was not good to have an enemy in these confined quarters. So he went to his opponent and offered him his hand.

"It is not good to be enemies while we are prisoners here. We may have to endure this cell and the people in it for some time, so we may as well be friends. It is our mutual enemy, the Bolsheviks who are keeping us here."

The Greek came to his feet and accepted Jacques hand.

"You are right. My name is Castor. You are a good fighter for a skinny man."

Jacques laughed and then cringed.

"You hurt me worse than what I did to you. You broke some of my ribs."

"Good," said Castor. "Now we are even for destroying my beautiful Greek nose."

And he laughed.

Some days later the guards announced that the prisoners would be allowed out for some air for a half-hour. They were taken out six at a time throughout the day to a fenced area in the rear of the building. It was good to feel the warmth of the sun for a change. Castor, the weight lifter suggested that they all needed exercise.

"We must keep ourselves strong," he said.

He organized a workout program, and most of the men were happy to join in. Time passes slowly when there is nothing to do.

They sat around in groups telling stories. Jacques mentioned that today he would have been boarding the 'Viktoriya', a fishing boat that was sailing out of Illichivsk bound for the Crimea. His final destination was Georgia and his fiancée, Irena. André told amusing stories of his childhood and delivering groceries in Paris on his bicycle. Then others began to join in with interesting antic-dotes from their childhood or their country of origin. Jacques translated for those who did not speak the language that the story was being told in.

"I am Polish" Alexander began. "I was born in a small town near Brest-Litovsk on the River Bug. Alexander means fisherman. My mother was an admirer of Alexander the Great, so she named me after him and my fathers name was Henry Rybak so that is where I got my name. Because Alexander means fisherman, I was intrigued by the river that ran not far from our little village. Two kilometers separated the village from the River Bug which was the border between Poland and Russia. As enticing as it was, it was very dangerous. But what do eleven year old boys know about danger? So one spring day, a group of us decided to take a look at the River Bug without telling our parents. They had forbidden each and every one of us from going to the river. Well, you know that boys will be boys. So off we went through the thick forest till we came to the river bank. It looked peaceful enough. Why were our parents so emphatic about us not going to the river? As we were walking along the narrow river bank, we noticed some men on the other side. With a closer look, we realized that they were Russian soldiers. They were sitting in a grassy place smoking cigarettes and talking among themselves. At first, they didn't notice us. But when one of my friends shouted to them, they immediately jumped up and started shooting at us; real bullets! Thanks to God that they were not expert marksmen. Several bullets thudded into the river bank beneath our feet and some went buzzing over our heads. We immediately dove for the cover of the forest! Then we ran as fast as our legs would carry us away from the River Bug and the Russian soldiers. We knew that the Russians would not cross the river into Poland to follow us. Their rifles became silent, but we kept on running until we were a safe distance from the river. When we regrouped we realized that my best friend Franz was not among us. A group of men from the village returned to the river cautiously where we told them we had been. They found Franz. He had been shot and killed by the Russian soldiers. It was a costly lesson for us boys. I missed my friend Franz."

"Being Polish, many of the young men in our village were conscripted into the German Army and sent for extensive training before the war began. Then mobilization rosters were posted all over Germany. They appeared in newspapers and in public buildings in every city and village. Millions of reservists arrived at our training camp. Just as we were, they were issued field grey uniforms, "Pickelhauben" spiked leather helmets, and new Mouser rifles out of boxes straight from the factory. After a few weeks of training, they paraded us through several towns with marching bands. The German populace cheered for us. They were eager for us to go to war. I was not ready to die for the Kaiser or the pride of Germany but we had no choice."

"In August of 1914, the battle for the city of Tannenbourg was under way. Our German forces were advancing rapidly toward the city in fierce combat against the Russian troops. We were far superior to the poorly trained Russian soldiers. Tsar Nicholas sent them to fight a war with not much ammunition and hardly any supplies. As we advanced through potato fields, and scattered wooded lots, we came upon rows of trenches that the Russians had deserted in their hurry to retreat. Smoke was rising from every village in our path. The Russians were burning everything as they retreated. They left what little artillery they had and several dead horses that looked like they had starved to death. It was a sickening sight. The smell was not nice either. In one of the trenches, we discovered a Russian soldier who was trying to hide rather than retreat. He was only a peasant boy of, possibly fourteen. He was scared to death, filthy, hungry and out of ammunition. My lieutenant ordered me to take the prisoner back to Colonel Hoffman at headquarters and be back in five minutes. Headquarters was twenty-five kilometers away. The boy looked so pathetic that I gave him some of my rations and when he had finished, I shot him in the head. Then I threw up. I can still see his face when I close my eyes. God forgive me." Alexander placed his hands together and looked to heaven for forgiveness."

"Several weeks later, I was captured by a new Russian offensive near the Masurian Lakes. We were marched east for two days. When we reached a railroad line, we were herded into cattle cars to be sent to the Ukraine. By the time we reached our destination, many of the wounded had died. We were told to take the bodies with us, and a short way from the rail stop we were handed shovels and told to bury them in shallow graves. Before our march to the prison camp began, they gave us some stale bread and water to share. There were not many guards and most of those had vodka in their canteens. So as the kilometers passed, the prisoners began to slip away, one at a time; those who had the nerve. I slipped un-noticed into the woods at a bend in the road and hid until nightfall. When I awoke, it was pitch black and with only the stars to guide me, I wanted to get away from the war and the intolerable cold weather of the Russian winter. So I wandered for days in a southerly direction until I found the Dniestr River and followed it down to Odessa. Now here I am a prisoner once again."

CHAPTER TWENTY-SEVEN

André had mentioned that he had a girlfriend in Naples. He had her picture in the breast pocket of his shirt that he had shown to Jacques and some of the other prisoners when they were sharing about their loved ones. The other men teased him about having a girlfriend so far away. Eli coaxed him,

"Tell us about this pretty Neopolitan girlfriend of yours."

So Andre told his story.

"When the Thasos, the ship I was working on, arrived in Naples, the captain asked me to go to the telegraph office to send a message to the ships home office in Athens. I went ashore. It was easy to get directions to the telegraph office even though my Italian vocabulary was very limited. As I entered the Ufficio Telegramme in Naples, I was surprised that the clerk was a very pretty girl with long black hair. It was a small office and I was the only customer. I tried to start a conversation but the girl was reluctant to talk to a sailor. Nice girls just do not trust sailors. I think that it was my warm smile and the awkward use of the language that won her over. I tried to explain that I was really not a sailor. 'I am artist, I said, 'a ballet dancer' and I gave her a shy smile. This young lady did not believe me but I was sure that she did like me a little from the way she smiled back at me. I told her I would like to visit the Opera House in Naples, but I did not know the name of it or the location.

'Ah yes, the Teatro di San Carlo. I know where that is,' she replied. 'Would you take me there?' I asked boldly?   'That would not be proper because I do not know you,' she replied.

As she went about the business of preparing the telegram to be sent, I tried to introduce myself. 'My name is André Basic and I am from Paris.' 'That is very nice, André from Paris, but my father will not be so pleased with me talking to a perfect stranger about anything other than the business of the telegram. My father manages this telegraph office and he is in the back room with my mother. It is his lunch hour. That is why I am tending to the office' she said.

"I do not know where I got the courage to ask if she would call her mother and father to the desk, so that I may ask permission to talk to their daughter." She laughed, hesitated for a few moments, and then she turned and knocked on the door to the back room. The door opened slightly and it was apparent that it was her mother that answered the knock. She whispered something to her mother, the door closed and she returned to the counter where I was standing. Later in the day, she said that she told her mother that there was a cute Frenchman in the office that wanted their permission to talk to her. There was a pause and then her mother came into the office followed by her father. They looked me up and down, and then the mother smiled at me. I said to them, 'I am André Basic and I would like your permission to talk with your daughter'. The mother looked at the father, said something in an Italian dialect, 'parlare', he nodded to his daughter and they returned to the back room, but left the door open. 'Well, my parents approved of me talking to you,' she said. 'I am Signorina Antoinette Bassolino and I live in Naples.' She laughed. 'Ah! Now that we are old friends' I said. 'Will you have lunch with me?' Antoinette thought for a moment, than she replied, 'No, but I will ask my parents if I may invite you to have lunch with us in the garden behind the office if you like'

"This was not exactly what I had in mind, but Antoinette was so beautiful that I could not turn down the opportunity to be in her company, even if we had to have her parents as chaperones. I had lunch with them in the garden, and her parents were very hospitable. They had a platter of assorted cheeses, salami and prosciutto with Italian bread and homemade red wine."

Eli broke in,

"Enough! Enough talk about food and wine here in this dungeon where we have none. Right now I would kill for a glass of good red wine. Now continue your story without the talk about food." André smiled, and continued,

"I enjoyed the lunch as much as I enjoyed the company. After lunch, her parents Raphael and Anna left us alone, but in plain view to chat in the garden. While I was with her, I had no thoughts of returning to the Thasos. I really wanted to visit the Teatro di San Carlo but I also wanted to spend time with Antoinette, and prove to her that I was a dancer, not a sailor. So, I proposed that she take me there to see the opera house that evening. It was agreed that she, and her mother, would be my guide for this evening."

"The Teatro de San Carlo was only a kilometer away from the telegraph office. It was a pleasant walk on this beautiful evening, and the company was even better. Anna, her mother, walked a few paces behind us. She could not hear all of the conversation, but I think she was enjoying the stroll. Half of our conversation was in French which her mother did not understand. As luck would have it, the theatre doors were all open to let in the cool evening air. There was someone playing music on a piano and there were several dancers rehearsing on the stage. When the three of us walked down to the first row of seats and sat, the piano player and the dancers stopped. I had a lengthy conversation with the dancers. Then they invited me to join them on the stage. I asked the woman playing the piano to play a piece from the Ballet 'Coppélia'. I did some movements with one of the young dancers. Then, with music playing, I danced the part of 'Franz' with the ballerina, which impressed Antoinette and her mother. They realized that I was not telling them a tall story. After I had thanked the piano player and the dancers for obliging me, we left the theatre. On the way home, I obtained Antoinette's address and permission to write her. Then I made Antoinette a promise to write as soon as I arrived in Odessa."

"Late that evening, I returned to the Thasos. The first person to greet me was Captain Constantine. He said 'Where have you been sailor? Did you travel to Rome to send that telegram or did you deliver it personally to the office in Athens? It's a good thing that we are waiting here with nothing to do until we sail. Or, we could have sailed without you.'

"I told him that I met a girl, and was detained. He said, 'You Frenchmen, always with the girls. You probably would have liked it if we did sail without you, but you know it is a long walk to Athens! Now get below. Tomorrow is another day' he scolded me."

"The next day came and there was still no work to do on the ship. So, when the Captain saw me, he told me to go ashore and find my new girlfriend. That suited me just fine. I went and had a very nice day with my Antoinette, under her parent's supervision, of course. She gave me her picture and promised to write to me. The next morning we loaded the ship and sailed for Athens."

Hans asked, "Do you still write to each other? How long has it been since you have seen your Antoinette?"

"It has been three years, but I receive letters every week, and I write to her every week," André answered.

Then Eli chided, "You better go back to Naples before she becomes an old lady."

Hans, the German soldier said, "I have not seen or heard from my girlfriend in five years. She is probably married with three children by now. At least you get letters from your Antoinette. I was with an artillery unit of the German Army. My unit was stationed in Sofia with stand-by orders. We were there to protect our ally. I was sent to Sofia as an advanced unit in 1913 to train the Bulgarian Army in the use of our latest artillery weapons. Toward the end of the war, the Bulgarian Army had been annihilated, the country was being over-run by refugees, and there was a severe food shortage. Their Government did nothing to help the situation. I could see that a revolution was brewing and I did not want to be caught up in it. By the end of March, I decided to defect from my unit and seek refuge with some of my distant cousins who had settled in the country-side somewhere north of Odessa. I knew that there were several German communities in that area. When I arrived in Odessa, I was surprised to find that the Bolshevik Government's control had reached this far south. I went to the market that morning to buy food for the trip north to find some of my family, and here we are."

CHAPTER TWENTY-EIGHT

Some weeks later, at the Red Army Headquarters in Odessa, a message was received from Commissar Trotsky`s office in Petrograd, on how to proceed with the prisoners. The message read: *To: Major Yurovski, Message: All foreign prisoners are to be shipped by train to Kharkiv, and then on to your old duty station in Kazakhstan. Signed: Commissar's Office, Red Army Headquarters, Petrograd*

This was a very surprising order. It created a large problem now for Major Yurovski. In the days when his private army roamed the great expanse of the Ukraine, he and his band of deserters had taken it upon themselves to blow up several sections of the railroad tracks that went north and west from Odessa. Destroying the rail road tracks facilitated the robbing of several trains with much needed supplies for his renegade troops. Now he would have to deliver his prisoners to a rail station more than two-hundred kilometers to the north. There were thirty-one foreign born men between the ages of seventeen and forty-five being held in the empty basement magazine.

"We need a plan," Major Yurovski said to his Captain.

"What we need to do is transport them away from the city on lories. Then they can walk the rest of the way north to a working railroad," advised Captain Stepanovich.

"Very good," said Yurovski! "Get it organized. Take forty men to guard them with a machine gun on a lorrie. Requisition supplies for your men and get enough horses for your men to ride. Do not forget enough rope to tie the prisoners together for the journey."

"Comrade Major, do you want me to lead the mission?"

"Nyet, I need you here with me. Find a trusted Lieutenant to carry out the job. Oh yes, one more thing Comrade Stepanovich, find any men who worked for the railroad and see if we can get the tracks repaired that we damaged in our tour of the Ukraine. It will make us look bad if the Red Army has no way of sending us supplies. I do not want to loose favor with our superiors, if you know what I mean. Give them enough laborers with shovels to fill in the holes. Put someone reliable in charge of the operation and give them trucks for transportation. Yes, and tell the man in charge to use rails from side tracks to replace the ones that we damaged. We need the main rail road lines open for our use."

"Yes, Comrade Major, I will take care of that also. I commend you for your foresight." Stepanovich replied.

Captain Stepanovich took two days to prepare the two missions. He ordered Comrade Subottin to take charge of the mission involving the prisoners. Together they requisitioned horses, a wagon, a machine gun, ammunition and supplies for his men. When the prisoners were being herded onto the lories, Eli whispered to Jacques,

"These trucks belonged to me a few months ago but they did not have big red stars painted on the sides like they have now. I bet that they were taken from the people I sold them to. Then Jacques said, "I hope you got paid for them."

"Oh, yes", was Eli`s quick reply.

The prisoners were driven ten kilometers outside of the city, where the Bolsheviks ordered the prisoners to form a column by twos. They tied a rope around each of the prisoner's waist, and then they tied each prisoner to the man behind him, spaced two meters apart, so that the group of prisoners were all tied together. Orders were given that anyone found with their ropes untied would be shot on the spot.

They marched for several days before one of the prisoners raised his courage enough to attempt an escape. He was shot and buried in a shallow grave close to the road. The group traveled in close proximity to the railroad tracks, even though there was no train traffic on this line. The tracks had to lead to an operating railroad station somewhere, hopefully sooner than later. One soldier rode ahead to assure that the group did not wander too far from the direction that the tracks were heading.

One day, the scout returned early in the day to report that he heard that the Czech Legion had mutinied against the Bolshevik regime and was headed east to join forces with the White Loyalist Army. Comrade Subottin did not relish the thought of running into the Czech Legion. They must proceed cautiously, but that will slow them down considerably. He did not like this situation.

Their next obstacle was a rain storm that lasted for three days. By mid afternoon of the first day of torrential rain, they came across a large deserted barn to hold up in. The barn was part of a Manor that they had destroyed some months before. All that was left of the Manor House were three charred up-rights standing in a pile of ashes. The prisoners were tied up securely in the loft while the soldiers waited for the rain to stop. The well deserved rest was welcomed by all, but Comrade Subottin who was not very happy with this assignment to begin with. The journey seemed to be dragging on with no end in sight. He had no idea when they would arrive at an operating railroad station to deliver his prisoners.

Comrade Subottin was a factory worker from Moscow, like his father before him, a member of the 'Proletariat'. Actually he was a lowly paid machinist apprentice when he was drafted into the Tsars Army. He was a private when he deserted the Army during a battle that was not going well for his side. They were out of ammunition and food. How can an Army run on an empty stomach? He had holes in his shoes and his uniform was in tatters. He hardly looked like a soldier.

Subottin was seventeen when the Army called him. Now he was twenty-one and not really qualified to be a Lieutenant in the Red Army. It was only by virtue of being a member of Yurovski`s original group that he achieved his rank. He was of stocky build, not too tall, but he was literate. That made him a favorable choice for Lieutenant in this Red Army. There was no love lost on these upper class prisoners. He would rather shoot them all and return to Odessa.

When the rain stopped they moved on. The roads were muddy, and there were places where they had to detour around flooded areas. Now some of the prisoners were sick from exposure to the wet weather and a lack of nourishing food. Occasionally, they camped on farmland where sugar beets were growing, and it was near harvest time for the beets. The prisoners were allowed to pull up the beets and eat them directly from the soil, raw. The weaker prisoners that could not keep up were shot. Their numbers were dwindling.

On their twenty-third day, they came to a large burned out Orthodox Church that was deserted. It was another casualty of the revolution. It had been stripped of all religious articles, and most of the stained glass windows had been blown out. A small portion of the front roof had been blown off from a mortar shell, but the remainder of the roof and the stonework were intact. The three-hundred year old Church was a little more than a kilometer away from a small town. It was solidly built with thick stone walls and was an ideal place to keep the prisoner detainees without too much effort on the part of the guards. Inside and out, the building was charred with black streaks, where the fire had scorched it. Most of the pews and woodwork were destroyed, but the flames could not quite reach the high ceiling beams or the roof. There was a large sacristy behind the alter that was large enough to house all the remaining prisoners. The sacristy had a door leading outside to the garden and the adjacent cemetery.

The cemetery and garden were completely walled in by a thick stone wall that could not be seen over by the average man. The cemetery had one large heavy solid wooden gate in the front, not far from the entrance to the Church to allow a wagon through for burials. The prisoners were ushered into the sacristy and both the doors to the alter and the door to the garden were barricaded and guarded by an armed sentry.

Subottin decided that this was a good place to stay while two men were sent ahead to find a railroad station rather than wandering with his men and the detainees, hundreds of kilometers without a destination. There was also the prospect of losing more of the prisoners, not to mention some of his own soldiers. Seven of his men had disappeared already. The scouts were ordered not to return until they found a railroad station that was in service. Several days passed, and two more men were sent out on horseback with the same orders. It was several days before the second scouting party returned with the news that the nearest station was seventy to eighty kilometers to the north-east of where this church was located.

Meanwhile, the prisoners who were still alive had nothing to do but complain about their situation, or tell stories about their experiences in life. These were the lucky ones. At least they were still alive to complain. Almost half of their fellow prisoners had not made it this far. It was 'survival of the fittest.' Then there were some who chose to escape knowing that they would be shot. They felt that death from a bullet in the back was better than going to the salt mines to die slowly.

They talked about their wives and girlfriends. A few of the men had children. They all worried that their families had no idea where they were, or may be targets for punishment, as they were. They were hoping that the word spread of their capture and interment. Some of the wives dared to stand outside the Headquarters building in Odessa and call their husband's names. Those men answered their wives and said that they were still safe, through the small openings high on the magazine walls. Several of the wives returned daily to call the name of their man to ascertain that they were still there. Now they would have to know that the prisoners had been taken way.

The Italian, Eli, mentioned that he had six children.

"My wife came every day to the prison to call my name. She will be lost without me. My wife is a Ukrainian girl. I hope that her family will help her. Our youngest is not a year old and I hope that she is not pregnant. Seven would be a very unlucky number for her and the children with no man to support them. I would hope that she will take the children and go somewhere safe, like Italy. I have enough relatives there that she knows would take care of her and the children for me. Unfortunately, I know that she will not seek help because, her family is here."

From their comments, the others were all surprised that this boyish looking Italian had that many children. His answer was,

"I know what you are all thinking. I can afford that many children because I make a lot of rubles." They joked about his answer, but it only enhanced their curiosity.

"What do you do for a living?" Daniel asked. Eli hesitated. He looked around and said in a whisper,

"I am a gun dealer. I sold Italian arms to the White Army. Please do not tell these Bolsheviks. They will show no mercy."

"Our lips are sealed," Daniel said.

They all nodded in agreement.

"Some people have interesting lives," Daniel said. "My business is boring. What I did before the revolution was import coal from my wife Minda is native Romania. I brought in trainloads of brown coal, lignite, for the furnaces of Odessa until the Bolsheviks blew up all of the rail lines coming into the city. I have a daughter. She is thirteen. My wife and I sent her back to Romania to live with her grandmother last year. We thought she would be safe there but who knows. It is just not safe anywhere these days."

Later, Eli confided in Jacques that the room adjoining theirs at the Military Attachés building contained a large amount of arms and ammunition that he had delivered personally, a short time ago.

"They are concealed behind crates of useless military equipment. I have to assume, from the looks of the guns our guards are carrying, that they have not bothered to look behind the crates that are stacked in front of all the new guns It was wise of the White Army Officer to hide them in that manner. These Bolsheviks are too lazy to look behind the front rows of crates."

"Yes," Jacques commented. "And they probably killed the White Army Officer without thinking of interrogating him first."

Castor, the Greek, was angry to be a prisoner. He could not wait to get even with these Bolshevik bastards. There was not one of them who were a match for him in a fight. But, they had guns. He would wait for his opportunity to strike back.

He said that he was not married. He had no time for a woman in his life. He was always training.

"I am on the Greek National Olympic Team," he said proudly. "I am a weight lifter and I do the shot-put. I have a gold medal back home in Athens that I won at the 1912 games in London, England, to prove it."

This was an interesting subject and the other men had all kind of questions to ask Castor about the games. This discussion lasted for hours. When the discussion about the games was over, someone asked about the women in England.

Castor said, "The women in London are beautiful. They are all fair skinned like alabaster dolls."

Then he related some stories of his adventures in the houses of ill-repute. They all had a good natured laugh. Jacques admitted that he had been to London when he was sixteen.

"My father took me there on a business trip. I was a rambunctious adolescent. He took me to a house of prostitution and told the 'Madam' that he wanted his son to be bred."

There was roar of laughter from the listeners.

"He told me to choose the girl I would like to be with. When I picked a young red-haired Irish girl, my father said that I should pick another because she was taken. Then another older woman stepped forward, took me by the hand and led me off to her room for my first experience with a woman."

There were many comments and questions, and that discussion went on for some time also.

CHAPTER TWENTY-NINE

The remaining inmates being held in the Church sacristy found that it was better to sit around, talk and share stories, rather than to feel sorry for themselves or think about what they did not have, or the fate that awaited them. The discussion on that day started with automobiles. Hraird mentioned that his parents allowed him to buy a motorcycle when they sent him off to live with his mother's cousin in Odessa.

"I left it outside the market on the morning that we were taken prisoner. I wonder if it is still there after all these weeks."

"Why did your parents send you to Odessa?" someone inquired. Hraird answered, "In 1915, the Turkish Government was systematically eliminating all aliens from their country. They considered all Armenian and Greek people to be aliens, even though they were born in Anatolia. Their rules were a little less stringent in the European portion of Turkey than they were in Asia Minor, but my parents were worried that they would find out that half of my blood is Armenian, and that I am a Christian. I am not sure if the motorcycle was a bribe or a consolation prize to leave my home in Constantinople to live in Odessa. My mother's cousin has two daughters that are several years younger than I am, and now I feel like they are my sisters. My mother is Armenian but she feels safe because my father is Egyptian. Both my parents are Christians. My father is Coptic Orthodox. Our sir name is Habash, which is Arabic, meaning 'The wise one'. My parents pray at home but they do not openly practice their religion for fear of being ostracized from the business community. They own a shoe store in the Egyptian Market in Constantinople. I bought the motorcycle used. It was a 'Trusty Triumph' that was made for the Army in England. I do not know how it ended up here but when I found it, I bought it. It ran very well and I was able to tinker with it to keep it going."

Jacques decided to add his motorcycle story to the conversation.

"My father bought me a Triumph also when I was fifteen. As soon as I learned how it worked, I took it for a ride up into the mountains. I was fearless and ran it at full speed, up and down hills and on the winding roads, with the wind in my face. I was enjoying the ride. When I was high up on a mountain pass the road in front of me took a sharp turn. At the speed that I was going, I was headed over the cliff, so I put the cycle down on its side and slid across the gravel while the machine went over the cliff. I heard it crash on the rocks below. I lay on the gravel near the edge of the cliff for quite a few minutes before I attempted to move. I could not tell how badly I was injured. My clothing was all ripped to shreds on the side that slid across the gravel, and I was bleeding, but I was alive. I had to walk about twenty kilometers to get home, all bruised up, and without the motorcycle. The only thing that I could think about was that my father was going to kill me when I got home."

Castor said laughing.

"You are still alive so I guess your father did not kill you."

They all had a good laugh from that story.

Daniel gave his account of an incident in his life that was not very pleasant He compared that incident to what they were experiencing now.

"I was born in a small Jewish farm community in the Ukraine. I met my wife in Chisinau. She is Romanian and her family is in the coal business, which is why I have been living in Odessa. The story that I am going to relate happened when I was ten years old. As I am sure you all know, Jews had no rights under the Tsar. We lived in a small out of the way village and kept to ourselves. One afternoon, a Cossack, one of the Tsars private army came prancing through our village on his big black stallion. The old man who lived across the street was almost run down by the Cossack. I was looking out the window, and saw the whole thing happen before my eyes. To me, it looked like the Cossack was trying to run the old man down. The old man jumped out of the way and cursed at the Cossack, who immediately reared his horse, drew his sword and sliced the old man's head off. The old man's headless body stood there for a moment before it collapsed to the ground. My father pulled me away from the window with his hand over my mouth, as the Cossack wiped his sword clean with his handkerchief and replaced it in the scabbard. Then I heard the horse ride off without another word. There was nothing any of us in the community could do without losing another life. The old man's wife saw the whole thing and fainted inside her house. No one made a move to pick up the body until we knew that the Cossack was far down the road. It was the most traumatic thing that I have ever witnessed in my whole life, up to now."

CHAPTER THIRTY

The Bolshevik guards waited five more days for the two original scouts to return, but they did not. Subottin had become very impatient. Late in the afternoon, he decided that his problem must be solved. It was the last week in July, and he was fed up. Now he was low on supplies. They had already killed one of the horses for the meat. He thought about the situation he was in. What he wanted to do was shoot the prisoners and return to Odessa. But that would create an entirely new problem for him. He was put in charge of a mission. If he returned to Odessa with his men, and no prisoners had been delivered, what would he tell Major Yurovski? He could say that they were delivered to a railroad station for further transportation to Kharkiv and then be sent to the salt mines in Kazakhstan. But that would be very dangerous for him to tell that kind of a lie. Suppose one of his men told the truth about what he did. He was not the most favorite officer of all of the men in this small command. If the truth was told, he would be shot for insubordination or worse. Major Yurovski was not a very patient man. He expected to have his orders carried out exactly as they were given. He could have his charges shot, disperse the men he commanded, and go home to Moscow. He missed his mothers cooking.

There was a tool shed in the rear of the cemetery with some rusty tools in it. There were shovels and rakes for digging graves and maintaining the cemetery grounds, although it looked like they had not been used for some time. The tools were rusted from lack of use. He could have the prisoners dig their own graves and shoot them with the machine gun. Then he could turn the gun on his own men and walk away the sole survivor. But some of these men were his friends, and then again, some of the men could turn on him before he accomplished the dirty deed. That was not a good idea.

He could send some of his guards back to Odessa with the excuse that he did not need as many men to guard the diminished number of prisoners. There were only sixteen of the hardiest prisoners remaining. It was hardly worth the trouble of delivering them to Kharkiv. He would select the men he trusted to stay. Then they could decide what they wanted to do after the prisoners were eliminated. He, along with others, had been deserters from the Tsars Army, so why not desert again. It made sense.

He missed Moscow. He was a city boy. He missed his friends, and the hockey games. God knows how many of his friends would still be around to ice skate with him when he returned. He had a girlfriend, but he doubted that she would be waiting for him to return. He was a long way from Moscow. Would he be able to make it back alive? All of these thoughts went through his head.

A plan began to formulate in his mind. Tomorrow morning, he would select a dozen of his trusted friends to stay with him to guard the prisoners. Then he would send the rest of the contingent back to Odessa. He would keep two horses and the wagon with the machine gun and several rifles for his guards. The rest of the horses would return with the dismissed troopers. They would have to take turns riding, because there were not enough horses to go around. He would appoint the soldier that complained the most about this mission to lead the group back to their home base. It would be a simple task to follow the railroad tracks south. Comrade Subottin did not sleep much that night. His thoughts were on the details of putting his plan into action.

At the morning muster, he explained the situation to all of his men. Then he selected the dozen men he wanted to stay, and told the rest of the men that they would return to their post in Odessa. Two of the soldiers he picked to stay requested to return with the contingent back to camp. That left him with only ten guards plus himself. All the better for him to carry out his plan, so he agreed to let the two volunteers leave with the contingent. It was noon by the time they divided up the remaining supplies and packed their gear for the return trip. The return to Odessa would take a lot less time without having those miserable prisoners to slow them down.

An hour after the contingent left, Comrade Sobottin explained his plan to the remaining ten guards. All were surprised by the bold plan, but agreed that it would be in their best interests. These men were tired of the fighting and wanted to go home. Like Sobottin, three of the other men were Muscovites; two were from Minsk and the rest from scattered parts of the Russian Empire. They had been away from their homes for almost four years now and longed to be back with their loved ones.

They anxiously brought the wagon with the machine gun into the cemetery yard and set it up facing the rear wall in the unoccupied portion of the burial grounds. They paced off sixteen plots with enough room for those making the supreme sacrifice to pile dirt on either side of their grave, and marked each with a shovel stuck into the soil. Then they returned to the sacristy and removed the barricade from the outside door to the garden.

The prisoners were surprised to hear the barricade being removed. There was something ominous about it. Were they being moved to another location? The sounds outside their enclosure were different today than they had been for the last week or so. There seemed to be increased movement and then the sound of horses being led away, and the creaking of the wagon being moved. Was it possible that they were being abandoned here? They were aware that Lieutenant Sobottin had been in a foul mood for the past week or more. They had heard the guards talking about returning to Odessa. Jacques had his doubts that anything good was about to happen here, but he did not want to discourage his fellow inmates.

When the barricade was down, and the door was finally unlocked and opened, one of the guards told them to form a single line and follow him into the garden. They were escorted toward the rear of the cemetery where they noticed the wagon with the machine gun mounted and facing the rear wall.

"You bastards!" Castor shouted! "Now you are going to kill us!"

As he charged one of the guards, a shot was fired and Castor went down.

"He is not dead," the Guard that shot him said. "Help him up, he ordered."

The next two men in the line helped Castor up. He was bleeding but no bones were broken. Alexander tore a piece of cloth from his shirt and tied it around the wound to stop the bleeding. Castor limped along, with help, to the row of shovels standing sentinel over their grave sites. Now the Bolshevik guard said,

"Dig! Or we will leave your bodies to rot on the ground."

Each of the prisoners took a shovel and reluctantly began to dig. The condemned men tried to converse but the guards put a stop to it by firing a shot over their heads to silence them. Several minutes later as the graves began to take shape, Jacques began singing in Italian. The guards told him to stop, but Sobottin said,

"Let him sing. He is probably saying his prayers."

Jacques knew that his captors understood only Russian. He continued the song in French, and then in Greek, then in Arabic, and finally in German. Each prisoner recognized the words as Jacques sang to them in their native language. He sang,

"Watch me carefully - When I give the signal - follow me over the wall."

Jacques` heart was pounding as he carefully watched, and waited for the guards to relax their vigil. It seemed like this took forever. He prayed to God for help. He prayed for his life and the lives of the other men. He knew that all of them would not make it. He prayed that God would help as many as he could to get over the wall, and he prayed for the strength to get him over the wall safely. When the machine gun operators were not looking and the other guard who knew how to shoot straight was completely distracted, Jacques said,

"NOW!!!"

He dropped his shovel and sprang for the wall, pulled himself up, and threw his body over the top. When he hit the ground on the other side, he ran at a crouch, parallel to the wall so as not to be shot in the back. André was the next one over the wall. When the guards realized what was happening, they began to curse and shout, but by the time they retrieved their guns, Alexander was over the wall, and when Hraird reached the top of the wall, the Bolshevik guards began shooting.

Although he was wounded, Castor grabbed Eli, and boosted him to the top of the wall. Now the machine gun opened fire. When two of the guards finally reached the top of the high stone wall, all they could see was the empty field and the woods beyond. Jacques and the others had disappeared into those nearby woods far to the left of where the guards were looking. Comrade Sobotton ordered the rest of the men to go out through the front gate and look for the escapees. By the time his men reached the outside portion of the rear wall, it was near dusk.

The escapees had scattered when they reached the woods, each man making his own way through the thick brush and trees. It was better that way. If one was caught, the others still had a chance to get away. Jacques ran in a zigzag pattern through the trees and brush. These woodlands were thick with blackberry brambles. His face and hands were scratched and bleeding. Speed and distance were the most important factors for self preservation, so he charged on. Winded, he dove under the thick bramble bushes and burrowed into the dried leaves that fell there the previous autumn. He lay down perfectly still, trying not to make a sound.

More shots rang out from the church yard cemetery. It was getting late now. The sun had set in the west. Jacques lay quietly under the thick bramble bushes. His face and hands were scratched and bleeding from the thorns of the blackberry bushes, but he lay there face down partially concealed in the leaves and dirt under the bushes. He could hear voices in the distance shouting in Russian, as other shots rang out. Then again, the chattering rat-a-tat of a machine gun confirmed that the remaining prisoners who did not escape were filling the open graves that each had dug for himself. All who were left that did not escape in the confusion were paying the price now for Jacques' life and his freedom. There was nothing he could do but pray for their souls and that those low life Bolshevik bastards would not find him.

When it was dark, maybe they would give up the search. His captors were not well equipped and not very smart. Thank God, they had only a few guns among the group, one of which was that machine gun set up for their assignation. Jacques doubted that the couple of lanterns his captors were using would be sufficient illumination to find all of the escapees in the darkness of that night. He lay there wondering how many of his fellow prisoners had made it into the forest and how many had been shot or re-captured. He wondered if his captors were motivated enough to pursue the escapees in the darkness or in the light of day tomorrow morning. He was the first over the wall and didn't look back to see how many others made it. The group was made up of Greeks, Germans, a Frenchman, an Italian, an Armenian, a Pole and a Check soldier, who was fighting against the Bolshevik's for the Tsar. They all wanted the freedom to return to their respective homelands.

As darkness fell, only the sound of the crickets chirping remained. The mosquitoes buzzing in Jacques' ears and sucking his blood was of little consequence compared to the fate he shared with his fellow prisoners only minutes ago. He knew that those mosquitoes smelled the blood from the bramble scratches and were eager to feast upon him. Patience was of the utmost importance, so he lay there motionless for, what seemed like, well over an hour. Then rising quietly from the brush in the darkness, he listened carefully for sounds of his comrades. Thankfully the night was pitch black and moonless. Though his eyes were adjusted to the darkness, it was still difficult to maneuver through the thick forest. Jacques tried a soft whistle but there was no response. Was he the only one who escaped? Or were some of the others still silently hiding in the woods.

After several minutes, he tried the whistle again, but to no avail. Moving on through the forest in a direction he believed to be away from his captors, Jacques decided that it was too dangerous to signal from the ground, so he looked for a tree with low hanging branches that would support his weight. He found the perfect one and pulled himself up. Groping for other branches, he managed to climb high enough to be hidden from anyone on the ground. Again he whistled softly. Listening for several seconds, he then heard a response. It was a soft whistle off to his left, maybe a hundred meters or so, but it was hard to judge the distance with all the trees, foliage and underbrush to muffle the sounds. Jacques moved his position in case it was not a friendly whistle. He did not relish the thought of being captured to face the firing squad again or just be shot on the spot.

In the distance, Jacques thought he heard the sound of footsteps crunching in the dry leaves on the ground coming closer, as a friendly French greeting asked, "Who is there?"

Carefully, Jacques worked his way, limb by limb, back down the tree until he felt the ground beneath his feet.

"Over here," Jacques said in a whisper.

Jacques and André embraced in the darkness.

"Did you make it over the wall before the shooting started, André?"

"Yes I did. Are you alright?"

"I am fine, only some bramble scratches and mosquito bites. We are a lot better off than some of our fellow prisoners."

"I am a little shaken but still alive, thanks to you. Jacques."

"Let us see if we can find some of the others. But we must put some distance between us and this place before morning, because they will be looking for us at first light. Let us stay quietly here for a few minutes and listen."

After some time, André whispered, "I think I hear something."

"Yes, I hear it too. It sounds like a heard of elephants. Whoever it is, they certainly are not light on their feet like you dancers. I doubt that it is our Bolshevik friends. I would guess that they would be carrying a light, not just wandering in the forest in the dark."

As the sounds drew nearer, they could hear a voice and wondered who it might be.

"It must be Alexander, our Polish friend. Leave it to a Polack to make such a ruckus and give away our position to those lousy Reds," said André.

"Ah, but he is so good natured, that we must forgive his minor flaws," said Jacques. And both laughed quietly.

"Who's there?" came the response from Alexander, first in his native Polish tongue and then in German. Jacques answered. "We are your friends, André & Jacques. Where are the others? How many made it?"

"Hans and Hraird made it over, but Hans was wounded because he hesitated on top of the wall before he jumped. Hraird was with him when they reached the cover of the forest".

Jacques suggested that they spread out and try to find them.

"But we can't waste too much time. At first light, the Red's will be after us. André you stay here. Alexander, you go to the left and I will take the right flank. We will meet back here in about ten minutes. André, in a few minutes you will have to chirp like a cricket so we will be able to locate you."

So off they went, and ten minutes later, they re-grouped at the location where they left André. Alexander had found Hans and Hriard in a gully where there was a small stream. Hraird had dressed Han's wounded shoulder the best he could in the dark after washing it with water from the stream. "Hans, how do you feel?" asked Jacques.

"I am a little weak, but my legs are still good. So let's get going out of here before those lousy Bolshevik's come looking for us. We must put enough kilometers between us and those Red's before daylight and then we may do well to hide during the day and move only at night until we are far enough away to travel in safety."

The small group headed west, concealed by the thick forest and the darkness of the night, leaving behind them the cemetery and five unfilled open graves.

CHAPTER THIRTY-ONE

Back in the church yard, after a half hearted search for the escaped prisoners, in the dark, Sobottin called his men together for an organizational meeting. He asked for a body count of the remaining prisoners. There were eleven bodies, so there must be five who escaped.

"Were any of the escapees wounded or did you sharp-shooters miss all of them?" Sobottin inquired sarcastically.

He knew that there was only one of his men capable of accurately hitting a moving target with a rifle. Sobottin looked at him inquisitively.

"I think I hit one of them in the shoulder when he was on top of the wall," the soldier replied.

Sobottin`s one leadership quality was that he was organized. That must have come from the meager training he had as a machinist apprentice.

"In the morning you three," pointing to the three men standing to his right, "will go outside the wall and look for a blood trail to determine what direction they went. Tonight we will drag the dead to the open graves and leave the rest of the work for tomorrow in the daylight. The rest of you men will fill in the graves early tomorrow morning."

With the light of two oil lamps, they collected the eleven bodies and dragged them to the open graves and dumped them in. It took four of them to haul the Greek's massive body to his final resting place. The machine gun had no respect for Castor's size, or the girth of his muscular body. With that accomplished, they retired to the inside of the church for the night. There was a lot to do tomorrow.

In the morning they began shoveling the dirt into the graves covering the bodies of the deceased. When that chore was finished, there were still six open graves. One of the soldiers counted:

"One, two, three, four, five, six, seven, eight, nine, ten! One of the bodies is missing! It was the little skinny guy; I think he was Italian."

Comrade Sobottin did not seem to be too upset by this discovery. At this point, he really felt bad about killing the prisoners, although he thought he probably did them a favor. Their fate in a prison camp would be much worse than the firing squad they faced. He almost wished that they all had absconded. The six remaining graves were left open in the event that some of the prisoners were re-captured.

At that moment they heard a horse galloping away. It was the sharpshooter. He was a country boy and he knew that a horse would get him home faster than he would get there on foot. Later, they discovered that his rifle was gone also. Sobottin was furious. He cursed and ranted. He kept two horses and now they only had one to pull the wagon. He cursed again. His men casually searched for the sixth escapee, but could not find him. Again there was no blood trail and no signs of where he had gone. None of the men could put their mind to the task now. All they could think about was getting out of there and going home.

They disassembled the machine gun, hid it under some blankets on the wagon along with the five rifles and ammunition that were left. Sobottin kept his pistol on him, but concealed it under his jacket. These items might come in handy on their journey home. Yet, they did not want to look like a military unit, or worse, the group of deserters that they were. By mid-day, the two men that were going east left on foot, as well as the one heading west. Then the six remaining deserters joyfully climbed aboard the wagon to head home toward Moscow and Minsk, leaving behind the burned out church and the unmarked graves of their victims.

CHAPTER THIRTY-TWO

Jacques and his friends wandered through the forest for several days. By now, they were beginning to feel safe from being re-captured by the Bolshevik soldiers. They were leery of building a fire. It may attract attention. There was another problem! They heard wolves howling last night and feared that they were being followed by a new predator. They had no food and no way to carry water although water was available. There were streams that bisected the forest. It was August now and the nights were getting cooler. None of them had jackets. They were all in shirtsleeves. Jacques had a jacket back at the burned out church and so did the others, but no one was willing to go back to retrieve them. Unfortunately, Jacques had more of a reason to go back to get his jacket. He still had a few diamonds sewed in the lining.

That evening, when they decided to stop for the night, they heard the wolves howling much closer than the previous night. It became obvious that the wolves were becoming aware of fact that there was food nearby. So that night, the five escaped men slept in the trees. It was not very comfortable, but it was better than becoming food for those wild dogs.

In the morning André found some snails.

"Ah," he proclaimed, "escargot! a delicacy."

He collected a handful and offered some to his four fellow wanderers. Alexander, Hraird and Hans cringed at the idea of eating the slimy creature and declined his offer. He and Jacques crushed the shells and ate the escargot raw. With not much other food available it was protein they needed to sustain their bodies.

While André and Jacques were eating their raw snails, the other three men found some fern sprouts and dandelion leaves to eat while they were still resting.

Alexander asked, "What are we going to do now? We cannot keep wandering in the forest with only what the forest offers for food. The nights are getting cooler, and the wolves are getting closer."

"Why don't we return to the church," Jacques suggested, "I doubt that Sobottin and his men are still there. With no prisoners to guard, they probably went back to Odessa. They may have left something behind that we can use. I left a jacket there and I would not mind having it to wear on these cool nights."

"Not me! I do not want to take the chance of returning and being captured again," Hans said. "I am weak from the wound in my shoulder and cannot run as fast as the rest of you, and I know that I cannot outrun a bullet."

"Hans and I have been heading toward the setting sun and home, so I really do not want to go back either. I think the two of us should keep going," Alexander offered.

"Very well then," Jacques said. "I am going back to the church to see what I can find, and then I will continue on to the Crimea to find my sister Emile and her husband Yuri. They have a house in Kerch and then I will continue on to Georgia to find my fiancée, Irena. I promised her that I would come back for her and I intend to do that."

"May I travel with you Jacques," Hraird asked? "I have relatives in Armenia."

André chimed in. "I think it would be best for me to go with Jacques because my girlfriend lives in Italy and there may be a ship sailing in that direction from The Crimea."

"So, it is settled then, the three of us will go back to the church. Very cautiously, I might add. The other two can travel west to their homelands, God willing," said Jacques.

They were all in agreement with this plan. Then Jacques excused himself and went into the woods away from the group. He scraped on the threads of his belt and removed one gold coin. Then he called Alexander who thought Jacques went into the woods to relieve himself. He could not imagine what Jacques' problem was. Jacques explained that he had three gold coins in his pocket when they were captured at the market in Odessa.

"The coins were to buy food at the market."

The explanation was not quite the truth, but it was a safe one.

"As you know, we never got to buy any food. One of these gold pieces will go a long way for your journey home. I am sure the two that I have left will be sufficient to get the three of us to the Crimea. My brother-in law will help us from there."

Alexander baulked at accepting the valuable coin but Jacques insisted.

"You have been a true friend on our brief journey together and I want you to get home safely," Jacques explained.

Alexander thanked him and they returned to the group. Then they bade farewell and went on their separate ways.

Jacques, André, and Hraird arrived at the small town where the church was located much sooner than expected, because they had brazenly taken to the roads. That made travel much faster. They could see the familiar steeple off in the distance and recognized it as the one where they were held captive. They decided it would be less noticeable if only one of them entered the town. Jacques was elected because he spoke the language the best, out of the three of them. He found a barber shop. Barbers knew everything that went on in a small town. He entered the shop and inquired where the church was, and received a wealth of information without even asking. The church was burned out by the Bolsheviks. For two weeks, some soldiers were holding prisoners there, but four days ago there was a lot of gunfire and then a wagon went through town carrying six or seven of the soldiers and they were traveling north in a hurry.

"Did you know that Tsar Nicholas and his family were assassinated by the Bolsheviks," the barber added.

This was shocking news to Jacques.

"When," He inquired?

"Only two weeks ago," one of the patrons replied.

He thanked the patrons and the barber, and returned to his friends.

When they arrived near the church, they held back and watched for some time before they ventured near. When they ascertained that the church was, in fact abandoned, they entered and searched for anything useful. Jacques found his jacket where he had left it, rolled up and tucked under a ledge. He made a sign of the cross and silently thanked God for his good fortune. Then he joined the other two in searching for things that were useful. Five more jackets were found. They recognized them as belonging to their fellow prisoners. They took them along. Their friends would no longer need them. Then they went out into the cemetery and there they found ten graves haphazardly filled in and six open graves.

"There were five of us who managed to get over the wall, so someone else must have gotten away also," André exclaimed. "I wonder who else it was that escaped."

They tried to remember who was digging the graves next to them but could not figure out the puzzle.

"Whoever it was may be lying wounded in the area," Hraird said. "Maybe we should look around to see if we can find anything."

They thoroughly searched the cemetery and the outside of the wall and then the edges of the forest, but to no avail. Then they moved on, leaving the church, the ten graves, and the mystery of the sixth grave behind them.

Two days later they reached a river and decided that they could swim across. Luckily, it was mid morning. That would give them a whole day of sunshine to dry their clothes for the cool night ahead. Now they were in the farm country of the Steppes, and it was nearing harvest time. They picked and ate raw beats, greens and all. In the wheat fields, they gleaned the wheat from the stalks and ate the chaff along with the kernels.

"Where did you get the idea of eating the kernels of wheat, Jacques," Hraird asked?

"Think about it, my young friend. Breads are made from flour that is made from wheat. Why not go right to the source and eat the wheat raw," Jacques explained "I am in the wheat business, but I really learned this from the Bible when King David's army was hungry they rested in a wheat field and ate the kernels for sustenance".

Several days later, they came to the Dnieper River. It was a much colder day, and this river was extremely wide here. As luck would have it, the banks were strewn with abandoned logs. They tied several of them together with wild grapevines that they collected from the riparian forest and fashioned a raft. It was decided that it would be too dangerous to cross the river in the daylight so they waited for the sun to set before they launched the raft out onto the river. They spent the whole night drifting downstream and paddling as best they could to get across in the dim moonlight. When dawn broke, they found themselves only a few meters from the bank on the other side of the river, several kilometers downstream. The raft was abandoned, but they were too tired to move on, so they rested most of the day. In the seclusion of the river banks forest, they built a fire and stayed the night. The three men resumed traveling with the first light in the morning, refreshed and eager to move on.

The three were making good time. They were covering as many kilometers by foot as they could each day. They were better nourished now than they had been in the last four months. Jacques was the oldest of the three and in fairly good physical condition, in spite of their incarceration. André was the next oldest and had very strong legs because of his ballet training. Hraird was the youngest, only nineteen and had youth on his side. The dirt farm road that they were traveling on was straight and almost flat. At times, it resembled a wavy arrow through a sea of wheat. On one rise they spotted two men walking in the same direction that they were, south-east. They were closing in on the two who they noticed were progressing slowly and not walking a straight line. When they approached the two men, they realized that they were drunk, and that they were the first two guards that were sent on a scouting mission to find a working railroad station. When Jacques called out to them, they were startled.

One of them said, "I think I know you?"

Jacques noticed that they were unarmed, so he asked them if they knew Comrade Sobottin. They looked at each other and broke out in a drunken laughter. One laughed so hard that he stumbled and fell down. The other man helped him up, still laughing. Then Jacques boldly inquired.

"What happened to your weapons?"

Still laughing, they explained that they traded their rifles for food, blankets and two bottles of vodka.

"And now, we are celebrating our return to Sevastopol."
"Good," Jacques said. "We are going to Yalta. We can travel together."

Then Jacques started walking at their regular pace and soon the two drunks were left far in the distance.

Hraird questioned why Jacques told the two drunken men that they were going to Yalta, when they were really going to Kerch? Jacques explained, "Who knows who else these drunks will be talking to and we may have a price on our heads."

"Clever," André said. "I am glad that we invited you to travel with us, Jacques."

Then all three had a good laugh.

As they journeyed across the Steppes, they passed through several small peasant villages. The news was that the anti-Bolshevik White Army was advancing in the north and the Crimea was under the control of the White Army. This was good news to the three weary travelers. It meant that Jacques' sister Emile and her husband Yuri would be in a safe haven. Now the territory began to look familiar to Jacques. The presence of the military became more evident as they got near the Isthmus of Perekop that connects the Ukraine with the Crimean Peninsula. A military caravan going north held up their progress, but gave them a well deserved rest for a few hours.

CHAPTER THIRTY-THREE

Jacques was not too familiar with the City of Kerch, so he asked for directions to Tomogennaya Street. When they arrived at the house, it was empty but locked up. Jacques went to the garden in the backyard and found a key in Yuri`s familiar hiding place under a rock. Once again, the house was well stocked with staples; rice, flour, yeast, tea and more. It was just as Emile and Yuri had left their house in Odessa. It was ready to be re-occupied when they returned. Surely, they planned on returning. Jacques wondered where they had gone and if they would come back. It had been eighteen months ago that he left this house with Dmitry to go back to Kiev. His sister Emile was pregnant and due in two months, so that would make her child a little more than one year old. It was a cheerful thought. He was an uncle. He wondered if the child was a niece or a nephew.

The smell of bread baking in the coal stove revived the three men's spirits after their arduous journey. They took baths, shaved and found clean clothes to wear. They almost didn't recognize each other from the transformation.

"Tonight we will sleep like kings in real beds, and tomorrow we will go to the water front and see what ships are in port."

The next morning, in a steady downpour of rain, the three walked down to the harbor. André immediately recognized one of the ships tied up to a pier.

"That ship tied up to the pier on our left is the one that took me from Athens to Odessa four years ago," he exclaimed.

"It is the 'Grand Duchess Anastasia' of the Bek Shipping Company, and it is owned by my brother-in law Yuri and his family," Jacques added. "We are in luck."

They approached the Anastasia and requested permission to board.

"We are very busy unloading," the sailor said. "Come back later this afternoon."

They found a place to eat. The cafe was crowded with military personnel from the White Army. The ships in port were unloading military supplies.

Later in the afternoon, they returned to the 'Anastasia'. The sailor guarding the gangway this time recognized Jacques and welcomed them aboard. They had worked together in Odessa repairing another Bek ship.

"Let me take you to our Captain. He will give you all of the news. We have been bringing in military supplies for the White Army since the beginning of the year, after the Bolshevik Government signed an Armistice with Germany in December," the sailor told them as they approached the bridge.

Captain Suslov was busy preparing the ship to sail on the morning tide the next day. He welcomed them to the bridge. He said to Jacques, "My mate tells me that you are Emile's brother."

"That is right," Jacques said with a smile. "How is my sister?"

"I am very sorry to tell you the bad news! Emile and Yuri were killed by the Bolsheviks along with Vladimir Sergeyevich and his wife and children."

"What happened to the baby?" Jacques asked in shock.

"Come down to the galley where we can talk. It is a long story," Suslov said.

They followed him down the ladder to the deck below. By the time Jacques reached the galley, tears were streaming down his face. He said,

"I can not believe my beautiful sister, Emile, is dead."

"Sit down and I will tell you what happened. I have sailed for the Bek's since I was a young man. Worked my way up to be a Captain. My ship was the 'Angelique' that sailed from Marselle to Athens with Yuri and Emile three years ago. Yuri was like a son to me. He started sailing on my ship when he was a boy. Yuri was a fast learner and he learned well. It was my honor to escort Yuri and your sister part of their way home to Odessa after their marriage. The 'Angelique' is in drydock in Athens and the Captain of the 'Anastasia' became sick, so I took command of this ship. This is my second trip to Kerch with military supplies from Greece for the followers of the Tsar. On our first voyage here to Kerch I met with Vladimir Sergeyevich Bek and he confided in me that he wanted to return to Odessa. He told me that he heard from several reliable sources that things were calm there and he wished to return to his home and revive his shipping business, and that he was willing to work with the Bolshevik Government. Now, I have not been to Odessa in the last four years, so I could not comment on the situation there. Then I asked some of my sailors. They told me that the Bolsheviks had control of the city, but it seemed to be calm there. I was not convinced that it would be safe there from the news that I have heard about the Bolsheviks. Vladimir is a very stubborn man when he decides to do something. That is what made him such a successful business man."

"When Vladimir came to me and told me that his family was returning home, I was surprised. He told me that his family would sail on our return to Greece and that this ship would drop them off there. It meant a detour of several hundred kilometers, but it is his ship, so I could not argue. It was one month to the day that we sailed for Odessa. When we arrived, I did not have permission to pull into the docks, so we anchored out in the harbor. There was no activity on the docks. Vladimir was impatient to get going, so I ordered our small boat lowered and my men rowed the family and their belongings to one of the piers. I was told that when the Bek`s were safely on the pier, with their belongings, that two soldiers came out to greet them. Vladimir explained who they were and one of the soldiers left to notify a superior officer about the situation. As the soldier returned with a group of officers and men, Vladimir told the sailors to leave. So they did. When they were almost out of sight of the pier, they heard gunfire. The sailors returned to our ship and immediately reported to me. Looking with my binoculars, I could see the soldiers leaving the pier with the luggage but I could not see the Bek`s".

Meanwhile, at army headquarters in Odessa, Colonel Yurovski was told that the owner of the Bek Shipping Company was waiting on pier number three for transportation to his home. He quickly assembled a group of soldiers and drove down to the waterfront. He greeted the Bek`s to confirm who they were. Then he ordered his men to shoot them all and bring their luggage back to headquarters. When the order was carried out, Colonel Yurovski ordered that the bodies be left on the pier.

"We must show our citizens how we treat the bourgeoisie who have crushed us with the heel of their boots for so many years."

Then he returned to his office.

Captain Suslov continued,

"That evening after dark, I went back with the small boat to see what happened. We cautiously approached the pier in the faint moonlight to find the bloodied bodies scattered on the deck. Three of my sailors immediately became sick. The rest of us stood there in shock looking at the carnage of these innocent people. They were all dead except for the child. Yuri and your sister shielded the boy from the bullets and fell on top of him to protect him. When I picked the boy up, he began to cry. At that moment, a woman appeared from the darkness and said that she was the boy's nanny and that she would take good care of Mihaylovich. I knew that was what they called the boy, the endearing term for Michael. She said that someone had told her of the shooting, but she was afraid to come out on the pier to see what happened. I sent the woman off with the boy with my blessings. We would not be able to take care of a baby on the ship. The woman said her name was Victoria Georgievna Moskalyova."

Jacques recognized the name. She was the young woman who worked for Emile and Yuri as their housekeeper.

"We lowered the bodies into the small boat and took them back to the ship for a proper burial. The next day we buried the seven at sea. You lost a sister and I lost a friend and a son, even though he was not my flesh and blood."

They sat in silence. Then André exclaimed, "Les un affreux, Yurovski."

Jacques added, "We know the man who did this. We spent time in his prison, and I suffered from the wounds of a hand grenade a year earlier that he threw at me and a friend. My friend was not as lucky as I was."

"So, what will you do now?" Suslov asked.

"I would like to go back to Odessa and kill that bastard

Yurovski and then find my nephew, but I know that would be very foolish," Jacques said.

"Actually, I am on my way to find my fiancée, Irena. She fled Kiev with her parents when the revolution broke out. They returned to their homeland in Georgia. Hraird will travel with me. He has relatives in Armenia. My friend André here, would like to go to Naples to find his girlfriend, and I believe that Athens is in the right direction."

André said, "I have sailed on a merchant ship before. I am a good sailor. Could you use another experienced hand?" Suslov laughed and said, "Yes, I could use another hand. Will you be ready to sail in the morning? André's answer was quick.

"I am at your service, my Captain. You see, all that I own is right here on my back."

"Excellent," said Suslov. "My mate will find you a bunk."

André was so excited that he kissed Suslov on both cheeks, in the French tradition, and embraced the Captain, who was a bit shocked at the sudden gesture.

André said goodbye to Hraird and Jacques. He thanked him for bringing him here and saving his life.

Jacques said,

"I hope you find your Antoinette waiting for you with open arms and stars in her eyes. Until we meet again in Naples or Paris, God be with you."

Then Andre turned and disappeared through the hatch to find a place to sleep.

Hraird and Jacques returned to the house on Tomogennaya Street, but before they left the ship, the Captain advised them to make it a voyage to Georgia because the overland route would be over very rugged terrain.

CHAPTER THIRTY-FOUR

Jacques and Hraird lived in the Bek`s house on Tomogennaya Street for almost two months. Each day they would go down to the harbor and watch the movement of ships and inquire about their next port of call. Unfortunately none of the ships, large or small were traveling east toward Georgia. Most of them were bringing in supplies from the west for the White Army. In the middle of November, the news came that the Great War was over when Germany sued for peace with the Allies. World War I had ended, and soon after, British warships streamed into the Black Sea in support of the White Army. One morning, Jacques noticed a Corvette flying the British Union Jack tied up to one of the piers. Jacques approached the Officer of the Deck who was holding court at the top of the gangway.

"Halt!" Came the order from a sailor holding a rifle.

Jacques stated that he was a Swiss citizen and business man wrongfully detained by the Bolsheviks.

"May I have a word with you Lieutenant," pointing to the officer?

The Lieutenant obliged and stepped nearer.

Jacques told him his tale of woe.

"Now I am trying to get to Georgia to find my fiancée who also fled the Bolsheviks from Kiev. I speak eight languages fluently and maybe of use to your ships Captain as an interpreter. I would barter my services for passage on your ship to Georgia. My assistant here also speaks several languages including Ukrainian, Georgian, Arabic, and Armenian. We have been here in Kerch for months trying to find a ship that can take us to Georgia."

"Well, that sure is a sad tale mate, but I am not the one to hire an interpreter. Sailor, take these two gentlemen up to the bridge to see the Captain, and stay with them until they leave the ship."

"Yes, Sir," was the snappy reply.   The sailor pointed and off they went in the direction of the bridge.

The British Captain was startled to see two civilians on his ship. He demanded an immediate explanation of this breach of security. The sailor explained,

"The Lieutenant thought that you may be in need of interpreters.

"Very well gentlemen. What languages do you speak?

"We both speak Ukrainian and Georgian, and I am somewhat familiar with the workings of ships. I spent five months re-fitting one of the Bek`s freighters that was damaged by Turkish cannon fire. I was in the wheat business in Switzerland and I am very good with numbers."

"I see that you speak English very well. We are having a problem explaining our needs to the dock workers here. One of our main pumps has broken down and we cannot get these Ukrainian's to understand our situation," said the Captain.

"I think I can help."

They were escorted below decks to the pump that had failed. Then the Engine Room Officer went with them to the ship fitters warehouse, dockside, and together they explained the problem. Now that they understood the problem, the Ukrainian ship fitters set to work repairing the pump along with some members of the ships black gang. In two days, they were prepared to set sail for the ships intended destination of Poti, Georgia.   Thanks to the two newly hired translators.

Before the British Corvette Orpheus left Kerch, Jacques returned by himself to the Bek family 'Summer House' on Tomogennaya Street to see if there was anything of value to take. Unfortunately, the Bek family would no longer need any of their valuables. He looked through the house thoroughly, but could find nothing of value small enough to carry with him.   The last place he looked was the fireplace in the large living room, knowing that the fireplace was another favorite hiding place of his late brother-in-law Yuri. Upon close inspection, he found some mortar that was blackened but not charred by fire. He located some tools and chipped away at the mortar. Two stones came loose and behind them he found a package wrapped up in heavy woolen cloth and tied up with a cord. He untied the cord and un-wrapped the package. It contained some silverware; knives, forks and spoons of various sizes, a rather large roll of gold coins and jewelry. There were several rings. One had a diamond that looked like it was larger than one karat. Another ring had three karat size stones; a diamond, a dark blue sapphire, and a ruby, the colors of the Russian flag. It was beautiful. It must have been a family heirloom. He re-wrapped the package and re-tied the cord around it and left the house not looking back. He remembered his sister Emile and was saddened to think of her and the nephew that he would probably never know. He said a prayer that his young nephew Michael would be safe and well cared for.

He returned to the ship with the package under his arm. The Officer of the day asked him what the package contained. Jacques said that it contained some of his late sister's private possessions. He was advised to bring it to the Captain for safe keeping. He and Hraird were given sailors work uniforms so they would not feel conspicuous on the ship, now that they were in the employ of the British Navy.

When they arrived in the port of Poti, Jacques and Hraird were assigned to the Commissary Officer to procure food supplies for the ship. They had been served mutton on this ship up until now, so Jacques decided to treat these brave sailors by buying beef and lamb here in the middle-east where mutton was not considered the delicacy that it was in England. The Commissary Officer gave Jacques the quantities to buy and told him how much he was allowed to spend. Jacques` bargaining for the food items pleased the Officer, especially when he was able to return to the ship with money left in his budget.

In conversation, while they were shopping, Jacques asked the Commissary Officer where he was from in England. He said he was from London. Then Jacques told the story about when he was sixteen, and he went to London with his father on a business trip.

"When we returned home, my Maman casually asked me what I learned in London and when I told her that I learned 'bloody bugger, bloody fool', she turned and slapped me across the mouth so hard I thought that she knocked my teeth out."

The British Office thought that it was so funny that he doubled over with laughter.

The next day, Jacques was summoned to the Captains quarters. He had no idea why he had been summoned. Did he do a poor job of assisting the Commissary Officer? On the contrary, the Captain complimented him on the good job he did.

"I really was becoming tired of eating mutton at every meal," the Captain said. "I mentioned to our Fleet Commander that I had hired an interpreter and that you had worked so well with our Commissary Officer. He suggested that I transfer you to shore duty to work with all of the six vessels in the fleet, if that is acceptable to you? In a few months, this ship will be returning to the Mediterranean and we will be able to take you as far as Constantinople, if that would be of any help to you to return to your homeland. As for your partner, he is welcome to stay on and help you, or he may leave at his discretion."

Hraird was as anxious to leave as Jacques was. He wanted to find his uncles and cousins in Armenia. He had no idea that a war was fought between these two countries less than a year ago. With the meager pay from the Brits and a small loan from Jacques, he boarded a train to Tiblisi and from there he would be able to make his way into neighboring Armenia. Once he found his relatives, he would be able to get word to his parents in Constantinople that he was alive and safe. As they said good-by, Jacques wondered how the other escapees had managed in their journeys home; Alexander to Poland, Hans to Germany, André to Naples or Paris, and now Hraird to Armenia. He wondered if the tenacious Italian, Eli, had made it to safety. Now he wondered where his journey would end.

CHAPTER THIRTY-FIVE

Jacques was assigned to an office in a warehouse at the port where the British ships took on their supplies. A Lieutenant Gibson was his new boss and was assigned to oversee his work. Jacques thought that it was much like having a puppy-dog following him around wherever he went. Lieutenant Gibson did not speak the language, so Jacques had to translate every word for him, on every transaction.

On May 26th of 1918, the Republic of Georgia was given its independence from Russia. Business would now be flourishing with the British fleet perched on their doorstep to help protect Georgia from the new Bolshevik Government of Russia, and there was the added incentive of the freedom their country had from Russian tyranny. It was harvest time for the grapes to make wine. The wheat was being gathered and the vegetable farmers were bringing their crops to market. That was going to make Jacques' new job relatively easy. The wheat business gained him the knowledge to bargain with the Georgian merchants and get the best deals. The first chore was to go to the Customs House to ascertain the current value of the British pound in relation to the Georgian coupon. With that accomplished, they could go shopping. This job suited him well. He went to each prospective supplier and introduced himself and Lieutenant Gibson, and announced that they were buyers for the British fleet. The merchants were very happy to accommodate them.

When they returned to their office, there was another ship tied up to the pier and its Commissary Officer was waiting with the list of supplies that he needed to feed his ship's company. The lists were divided up and delivered to the various merchants in the produce market, the slaughter house, and the flour mill to be delivered to the pier the next day. When each of the ships had their allocation of food aboard, their job was done for the next week, until the process would start over again with the first ship back in port for supplies.

"A job well done," said Lieutenant Gibson. "Now we deserve some time off."

Jacques was in full agreement with that. He was anxious to go to the Baratashvili Vineyards to find his beautiful Irena. He prayed that he would find her there, but if she was not there she certainly could be found at one of her relative's homes in Tbilisi.

The train ride through the lowlands of western Georgia was magnificent. With the Lesser Caucasus Mountains rising to his right, and the snow capped Caucasus Mountains to his left, it was a breathtaking scene adorned by azure blue skies. It reminded him of his home in Switzerland, and made him a little home sick, but the thought of finding Irena erased his thoughts of home. He had not seen her in over a year and a half. Would she be happy to see him? Would she be waiting for him to find her? Would she feel the same about him? Maybe she has married to another in his absence. These thoughts went through his head as he left the train in Kutaisi.

He hired a driver to take him to the Baratashvili Vineyards where he was greeted with shock and surprise by Irena's uncles.

"Where have you been? Irena has been waiting for you," they said. "We had doubts, but she knew that you would come for her." That was music to Jacques' ears.

"Where is she," he asked?

"Denys and Inessa decided that they would rather live in Tbilisi and they took Irena with them. She was reluctant to leave but her mother insisted that she go with them," one of the uncles said.

"They left here three months ago. We have not seen them since. Their letters said they arrived safe. They are staying with one of Inessa`s sisters, but I do not remember which one. You are welcome to stay here as long as you like, but I am sure that you are anxious to see our lovely niece, Irena."

"Thank you for your hospitality." Jacques said. "May I stay for tonight? I would like to take the train to Tbilisi in the morning."

"Yes, we understand," the brothers said in unison. It will be our pleasure and one of us will drive you to the train in the morning.

At the evening meal, as Jacques began relating the story of his adventure, they told him that they hardly recognized him because he was so thin. The women in the family urged him to eat more.

"We do not want you to leave here looking so thin. The neighbors will think that we did not feed you. It would make the Baratashvili family look like misers, so eat," one of the brothers wives said. Another suggested that he stay, "We will fatten you up, and we will send for Irena to come here. Then she will find you as the man you were when you parted in Kiev." They all laughed.

Jacques said, "I appreciate your concern for my well being, but Irena will have to accept me the way I am." When I left Kiev, Irena expected me to return in a month or more. But when I reached Odessa, I found that my sister and her husband with his family were preparing to sail on one of the Bek ships to go to their summer house in Kerch because they felt that it would be safer there."

Then he told them of how he met Dmitry and the journey from Kerch to Kiev and the hand grenade that injured his leg, and how the farmers saved his life and kept him until he fully recovered.

"When I finally returned to Kiev, Irena had already left to come here. Then I went back to Odessa. I planned to come here by boat and I had made arrangements to do that when I was captured by the Bolsheviks. The leader of the Bolshevik Army was the same man that left me wounded in the road to die. The prisoners I was with were all foreigners and they were sending us to a prison camp in Siberia. When he had taken us half way to an operating railroad station, the leader of the guards thought it was too much trouble to deliver us, so he decided to have us dig our own graves in a cemetery but we scaled the cemetery wall and ran along it so we would not be shot in the back. There were five of us that made it into the forest and got away."

"What happened to the other prisoners?" one of the brothers asked.

"They were executed," was Jacques shocking answer. "Two of my fellow prisoners went west and three of us managed to get to Kerch, where I found out that my sister Emile and her husband and his family had all been murdered by the same butcher that left me to die. I managed to get aboard the British Corvette Orpheus that brought me from Kerch to Poti, and here I am. Thank you for listening to my sad tale. Now that I am so close, I need to find my dear Irena."

The next morning, Jacques was on the train going to Tbilisi. The scenery was still magnificent as the train began its climb into the foothills. He took out the picture he had of Irena that he had been carrying in his breast pocket. It was well worn from the arduous journey of the past two years. His heart raced with joy at the thought of seeing her again. He tried to remember the location of Aunt Sofia`s house where they had stayed two years ago. He was not sure how to get there from the railway station, so he asked a porter for directions.

"The house I am looking for is a short distance from a pie shaped grey stone building two or three stories high and the streets were narrow in that part of the city. If I find the building I will know where to find the house."

The porter said, "I know the building," And gave him directions.

As he approached the house of Irena`s Aunt Sofia he became nervous. He knocked on the door and held his breath. What if they moved or if he was mistaken and had the wrong house? He could not remember her Aunt Sofia`s last name. Then the door opened and Irena`s Aunt Sofia said,

"Can I help you?"

"Good afternoon! I do not suppose that you remember me. I am Jacques Vesery, Irena`s fiancé, and I am looking for Irena Baratashvili?"

Aunt Sofia stood in the doorway with her mouth open for a moment. Then she said, "Oh, my dear boy, I apologize for not recognizing you. Please come in."

"Where is Irena? Is she here?" Jacques inquired.

Aunt Sofia invited him to sit in the sitting room while she explained the situation.

"I am sorry to tell you that they have gone. My sister Inessa, Denys and Irena decided to go to America and start a new life there. Irena was almost resigned to the fact that you were dead, because you had not come to get her. They left over a month ago. They booked passage on a small Black Sea Freighter. I do not know the name of the ship, but I believe it was going to Constantinople."

Jacques' heart sunk. He put his face in his hands and cried.

"I am so sorry for you and for Irena. She has been waiting for you for so long. Stay here with us. I know that we will receive a letter from my sister when they arrive wherever they are going," Aunt Sofia suggested.

"I cannot stay," Jacques explained. "I have been offered passage to Constantinople by the Captain of the British Corvette Orpheus. That is the ship that brought me to Poti. They hired me in Kerch as an interpreter and I am working with their Supply Officer to purchase food for the British fleet. I would like to return to Poti on the next train which will leave a little after noon tomorrow."

"Good," said Aunt Sofia. "Then you will stay with us tonight and catch the train tomorrow to return to Poti.

That evening Aunt Sofia served Khinkali because she remembered how much he liked that meal. While they dined, Jacques told Irena's aunt and uncle about his experiences as he did with Denys Baratashvili`s brothers. They were amazed that he was still alive and here to tell the story. The next day he boarded the train to return to Poti. He was anxious for the Orpheus to return to port for supplies. They had been out on patrol for more than two weeks and were due back soon. Jacques knew that it was urgent for him to get to Constantinople and catch up with Irena. The more time that passed, the harder it would be to trace the Baratashvili`s steps.

The next few weeks passed slowly for Jacques. He had established that Lieutenant Gibson was the man for the merchants to deal with. He even taught the lieutenant enough Georgian to be understood in dealing with his suppliers. Jacques found a Georgian dock worker that spoke good English to assist with translating on any mechanical problems the small fleet might have, and told him to stay in contact with Lieutenant Gibson.

Early one morning, the Orpheus pulled into port for supplies. Jacques immediately went aboard and spoke to the Captain, who informed him that the Orpheus was being replaced by another Corvette within the following two weeks. Jacques was overjoyed. He thanked the Captain. Then he went to the Commissary Officer and together they worked it out that the ship would have to be re-supplied before they sailed for Constantinople. Jacques did not want to miss his ride. Un-be-known to Jacques, the last freighter to leave Poti a few months ago was on its way to Athens, Greece with a shipment of Georgian wine, and wheat. And the Baratashvili family!

CHAPTER THIRTY-SIX

On a sunny winter day the Corvette Orpheus was cruising at sixteen knots half way across the length of the Black Sea, heading west. Jacques could not believe that within the next day he would be in Constantinople. He was happy and excited. The azure blue sky reflecting on the water, and the bright sunshine gave Jacques a warm feeling even though it was cold on deck.

The next day, the ship entered the Bosporus and docked near the ferry slips that brought passengers from the European to the Asian side of the city. Before Jacques left the Orpheus, he retrieved the package that the Captain was holding for him. He thanked the Captain and said good-by to the Commissary Officer and some of the crew members that he became friendly with. He asked permission to go ashore from the Officer of the Deck, saluted the Union Jack and left the ship. Jacques was vaguely familiar with Constantinople. He had been there several times before, but only for short visits while passing through. He sought directions to Istiklal Avenue and found a hotel. He remembered that there were many good places to eat on this Avenue, and having been deprived of good food for so long, he felt that he deserved some delicious fattening Turkish food. .

In the morning of the following day he went to the Ministry of Marine on the shore of the Bosporus to inquire about a vessel that had arrived from Poti, Georgia in the last few months. He was taken aback by the answer. There were none.

"There must be some mistake," Jacques said incredulously. "Maybe it sailed from another port in Georgia?"

"No, none from Georgia," the clerk said un-mistakenly.

Jacques left the office in shock. How could this be? Did the ship sink? Did it go to another port? He did not know the answer, or what to do about the problem. It was not very often that Jacques could not come up with an answer to a problem, especially a problem of this proportion.

Jacques sold the silverware that he found from Yuri`s catch in the house on Tomogennaya Street. He could use the Turkish lira to live on while he was here in Constantinople. The remaining contents of the package, he put in a safe deposit box, in the Turkish bank along with two remaining diamonds that were sewn into the lining of his old jacket. He inquired about the location of the Swiss Embassy, but first he owed it to Hraird to find his parents and tell them that their son had returned to Armenia. He could not remember where Hraird said the store was. He went to the Armenian section of the city and after several inquiries, he found someone who knew the Habash family. "They operate a shoe store in the Egyptian Bazaar," the man told him. Now Jacques recalled that Hraird mentioned that his parents owned a shoe store in the Egyptian Bazaar.

The Egyptian Bazaar was a large market place with many shops selling everything you could imagine. The Habash`s shoe store was located next to a haberdashery. Jacques realized how poorly he looked in these old clothes, and how badly he needed some new clothes. He wanted to look like he fit in, in this cosmopolitan city. His old jacket was threadbare, the pants and shirt were British Navy issue work clothes, and his shoes had holes in the soles. Jacques made a wise decision to stop at the haberdasher before attempting to meet Hraird`s parents. After he had purchased the new clothes, the clerk made a kindly offered to dispose of his old clothing. To the surprise of the clerk, Jacques kept his old jacket and belt for sentimental reasons, and thanked the clerk for the offer.

When he entered the adjourning shoe store, there were two customers being waited on, so Jacques took a seat and waited. As he looked down at his shabby old shoes, he realized that they strangely did not quite go with his new outfit. When the gentleman came to wait on Jacques, he rose from his seat and introduced himself.

"My name is Jacques Vesery and I am a friend of your son, Hriard. I came here to let you know that he was on his way to Armenia when I last saw him in Georgia." Hraird's father was a thin man with a full head of gray hair.

"Ah, then you must be the one that Hraird told us about in his letter. We received a letter from him a few days ago. It was the first time we heard from Hraird in over a year. We were very worried about him. He arrived safely at my brother's house in Yerevan. When the ostracism of Christians began to be oppressive in Anatolia on the Asian side, we became worried about the future, and sent our only son Hraird to live with a cousin in Odessa. Little did we know, at that time, what would happen in Russia. My wife and I did not want to leave here. We have our business here. We both have put our sweat and blood into this business, and did not want to just give it up, so we stayed.

"Nairy," he called to his wife. "Come here and meet the man who saved Hraird's life." She came quickly and threw her arms around Jacques and kissed him on both cheeks. "Thank you for saving my baby," she said.

"No, no! Do not make me a hero," Jacques explained. "We escaped together with three other men, and your brave son saved one of the other men who had been wounded."

Nairy said,

"Do not be so humble. We read Hraird's long letter, but we would like to hear about the ordeal from you if you would join us for dinner at our home tonight? Looking down, she said,

"But first, we must get you into a decent pair of shoes."

Sitting down in the chair, Jacques laughed and said,

"These shoes have served me well. They have traveled many kilometers, and I have to admit that are a little thin on the bottoms." Louis picked up the shoe with Jacques' foot in it. He laughed and exclaimed.

"Thin bottoms! What bottoms? They have large holes in the soles."

Louis also noticed that Jacques walked with a slight limp, so he fitted the new shoe with a lift to correct for the limp. Jacques wanted to pay for the new shoes, but they would not accept any payment.

That night, Jacques had dinner at the Habash's home and again related the story of his journey, their confinement, the escape, and the way he and Hraird arrived in Georgia; compliments of the British Navy. The meal was a traditional Armenian dinner consisting of molohkia, (a dark green soup) with chicken and rice, tabbouleh, hummus, pita bread, and baklava for desert. Nairy said that it was Hraird's favorite meal. Jacques laughed and said,

"I know, Hraird spoke of it many times. He kept our spirits up on some of our darkest days talking about his mothers cooking."

At the end of the evening, Jacques thanked them for the delicious meal and their hospitality. Nairy said to Jacques,

"You are welcome in our home any time. I will write to Hraird and tell him that you are here in Constantinople."

Then Jacques retired to his hotel for the evening.

In the morning, he went to the Swiss Embassy to renew his passport. He explained to the agent that he was in Kiev on business when the Russian Revolution broke out and that the Bolshevik's had taken all of his credentials.

"I am a Swiss citizen."

He gave the agent all of his information, including his home address in Lausanne, his mother and father's names and those of his brother and three sisters.

"You have been out of our country for more than three years," the agent said with shrug. "We will have to verify this information. Come back next week to check with us."

During the week Jacques tried to find out if a ship from Poti passed through the Bosporus destined for another port, but to no avail. Hundreds of ships had gone by here in the last few months bound for the four corners of the world. It was very frustrating.

A week passed and he returned to the Swiss Embassy to get his new passport. The agent told him that the address that he gave was false. No one with the name 'Vesery' lives there. Jacques stood there in shock.

"This is not possible," he exclaimed! "My Maman, Mary Anne Vesery, and two younger sisters, Olga and Lilly must still live there. It has been our home for many years. There must be some mistake. Did you get the numbers correct on the address in Lausanne?"

The agent read back the address and asked, "Is that correct?"

Jacques was dumfounded. It was the correct address.

"I am sorry," the agent said. "We cannot issue you a new passport without a relative to collaborate the information that you gave us."

Without a word of thanks, Jacques turned and started to walk down the hall toward the front entrance of the Embassy, in shock and disbelief. This was not like Jacques at all. He was taught to be polite, no matter what the circumstances. He was deep in thought. What do I do now? Where did my Maman and sisters go? Without a passport, will I have to stay here in Constantinople? I cannot find my family. I do not know where my Irena is or where she is going."

"Excuse me, Mr. Vesery," came a voice from behind him. "I could not help but overhear your conversation with the Swiss passport agent. After a war and with several revolutions going on nearby, there are many people left without a country to return to. Allow me to introduce myself. My name is Edgar Sealander. I work for the American Embassy here in Constantinople. This Swiss Embassy is very particular about who they let into their country. They insist that all papers be in order before they allow someone to pass their borders. It is almost lunchtime. Would you like to get something to eat? I may have some suggestions to help you get back home."

At lunch Edgar explained that he worked under the American Ambassador, Mr. Henry Morgenthau.

"Right now I am in the process of helping two friends of mine, A Greek couple, who wish to go to America. These things take time. Explain your circumstances to me and we will think about a solution to your problem. I overheard that you are from Lausanne, a very nice city but extremely hilly." They laughed. "Do you have any other relatives there?"

"I have only one cousin in Lausanne, Marie LaManna. She is the office manager in our family wheat business. My mother came from Milan and I have family there. My father, rest his soul, came from a wheat farm in the Loire Valley of France. We have family there also. My older brother Michael was killed in the war at the Battle of Neuve Chapelle, fighting for France. My sister Emile and her Ukrainian husband were murdered by the Bolsheviks in Odessa. My Maman and two younger sisters, Olga and Lilly are apparently no longer living in our family home in Lausanne. There was also our family housekeeper for many years, Margarette Cogny. I wonder if she went with them."

"That is very interesting," Edgar said. "Why was your brother Michael fighting with the French?"

"France called for French speaking volunteers when the war broke out," Jacques replied.

"And your sister in Odessa," Edgar asked?

"They were the bourgeoisie in the 'New Workers Paradise'," Jacques explained. "They murdered her husband's whole family, just like they did to the Tsar."

"I am sorry to hear of all of your lost family members."

"Thank you! Aside from that, I became engaged to a Georgian girl while I was in Kiev. Her name is Irena Baratashvili. Her father was in the wine business. His brothers operated a large vineyard in Georgia. I had to return to Odessa on family business, and needless to say, I was delayed. When I arrived back in Kiev, quite some time later, she had gone home to Georgia with her parents and now, I believe, they are on their way to America. I have no idea how they were going there or where their destination was in America. I need to find her also."

"Well! You have quite a list of things to accomplish. Do you know the address of your cousin in Lausanne?"

"Yes."

"Then you must write her a letter and inquire about your Maman and sisters. Also write to your people in Milan and France. It may be easier to obtain a French or Italian passport. I know people in both Embassies. As for Irena, a ship from Georgia would probably not be very large, so it would most likely come here to Constantinople or go to Athens. Write a letter to the Maritime Office in Athens for information about a ship from Georgia and any ships going to American ports from Athens. I think that would be a good place to start, but remember, as I said before, these things take time. Give me the name of the place where you are staying. I would like to know what progress you are making. Here is my card with my home address on the back or you could contact me at the American Embassy.'

Jacques wrote the address of his hotel on a slip of paper that the waiter provided, thanked Edgar Sealander for all of the advice that he received and returned to his hotel.

The desk clerk at his hotel was kind enough to furnish Jacques with hotel stationary, envelopes, a pen, and a bottle of ink. He took them to his room and began writing.

November 15, 1918

My dear Cousin Marie:

I am sure that you are surprised to receive a letter from your long-lost cousin Jacques. I am alive and well in Constantinople. The business trip to Kiev was time consuming. However, it was successful. I did accomplish all that was intended, with the exception of bringing more shipments of wheat to our warehouse. I wonder if any of my letters reached the Wheat Exchange. They told me at the Swiss Embassy that Maman, Olga and Lilly are no longer living at our family home. Is this true and where did they go? I need to contact them. Is the Wheat Exchange still operating?

I sincerely hope that you and Roberto are in good health and doing well.

With best regards,

Your cousin, Jacques

PS - Enclosed is the address of my hotel here in Constantinople.

The next letter went to his Uncle Gusstaf Tomasini in Milan, inquiring about the whereabouts of Maman, Olga and Lilly? Then he wrote another letter to Valerie and Anton Vesery in Chemille, France, his paternal grandfather and grandmother. Last but not least, was the letter of inquiry to the Maritime Office in Athens about a ship that came from Poti, Georgia and any that were bound for the United States of America around the same time period. He posted all four letters and now all he could do is pray and wait.

CHAPTER THIRTY-SEVEN

With nothing to do but wait, Jacques decided to obtain information on trains through Eastern Europe to Paris. He found the way to the Sirkeci Terminal. It was the last destination east on the celebrated 'Orient Express'. He had traveled it several times with Papa and once with the whole family. The farthest destination going west was Paris but the Vesery's boarded the Express in Bern. It was a long journey to Constantinople. At the terminal, he inquired about trains going to Bern, and was told that there were none going there lately, due to the uprising in Bulgaria. He was told that the 'War' had disrupted rail traffic in other parts of Europe also. This was more disheartening news, but it came as no surprise.

When he arrived at his hotel the desk clerk gave him a message from Edgar Sealander. It was an invitation for lunch the next day at the American Embassy. Edgar was waiting at the reception desk when Jacques arrived, on time, of course. Edgar greeted him warmly and then escorted him to the Embassy cafeteria where mostly American food was served. Edgar said,

"I hope you don't mind eating here, I have a very sensitive stomach and cannot tolerate too much of the Turkish food. I try to dine here as much as possible."

They were seated in a section where they were served. The Turkish waiter brought them menus.

"Now, how are you doing? I am sure that you have not received any replies from your letters as yet."

Jacques nodded no.

"I made another visit to the Swiss Embassy this morning and inquired about your status. They are very stubborn people at your Embassy. They have rules and don't bend them."

"Thank you for trying to help me," Jacques said.

Then he told Edgar how he lost his passport and his ordeal becoming a prisoner and his escape, and his brief employment by the British Navy.

"Now that you have been bored with the details of my life, tell me something about yourself. All that I know about you is that you are an American and work here at the Embassy. You must have many important things to do here. Why are you helping me?"

Edgar laughed,

"I enjoy helping people with their problems when I feel that I can be of help. My job allows me to be of service in ways that others cannot. I am forty-five years old and I was born in New York City. I was an athletic young man. I attended New York University and earned a Masters` Degree in History and Foreign Languages. After college, I joined the Army and went to Officers Training. I had the honor of serving with Teddy Roosevelt at the battle of San Juan Hill, in the Spanish-American War. He took a liking to me as a fellow New York City boy, and convinced me to go into public service. I started my public service career in the Capitol in Washington. That is where I met my wife, Sarah. She was a beautiful, southern girl from South Carolina, with blond hair and a sweet southern accent. We had two children, a boy and a girl. We were sent to Panama for diplomatic purposes while the Panama Canal was under construction. We lived there for four years. It was wonderful. We had a beautiful house to live in with a tropical garden. The children were schooled by American teachers. We had wonderful servants. Sarah said that she always felt like she was on a long vacation."

"In October of 1912, the United States Government re-assigned me and my family to Turkey. We had very nice quarters here and the best schooling for the children. They had American teachers just as they had in Panama. Six months after we were posted here, they sent me to see the Greek Orthodox Bishop in Smynra on the Aegean coast of Asia Minor. It was summer and the children were on their summer vacation, so I thought it would be nice to take a family trip. We had the new Ford car that was assigned to me shipped to Smyrna on the same vessel that we sailed on. It was a very nice experience, especially for the children. There was a very large community of Greeks in Smyrna. My wife and children hired a guide and went sight seeing while I took care of my business with the Bishop. We all had a wonderful time."

"On the last day when we were to return to Constantinople, there was a terrible thunder storm. It was pouring rain and I was to deliver some papers to the Bishop. I parked the car across the street from the Cathedral and ran in to deliver the papers while Sarah and the children waited in the car. The church was empty except for a couple in the front row praying. I hardly noticed them. While I was with the Bishop, there were several loud cracks of thunder and lightning. Then there was a roaring crash. We leaped to our feet and rushed to the street."

Edgar hesitated, then with tears in his eyes he continued.

"Lightning had struck the chimney on the building across the street." He paused again. "And the chimney fell on my car and crushed it." Jacques put his hand on Edgar's shoulder and said, "I am so sorry."

"A few moments passed. Edgar composed himself and resumed the story.

"The woman from the church said that she was a nurse. As the four of us removed the pile of bricks, we realized that there was very little hope that my wife and children had survived. Now I am here all alone. My only pleasure is helping others. Life goes on."

"How old were your children,"

"The boy, William was ten and the girl, Barbara was eleven," Edgar replied.

"You are a brave man to carry on after that kind of a catastrophe," Jacques said, shaking his head. They finished their lunch in silence. When they parted, Edgar told Jacques to keep in touch. He would be interested to hear the replies to the letters that went out.

The mail service in Turkey was especially poor. After a few weeks, Jacques sent out a second letter. They were copies of the first letter with a note to ignore these letters if they had received the first original letter. Maybe it was time to look for a job before his money ran out. He went to several tobacco shops but they all told the same story. They would only hire Turks. He found a shop with a Jewish name, 'Hirsch Brothers'. The man behind the counter asked if he was Jewish. Jacques smiled and said,

"I could be if you hire me."

The salesman told Jacques that his brother-in-law owns the shop.

"My name is David Triandafillou and this was my business but they do not allow Greeks to own a business here any more. Because you have experience in the tobacco business, I will give you a job. I can use the help. I will not hire a Turk because I do not trust them. My brother-in-law knows nothing about tobacco. He is no help to me at all. I hope you will be." Jacques assured his new boss that he would do well.

During the next week, when Jacques returned to his hotel there was a letter waiting for him. It was from his uncle Gusstaf in Milan, dated January 10, 1919.

Dear Nephew,

I was surprised to hear from you. It has been almost two years since your mother told me that she heard from you. She had given you up for dead. It broke her heart to loose your father, two sons and a daughter who she was out of touch with because she moved so far away. It all happened in such a short period of time.

In her weakened condition, your mother came down with consumption, like your father had. It is now known as 'Tuberculosis'. She passed away in October of 1916. I am so sorry to bring all of this news to you at one time. You have been out of contact for so long.

Your sister Lilly married a Frenchman, Basil Debbas. He works for a French automobile manufacturing company. I believe he was being posted to Egypt, but I do not know where. The two girls decided to sell your family home, and Olga went to live by your grandparents in France. The Wheat Exchange has been out of business for well over a year with no one to operate it and no wheat coming in to sell.

I am extremely sorry to give you all of this tragic news at one time, but I am sure you will understand. I am deeply sorry about the loss of my sister Mary Anne, your mother, and all of your family.

Please come and stay with us here in Milan. You are always welcome in our home for as long as you wish to stay. I will understand if you are anxious to return to Lausanne, but please keep us advised of your plans.

Sincerely,

Uncle Gusstaf

Jacques read his uncle's letter over many times. He could not comprehend that his family was gone; that they no longer lived in the city where he was born, Lausanne, that his mother was dead, that their family home was gone, that his two little sisters, one married and the other gone to live where their father came from, Chemille, France. There was nothing left there for him. There was nothing to go home to. No family, no business, no home! He felt so alone. He put his face in his hands and sobbed. Then he asked God, why Lord, why? What did my family do to deserve this? Why am I still here? I should have been killed by a firing squad or a hand grenade. Why not me, Lord? There was no answer.

He did not sleep much that night. The next morning, when he went to work at the 'Hirsch Brothers' tobacco shop, he told David, his new employer about the letter he received the day before and asked for some extra time when he went out for his lunch. David readily agreed

"Take as long as you need. You poor man, I am so sorry for your loss."

When Jacques went to lunch that day, he was so upset that he could not think of food. He went directly to the American Embassy and asked if he could see his new friend Edgar Sealander, and was ushered into the office. Edgar rose from his desk which was piled with papers, and greeted Jacques with a firm handshake.

"You look upset. What happened?"

"I received a reply yesterday from my Uncle Gusstaf in Milan," handing Edgar the opened letter to read. After reading the letter Edgar said,

"You poor fellow, this is devastating news. I am so sorry that your mother passed away. It is very hard to lose the ones that you love. But, like me, you are a survivor. Now, you have to go forward. You will find your sisters and your fiancée and life will go on for you, just as it has for me without my family."

Jacques thanked Edgar.

Then Edgar said,

"Now you will have to wait for responses to the other letters that you sent out. They may have better information about where your sisters are and where your fiancée has gone to in America. Come to my house on Sunday for dinner. My Greek cook will make us a nice dinner. It will cheer you up. Come early. Spend the day. We would enjoy having your company."

"Thank you again. What time shall I arrive?"

"You may arrive any time after eleven in the morning. I like to sleep late on Sundays. It is my only day off from work, and there is no Catholic Mass to attend in this city. There are Greek Orthodox Churches in this city but I was advised not to attend any of them, from my superior at the Embassy."

CHAPTER THIRTY-EIGHT

Jacques arose early on Sunday, as he always did. He went to a bakery and purchased a box of assorted Turkish deserts to bring to his friend's house. He arrived at his destination just after eleven in the morning. Edgar's apartment was in a large house in Pera, a residential section overlooking the 'Golden Horn', on the north side of the city, and near the American Embassy. He knocked and the door was opened by a Greek gentleman.

"Welcome to the Sealander residence. My name is Timis. Come in and make yourself at home." Jacques entered the spacious room decorated with beautiful tapestries on the walls and very comfortable looking furniture. Before Jacques could sit down, Edgar entered the room and greeted him with his traditionally firm hand shake.

"I am glad that you could come for dinner, my friend. Can I get you a cup of coffee? But before we sit down, I would like you to meet my two good friends Tata and Timis Kappas. I believe you have already met Timis. Tata, will you come in here for a moment?" he called. "Tata is busy preparing dinner in the kitchen. She will be here in a minute," he whispered. "Technically, they are my cook and my valet, but actually they are my best friends. They reside here in this large apartment with me as servant staff. My Embassy pays their salaries, but I will tell you about that later."

Tata entered the room with Timis right behind her. Edgar introduced them, "Jacques, I would like to meet my good friends, Tata and Timis Kappas."

Jacques greeted them in their native tongue and both broke out in a broad smile. He kissed Tata`s hand and shook Timis`s. Tata said to Edgar,

"I like him already" and they laughed.

They were an older couple in their late forties or early fifties. Tata was a short woman with a round face and a broad smile. She had a deep voice for a woman, the voice of authority. Timis was more than a head taller than his wife. He was slim with a very pronounced Greek nose and soft spoken. After pleasantries, they excused themselves. Before they left the room, Edgar asked.

"Timis would you please bring us each a glass of Raki? I feel like having a drink before dinner." Timis acknowledged and disappeared into the kitchen.

While they made themselves comfortable in the sitting room, Jacques began the conversation by telling Edgar that he had gone to the Sirkeci Terminal to check on trains to Switzerland and found that there were none.

"The Valdaya uprising in Bulgaria is the cause of some rail disruptions in that country, Edgar said. "But there are other factors involved. The war has caused many problems with the rail transportation all over Europe."

"Before we go into the dining room for dinner," Edward began quietly, "I would like to explain the situation here with my housekeeper and valet. Tata and Timis were the couple praying in the Greek Orthodox Church in Smyrna, in my darkest hour of my life. They were the 'Good Samaritans' that came to my aid when my family was killed. Together, with the Greek Bishop, the four of us pulled broken bricks and cement from the chimney that fell on my car until our hands were bloody. We worked until we recovered the crushed bodies of my wife and children. After the Bishop gave my family the last rights of the Church, they carried the bodies into the rectory where they cleaned them up and prepared them for burial, while the Bishop prayed with me in the Church. The Papas` took me to their home that evening and sat up all night with me in my grief. The next day, they made arrangements to have the bodies sent back to my Embassy in Constantinople. We have been true friends ever since that day. I will ask them to tell you their story at dinner."

When Tata announced that dinner was served and they went into the dining room, Jacques noticed that there were four places set at the table. They all sat down and Edgar said grace. He looked at Jacques and said,

"This is my family now. Today we are having Greek food in your honor. Tata is an excellent cook. She usually makes American food for me because of my finicky stomach. She always watches out for my health. Then Tata spoke up,

"That is because Edgar eats the wrong things or sometimes he gets so involved with his work that he does not eat at all", she scolded.

Edgar laughed, "There are times that Tata acts more like my mother than my own mother did, God rest her soul."

Tata added, "You see Jacques, we must look after this man because he saved our lives."

"I did nothing of the sort," Edgar argued.

"It was you that saved me!"

Tata began,

"Timis and I were praying in the church when the lightening struck the building across the street and the bricks from the chimney fell on Edgar's automobile. When we ran to the front door of the church and saw what had happened, a man pushed us aside and screamed, 'My family is in that car'. We rushed to their aid and as Edgar must have told you, it was too late. His family did not survive the terrible accident.

"Timis and I had gone to the Church that rainy morning to pray for our safety and guidance. The situation in Smyrna was not good. The new Turkish Government had passed an edict to remove all Greeks from Anatolia. More than half of the people who lived in Smyrna were Greeks. Even though the both of us were born there, they considered us aliens because we were not of the Muslim faith. Our parents and grandparents were born in Smyrna. Timis was a soldier in the Turkish Army and I was a Turkish Army nurse. That is how we met. Timis was wounded in battle, fighting for Turkey when the Italians seized the Isle of

Rhodes. I was his nurse, and we fell in love. It almost seems silly at our age, but it happened."

They looked at each other lovingly and smiled.

"When we were both dismissed from the Army, we returned to Smyrna to live. We were married in that Greek Orthodox Church. I got a job in a hospital and Timis went to work at the Singer Sewing Machine factory near our home. Soon after he started working there, he was let go. It was not because he did not work hard or do a good job. The manager said that he was ordered to fire him because Timis was not Turkish. Timis protested that he was born in Turkey and served for eighteen years in the Turkish Army. He told the manager that he was wounded and almost died for his country and now they would not let him work because his parents spoke Greek! The manager said that it was not his decision to make. It was an order from the new Government. It was said that people who spoke any language but Turkish were disloyal to the country and were aliens. He said that all Greeks were suspected of concealing guns in there homes to start a revolution and overthrow the Turkish Government. That was an outright lie. "

"Soon after, the new Turkish Government began deporting all Greeks from Asia Minor. They were being sent to the Island of Chios or to the mainland of Greece. We were in great danger of being deported. Some of our neighbors had already been taken away, but because I am a nurse, we were allowed to stay a little longer. We went to the Church to seek guidance from our priest. We prayed together. Then our priest told us that he too was prepared to leave in the very near future. It was inevitable that we would have to leave our home also."

"Meanwhile, Edgar went back to America to bury his family. When he returned more than two months later, there was a new Ambassador at the American Embassy, Ambassador Henry Morgenthau. On his return, Edgar was shocked to hear that all Greeks were being deported from Asia Minor. He immediately came for us. He insisted that we pack our things and go with him to Constantinople immediately. He explained that if we worked for him, we would be protected by the American Government.

Now I know that when God made us go to the Church to pray, it was really to save our lives."

"Our plight is nothing compared to that of the Armenian citizens of Turkey. Some Greeks who resisted were killed but most were deported. The unfortunate Armenians were systematically annihilated. Armenian soldiers in the Turkish Army were disarmed and used as pack horses until they dropped. Many of them were decorated brave fighting men that Timis served with in the Turkish Army. Some fled to Russia, and escaped. Women, children, and the elderly were relocated to the Syrian Desert. None of them ever reached that destination. Millions perished. It was a crime against civilization. We will never know the half of what went on."

CHAPTER THIRTY-NINE

Two more months passed. Jacques was becoming very depressed with the thought that he had lost contact with all of the people he loved. Now he thought that he would be forced to stay here in Constantinople. Without a passport or any papers to prove who he was or where he came from, it would be difficult to go anywhere. He could not fathom how easy it was to walk into Constantinople from the British Corvette, and how difficult it would be for him to go anywhere from here.

He spent his time working in the tobacco shop six days a week. It paid for his living expenses. Almost every Sunday, Edgar would invite him for dinner. He enjoyed the company of Edgar, and the Greek couple. It was good to have friends in a foreign place, or for that matter anywhere you have to spend your time. He often told his friends how discouraged he was because of his situation, but Edgar encouraged him to be patient.

"Don't worry. Everything will work out for you. Just be patient and pray. God will answer your prayers."

On one weekday when he arrived home from work, there were two letters waiting for him. The first was from the Maritime Office of Greece in Piraeus. No wonder the reply took so long. He had addressed it to Athens. The second letter was from his cousin Marie in Switzerland. That is strange, he thought. It too, had a different address from where he sent it. He quickly went to his room and opened the first letter. It could give him a clue as to where Irena went.

Dear Sir,

In reply to your request for information on ships entering and leaving the port of Piraeus, in the month of October 1918, one ship under Georgian registry arrived from Poti, Georgia on the 4th day of October, 1918 and departed 7th day of October to return to Poti. Several ships of the Cunard Lines departed from this port in October of 1918 bound for various ports in the United States of America; On 2nd of October to New York, on the 8th of October to Boston, on the 9th of October to New Orleans, on the 15th of October to Boston, on the 21st of October to New York, and on the 27th of October to Boston.

We hope this information will be helpful to you.

It was signed by the director of the port of Piraeus. In Jacques' thoughts, he imagined that Irena's family must have gone to one of these three ports in America. Then he quickly opened the second letter from his cousin Marie dated 15th of March 1919 and read.

Dear Cousin Jacques,

Where shall I begin? First, let me say that I am so very happy to hear from you, and that you are still alive and well. We all assumed that you had been killed over there in the Revolution. The last letter your Maman had received from you was in May of 1916 telling her that you met someone whom you were very fond of, and that you were thinking of asking for her hand in marriage. You mentioned that you were going to stay for a little longer than you expected. That was around the same time that your Maman started with the coughing spells. I urged her to go to the doctor, but you know how stubborn your Maman could be. She refused to go. Your Maman had come down with tuberculosis like your Papa had. In the following months your Maman became very sick. I could not handle the business at the Wheat Exchange by myself and she was too sick to work. Olga took care of her with help from Margarette Cogny while your sister Lilly finished school. Due to your mother's sickness, the banks would not lend us more funds to keep the business operating, so at that point Olga and I decided that we should dissolve the business.

Your Manam passed away that October 4th. It was a very sad day for all of us. She was buried next to your father. Your two sisters had no choice but to sell your family home. They just could not maintain that big house. There was also some money owed by the Wheat Exchange that had to be repaid from the proceeds of the sale of the house. With the francs that remained, they rented a small apartment. Lilly went to the University and Olga trained to be a nurse. You can be proud of your sisters. They are strong girls, just like your Maman.

At the Lausanne University, Lilly met Basil Debbas. They were married on the 12th of May 1918 at Our Lady of Faith Church with a small reception of family members only. Basil's mother and father came here from Paris for the ceremony. The next day, the newlyweds left to go to Basil's new assignment in Alexandria, Egypt where he represents the Renault Motor Car Corporation.

After the wedding Olga went to France. There was an urgent need for nurses because of the war. She said she would probably stay in France and take up residence somewhere near your father's side of the family. I received a letter from her a month later. She was working in an Army hospital. She also mentioned that she had met with Michael's girlfriend Larisa, from Cholet, and returned the letters she had written to him along with the sad news of his being killed in action at the Battle of Neuve Chapelle. Olga sent me another letter saying that she had fallen in love with a wounded American soldier and was going to marry him and go to America. That was the last I had heard from her.

I imagine that you have noticed our new address. Roberto and I have moved to Versoix. We both found work at the Lindt and Sprungli Chocolate Manufacturers in Versoix. Roberto was hired for his expertise with chocolate and I for my experience with import and export. Thanks to the Wheat Exchange.

Please write and tell me of your plans. How are Emile and Yuri doing?

You're loving cousin,

Marie

Jacques read the letter several times. He had to let all of the information sink in before he picked up the pen and began his reply. It was a very long letter also. He had so much to tell his Cousin Marie. How he met Irena, his journey from Kiev to Odessa, the hand grenade attack, the escape from the firing squad, how he found out about his sister Emile's death at the hands of the Bolshevik soldiers, along with Yuri's entire family and how he arrived in Constantinople. Then he brought his cousin Marie up to date on what he was doing and the friends he made here. He wrote, 'The situation that I am in now, without a passport or any proof that I am a Swiss citizen, I cannot return home to my own country. If there is anything you could do to help me, I would appreciate it. I will keep you posted.

P.S. Please send Olga and Lilly's addresses to me when you can. Thank you.'

Now he read the letter from Cousin Marie again. He still could not believe that his mother was gone. He fell to his knees at the side of his bed and prayed. His heart was heavy. He prayed for his Maman's soul as he did each day for Papa, Michael, Emile, Yuri and their son. Then he prayed for Lilly and Basil, his new brother-in-law even though he never met him. He prayed that Basil would be a good husband to his baby sister. He prayed for Olga, that God would keep her safe from harm, and that she would find happiness in her life. Then he asked God to help him find his love, Irena.

He would have to wait for Sunday to tell his new friends all of his news. At least now he knew that Irena and her parents went from Georgia to Piraeus in Greece and then on to America. The question is where in America. America is a very large country, and he did not know much about it. He would ask his friend Edgar if the Embassy had a library that he could use to acquire information about the country that Irena had gone to. He wondered if the people there were really cannibals. He had heard that they ate hot dogs in America. That could not be possible. America is a civilized country.

Sunday morning, Jacques woke before dawn. The sun arose on a beautiful day. Spring was in the air; the sky was blue. He left his room early to walk along the Bosporus. It was a busy waterway. There were always large ships mingled with small boats going in both directions in the fast current. The sun glistened on a high spot on the Topkapi Palace in the distance. This bright new day had raised his spirits from the sad news of the past few days. He lingered along the waterfront for a few hours, enjoying the sights and sounds of the day. He stopped at the Turkish bakery to purchase some halvah, honey and baklava because he knew that they were everyone's favorite. Then he headed to his friends house for their regular Sunday get together.

When he knocked on the door, he was welcomed into the house by Timis who said, "Come in, Come in, Jacques. You are looking good. You are no longer the frail skinny man who first came into the house a few months ago."

"Thank you, Timis. It is mostly due to Tata`s cooking."

At dinner, Jacques told them about the two letters. First the one from his cousin who he explained was very close to him and worked in the family's Wheat Exchange. He mentioned that his family business was gone and that his two remaining sisters had left Lausanne also. His baby sister Lilly had married and gone to live in Egypt with her husband. The other sister became a nurse and went to France to live near his father's side of the family, but now I hear that she is going to marry an American soldier that was wounded. She met him in the hospital where she was working in France.

"That is wonderful news, Jacques," said Tata. "Your two sisters are grown up and both are spoken for. Be happy for them."

"Yes," he said with a tear in his eye, "but now I have nobody to go home for."

"Cheer up." Tata retorted. "Life goes on and you are young. Go find your Irena in America. Start a new life."

Then Edgar chimed in. "Yes, go to America and look for Irena and you may find your sister Olga there too. You know, our embassy has a wonderful library with maps and pictures from all over our country. I will give you an invitation to use that library any time you wish. The people who work there will be more than willing to answer any questions you may have."

"Thank you Edgar. You read my mind. I was thinking about going to your Embassy to find out more about your country. And, by the way, I have heard a rumor that you Americans eat hot dogs. Is that true?"

Edgar burst out laughing at Jacques' question. Jacques blushed with embarrassment. Edgar, still laughing, said,

"We don't eat dogs in our country. 'Hot dog' is a nickname for a type of sausage on a long roll that is usually eaten at sporting events."

Then they all had a good laugh together. Tata chimed in,

"I am so glad you asked about 'hot dogs'. We heard the same rumor but we were too embarrassed to ask about them".

After dinner Jacques showed Edgar the letter from the Greek Maritime Office about ships sailing to America.

"This is wonderful news," Edgar said. "There were three ships that went to Boston, so I would start looking there. If you don't find your Irena there, New York is not far from Boston and two of the ships went there. Only one ship sailed to New Orleans. That is a good distance from New York, but that is five out of six cities where the ships have landed. They will have records of all immigrants that arrived on those ships."

Before he left that evening he thanked his friends for the meal and most of all for the encouragement and support they had given him.

CHAPTER FORTY

Jacques made good use of the library at the American Embassy. He found a wealth of information and had many questions answered. He studied the maps and figured out the distances between the major cities. He was especially interested in the distance between Boston, in the state of Massachusetts, and New York City. He found that there were regularly scheduled trains that ran between the two cities. That was good news.

The librarian reminded him that the United States of America had quotas on immigration. Each foreign country was allotted so many people each year. As his luck would have it, the Swiss quota was full for this year and had a waiting list for the next two years. Young Swiss citizens were encouraged to leave their country to avoid over populating their small nation. Not that it would make a difference for him. He did not have Swiss papers either. His only chance of returning to his native country would have to come through his Cousin Marie's efforts, and that may take time. He did not want to stay here in Constantinople any longer than he had to. Now he was not even sure that he wanted to go home to Lausanne.

Jacques was not very happy about working in the tobacco shop. It was just a job. He did his work well and was liked by his employer, but he was used to being his own boss. He learned the tobacco business from Jozsef Dobryakov, Nikita`s uncle, back in Kiev. He could run a business like this anywhere, and make a living at it. There were smokers all over the world and he knew his tobacco, just as well as he knew the wheat business from the sowing of the seeds to the making of the bread. Jacques was resigned to be patient.

The next Sunday before dinner at Edgar`s home, Jacques produced a list of questions to ask his friend that he did not feel comfortable asking the Embassy librarian. Edgar laughed when he saw the list that Jacques had made up.

He said,

"I think that you have enough questions here to keep me up all night. Then again, I may not have all of the answers. But before we start with your questions, I have some questions to ask of you. Have you decided to go to America? Are you sure that is what you want to do? Or will you return to Switzerland? Will you have enough funds to get you to the destination of your choice?" Then he waited for Jacques' answers.

Tata and Timis were working in the kitchen preparing the meal. Edgar felt more comfortable asking these questions of Jacques in the privacy of the sitting room.

Jacques began,

"Yes, I have decided to go to America and look for Irena. That is my definite decision. Yes, I am financially able to make this move. When I went to Kiev on business, I carried with me several thousand Swiss francs worth of diamonds to pay my supplier for a lost shipment of wheat, and the transfer of two ships. Diamonds travel much easier than a satchel full of gold. When I went to sell them in Kiev, I found that they were worth much more than I had paid for them, because of the War and the Revolution. I sold enough to settle my debt. Then I had one of the larger stones that remained made into an engagement ring for Irena. The rest of the stones were sewn back into the lining of my jacket. They came in handy at times and I still have two stones left, along with some jewelry and gold that I retrieved from my sister's in-laws house in Kerch. They are in a safe deposit box in the bank along with some gold coins that were sewn into the leather belt that I traveled with. I used some of those in my travels also. I am sure that these assets would get me to my destination with some funds to spare. My job at the tobacco shop gives me enough to live on here without going into my savings. So, I think that is a 'Yes' to all of your questions."

"Excellent," Edgar nodded and said, "Very well. Now I can try to answer your questions and solve some of your problems. Tata and Timis are going to the United States under the Turkish quota, and with my sponsorship. They are technically Turkish citizens because they were both born here in Smynra, and they have papers to prove that."

"As you know my Embassy has handled the business here in Turkey for the Allied Countries of Britain, France and Russia for the duration of the War. I still have some influence at those Embassies even though the War has ended. We could arrange to get you to France, if that were your choice. But now that I know your heart is set on going to the United States, we will have to work something else out."

"The Russian Embassy is a shambles. The new Bolshevik Government is having enough trouble bringing their own country under control without entering the world of foreign relations. The residents of the Russian Embassy here are mostly remnants from the Tsar's Government and they don't want to return to their homeland for fear of the same fate that the Tsars family endured. If we could tell my friends at the Embassy, a small lie; that you were born in Odessa, they could make a new official birth certificate for you stating that you are a citizen of the Russia Empire. The American quota for Russian immigrants has not been filled since the Revolution broke out. Prior to that there was a small influx of Russian Jews who fled the persecution of the Tsar's Government. So, if we have any luck and I still have some influence at the Russian Embassy, we may be able to get you into my country by that route. If you would be willing to agree to that situation, it would be like renouncing your Swiss Citizenship. Would you be willing to say that you were born in the former Russian Empire?"

Jacques nodded,

"Yes."

"If we can work this out with a Russian birth certificate, I would be willing to sponsor you for your Visa. Visas come with different conditions. Some are for an extended visit with the stipulation that you would return to your country of origin after a certain time period. Others are for permanent immigration. I am going to assume that you will apply for a permanent immigration Visa."

"Yes, I would like to stay in America."

The remaining questions were quickly dispatched by Edgar. The most pressing problem, of course, was the one that Edgar may have just solved, if all went well. There were questions Jacques asked about some cities, especially New York. That was easy for Edgar to talk about because he was a native of New York City. Talking about his beloved Manhattan made him realize how much he missed home. He was eager to return in September when his tour of duty here was over.

Edgar became curious when Jacques began asking where the wine making regions of the country were located and how far from New York they were.

"Why do you want to know where wine is made," Edgar finally asked.

Jacques explained, "My fiancée's family are wine makers. Irena's father and his five brothers owned and operated a large vineyard in the Republic of Georgia. Irena and her parents were living in Kiev when I met her. Her father was the importer of their wines to the Ukraine. So, I would imagine that he would look for a place to live where wine was being made. If I want to find her, I would start looking there. Oh yes, and her Grandfather was Nikoloz Baratashvili, a famous Georgian poet."

"That is very interesting," Edgar replied. "Jacques, you amaze me. Or, as my mother used to tell me, 'You are a lot smarter than you look'."

They had a good laugh over that one.

"As for wine country back in the States, there are only two regions that come to mind; the Hudson River Valley and the Finger Lakes of upstate New York, or the Napa Valley out in California. The upstate area is close enough to Manhattan, but California is three thousand miles away. That is very far, almost five thousand kilometers. On the other hand, if you get to New York, from this side of the world, what is another five thousand kilometers to find the love of your life? I envy you Jacques. You still have your life to live. You are a survivor and a persistent one at that. My life ended when I lost my Sarah and the children. I feel like I am too old to start over again. My work occupies my entire life."

"Nonsense. You are never too young or too old to live your dream. My Maman told me that."

Before the evening ended, they made arrangements to meet at the Russian Embassy the next day to work on their plan to get a Russian birth certificate for Jacques.

At the Russian Embassy the next day, Edgar was greeted with open arms. They owed him much more than one favor. Any friend of his was a friend of theirs. They were very willing to make up a new birth certificate for Jacques to replace the one that he had lost. They also knew that Edgar would be more than wiling to help several members of their Embassy to immigrate to America in the near future. Edgar had to remind them that his tour of duty here would be over in September when he would be returning to his home in New York City. He told them that they had better start making plans soon. "

"Once I leave Constantinople, I will not be able to help in any way." For their sake, he hoped that they took his suggestion seriously.

Jacques gave the secretary all of his information; his name - Jacques Mickelovich Vesery, (he added the Russian pronunciation of Michael to make his name sound more believable), date of birth - 22nd October 1892, address - (he gave his sister Emile's address) Stroganovskaya Street #336, Odessa, Ukraine, father- Michael Vesery, mother - Mary Anne Tomasini Vesery. That was all of the information that was necessary. The secretary went to a file cabinet, retrieved the proper form, and typed in the information. When she finished typing, she removed the form from the typewriter and gave it to the Ambassador's aid to be signed and a seal placed over the signature to make it official. Jacques was now a citizen of the Ukraine, born in the Russian Empire. Both Jacques and Edgar thanked them graciously for the trouble they had gone through for Jacques. Then they left the Embassy.

"Well, that went well. We will see you this coming Sunday at my house?" Edgar said casually as they crossed the street in front of the Russian Embassy

"Yes," Jacques said. "Thank you again, and I will see you around eleven o'clock Sunday morning."

They shook hands and both went their separate ways to return to their respective places of employment.

CHAPTER FORTY-ONE

Jacques penned another very long letter to his Cousin Marie, dated the 7ᵗʰ of May, 1919. This time he told her more about Irena, and more details about his sister Emile's death and burial at sea, as it was related to him by Captain Suslov. Then he explained that he had managed to get a Russian birth certificate and that he was planning to go to America within the next few months to find Irena. He ended the letter with 'I will keep in touch, Love, Jacques'.

One day in that week, when business in the tobacco shop was slow, Jacques asked for some time off to take care of a personal business matter. The proprietor told him to take the rest of the day.

"It seems like such a lazy spring day, I do not expect many customers on a day like this," he said. Jacques thanked him, left the shop and found his way to the office of the Cunard Lines, a freight forwarding company. He knew that Cunard Lines were a reliable carrier and that they took a small amount of passengers on every trip.

At the Cunard Lines Office he found the ticketing agent and inquired about taking a voyage to America.

"Do you have regular departures from here to New York and Boston?" Jacques inquired.

He was told that the departure dates were always approximate because there were times that ships were delayed because of bad weather at sea, or sometimes a shipment of goods was delayed getting to the port.

"It takes twenty-five to thirty-five days for a ship from here to arrive in the United States at either of the ports of New York or Boston."

The clerk checked the schedule.

"The next voyage to New York is scheduled for the seventeenth of May. You would arrive approximately a month from that date. The one after that would be on the thirty-first of May. There is a ship going to Boston tomorrow but that passenger list is full. The next one going to Boston is leaving on the twenty-eighth of May, and we have some openings for passengers on that trip."

Then the clerk looked at Jacques and asked which date he would like to book his passage? Jacques thought for a moment then replied,

"I would like to go to Boston on the twenty-eighth of May."

Jacques gave the clerk his name and a deposit to hold his booking and asked when full payment was due.

"Full payment is due ten days prior to your date of departure," the clerk replied.

Now that Jacques had booked passage. He had to make sure that his papers were all in order and that he would be able to get a Visa to the United States. He went directly to the American Embassy and applied for the proper papers, showed his birth certificate, and was told to come back tomorrow with the application filled out and the name of his sponsor in the United States. When he was told that the process would take several months, his heart sank.

"But, I have booked passage to Boston on the twenty-eighth of this month." Then he said, "My sponsor, Mr. Sealander, works here in the Embassy."

"Oh, that's different," she said "Fill out your form and give it to Mr. Sealander to sign and you will have your Visa by tomorrow at noon."

He thanked the clerk and then asked if Mr. Sealander was in? Edgar was busy with someone in his office, so Jacques had to wait. After a while, the door to the office opened and Edgar escorted two of the gentlemen from the Russian Embassy, that Jacques had previously been introduced to; Mr. Ivanov and Mr. Bubovay. The Russians recognized Jacques and greeted him warmly. When the two gentlemen left, Edgar showed Jacques into his office.

"To what do I owe the presence of your company today, Jacques?" he asked. "Please sit down." Jacques sat in one of the chairs across from the big desk. Then Edgar pushed back his chair and put his feet up on the desk in a relaxed mode and offered Jacques a cigarette. It was an American cigarette. He enjoyed American cigarettes, they were even milder than the ones made with Turkish tobacco.

"I took your advice and booked passage to Boston on the Cunard Lines, and I have an application to fill out for a Visa. I will be sailing on the Martha Washington on the twenty-eighth of this month", Jacques announced proudly. Edgar jumped to his feet and shook his hand.

"Congratulations. That calls for a drink."

He reached into a desk drawer and produced a bottle of Jack Daniel's No. 7 Tennessee Whiskey, and two small glasses. He filled the glasses and proposed a toast, "To a new life, in a new land, a smooth voyage and prosperity."

Jacques touched his glass to Edgar's and said, "To good friends! Thank God for good friends." Then they tipped up their glasses and Edgar poured another.

"By the way, who are you going to get to sponsor you for your Visa?" Edgar said with a questioning look.

Jacques replied with a sheepish grin, "I have a very good friend who promised to sponsor me."

"Oh yes! I did say that I would do that for you, didn't I? Give me the forms and we will fill them out together right now."

And he tipped up the glass with his second drink.

"Now, let's get to work filling this out so you will be able to catch that ride to the States. Question number one........."

When the form was completely filled out to his satisfaction, Edgar said, "Let's walk this down the hall to the clerk so she can file it and prepare your Visa.

"How can I thank you enough for all that that you have done for me?"

"Luckily, I told Tata that I would not be home for dinner

tonight so I think that we should go out and celebrate. You can buy me dinner."

"It will be my privilege and an honor to buy you dinner."

At dinner they talked about the journey by ship to America.

"You picked a good time to sail. Isis, the Goddess of Navigation keeps the seas calm from March until winter, if you have any faith in Greek Mythology. Now, when you arrive in Boston, you will have to go through immigration. Don't forget to ask about your fiancée Irena and her family. You should also inquire about your sister Olga. If she is not married yet, they will have her name in the books. If she is married, that may be another situation, but they should have her maiden name listed in the books. Tell them that you believe that she married an American soldier. You will find that information at the port where they entered the country. If, by chance they did not sail to Boston then you will have to go to Ellis Island in New York City for the information. Ellis Island is part of the City but it is across the Hudson River on the New Jersey side. You have to go to the Battery and take a ferry boat to get there. The Battery is at the southern tip of Manhattan Island. All immigrants enter the Port of New York through Ellis Island. You should be able to trace Irena and Olga through one of those Offices. I doubt that they would book passage to New Orleans."

"When will you be going home to New York," Jacques inquired.

"We will be leaving in the first week of September," Edgar said. "I said 'we', because Tata and Timis are leaving with me. Because they are my servants, the United States Government will pay for their passage along with mine. We will be sailing on a passenger ship. When I arrive in New York in the beginning of

October, I will be staying at The Plaza Hotel, located at Fifth Avenue and Central Park South until I can find an apartment. I hope that it will not take long to find a suitable apartment. Then I will have a telephone and you will be able to get my phone number by calling the Telephone Company Information. When you find a place to live in the city, you should get a telephone and have your number listed with Information. Then anyone who comes from Europe to New York City can look you up. I will make sure that Tata and Timis are close by wherever I find a place to live. I don't expect you to remember all of this information. I will write it down for you before you leave."

"I would appreciate that. I want to be in touch when we are both in New York"

When the meal was over they toasted to New York City, to good friends, to a safe trip on the Martha Washington, to the Russian Embassy, to the American Embassy, to finding Irena, and last but not least, to leaving Constantinople. Then they thought it best to take a taxi home, because neither one was capable of walking any distance.

CHAPTER FORTY-TWO

After a few days passed, Jacques decided to notify David Triandafillou that he would be leaving in two weeks. David was very disappointed, but he knew it was inevitable. He knew that Jacques was just biding his time here in Constantinople.

"I imagine that you finally got all the proper papers and now you want to go home. I am sorry to see you leave, but I understand. I will not be able to find another worker in this city that knows as much as you do about the tobacco business".

"I am sorry that I have to leave you. You have been good to me and gave me a job when I needed one. I am not going home to Switzerland though. There is nothing left there for me to go home to. I am going to New York, in America. I am going to try to find my fiancée Irena."

"Well I wish you all the luck in the world, my friend."

That week, Jacques sold the last of the diamonds to pay for his passage on the ship, and give him something to live on for a several weeks when he arrived in the United States. Before he knew it, it was the twenty-seventh of May. It was his last Sunday in Constantinople and his last Sunday to spend with his friend before they would be reunited in New York City in the coming months. Tomorrow he would be on his way to a new land, and a new life. He was excited and sad at the same time. He was unsure that his European culture would be acceptable in the 'New World'. But, he thought, why not. The American population came mostly from Europe.

There was an air of excitement in Edgar's house today. Tata was preparing one of her special Greek meals that she knew Jacques was fond of, roast rack of lamb with all of the trimming. Timis was excited because Jacques' departure would bring them closer to their own exodus. Edgar was glad that his foreign service would soon be coming to an end, and he would be returning to his beloved New York City, the plays, and the sporting events, especially the Major League baseball games and, of course, his beloved Yankees. He hoped that he could be able to leave all of the bad memories of that fateful day in Smynra behind. All three of them would miss Jacques but they were happy for him. Jacques brought thoughtful gifts for each of then in gratitude for their help and friendship. He also brought their usual favorite deserts and a bottle of 'Ouzo', the national drink of Greece to celebrate the occasion.

Parting was emotional that evening. Tata hugged him, kissed both cheeks, and then patted his cheeks like a Greek mother would do to a departing son. When Jacques was ready to leave the three of them gathered outside the front door of the house, Tata had tears in he eyes. Then Edgar said,

"Oh, I almost forgot to give you this."

He reached into his jacket pocket, withdrew an envelope, and gave it to Jacques.

"I have enclosed directions for you when you get to New York."

Jacques thanked him, and placed the envelope in his pocket. As he walked down the street, he turned back, waved, and called out, "I will see you all in New York."

Then he disappeared around the corner.

When he arrived back at his hotel, he opened the envelope that Edgar had given him by the front door of the house. Jacques began to laugh. The document was three typewritten pages long. Evidently, Edgar had a secretary type up the pages. It read,

Hello Jacques:

Welcome to America. To take the train from Boston to New York, you will have to go to the Boston South Station located at Atlantic Avenue and Summer Street in Dewey Square. When you arrive in Manhattan, you will be in Grand Central Terminal. Exit the terminal onto Forty-Second Street, turn right and walk two blocks. Diagonally across the street, you will see the New York Public Library. I believe they have free maps of Manhattan to help you get around. Manhattan Island is long and narrow. It lies north and south. Like the Island, Central Park is long and narrow in the middle of Manhattan running from 59th Street to 110th Street. The numbered streets run East and West, starting at 3rd Street in the Greenwich Village section up to 220th Street at the Inwood section of the city. The Avenues run North and South. Fifth Avenue starts at Washington Square in Greenwich Village and runs along the East side of Central Park and is the dividing line between the streets that are numbered East and West. Eighth Avenue runs parallel to Fifth Avenue on the west side of Central Park. Below Greenwich Village, all of the streets are named streets but that portion of the city is only one fifth of the city's area. I hope this is not too confusing to you. It is really a very simple system. Manhattan is very easy to get around in, once you become accustomed to it.

Edgar continued to give specific directions to his hotel, the Battery, and City Hall along with elevated train routes that ran the length of Manhattan Island, how to obtain information from the Telephone Company and many other tidbits of useful information about the city.

After he read through the three pages of information, he was still a little confused, but he was confident that it would all make sense when he arrived there. Jacques packed his meager belongings in two small suitcases that he had purchased at the Egyptian Bazaar that past week. While he was at the Bazaar, he took time to say good-by to Hraird's mother and father, Nairy and Louis. He told them that he was going to New York City in the United States to live. If they ever came to New York, they would find his name in the Telephone Directory.

He did not sleep well that night, anticipating the long journey ahead of him. Up early, he shaved and went out for a hearty breakfast. Then he returned to the hotel to pick up his bags and check out. He arrived at the docks early but was allowed to board and get settled into his very small quarters. The single bunk had clean sheets and blankets and there was a night stand with a basin and pitcher of water. The night stand was constructed to hold the basin and pitcher firmly in rough seas. He laid down on the bunk to rest and regroup his thoughts but he fell asleep.

He was awakened by the sounds of the ship preparing to leave the port. The Martha Washington was leaving on an early afternoon tide. The sailors on deck were untying lines and shouting. There was a tug boat bumping the side of the ship and the throb of the steam engine was much louder than before. He arose and went out on the deck to watch the operation of the ship leaving the port of Constantinople, but they were no longer calling the city by that name. Now the new Turkish Government was calling the city Istanbul.

As the ship pulled out into the Bosporus, the lines from the tugboat were cast off, and the ship sailed freely around the 'Golden Horn'. Soon they were out in open water. When the sun was sinking in the west, the steward came around and announced that dinner would be served for all passengers, in the dining room in fifteen minutes. Jacques went to his room to quickly freshen up, and then found his way to the dining room. The Captain was already seated at the head of the long table with five chairs and place settings on each side for the ten passengers that the ship carried. Jacques was the first passenger to enter the dining room. He was greeted by the Captain who put down the book he was reading and shook Jacques hand.

"I am Captain Walsh. Thank you for joining me for dinner this evening."

He was a portly gentleman with a full head of graying hair and a full beard. Without thinking about it, Jacques automatically took the seat on the left hand side next to the Captain, as was his place at the table at home in Lausanne. After he sat, he realized that it was habit that placed him there.

The next two persons to come into the dining room were young, teenaged girls who called back to their parents speaking in Russian that they had found the dining room. Then they waited for their mother to enter the dining room to tell them where to be seated. Behind the mother, Jacques was surprised to see one of the gentlemen from the Russian Embassy, and behind him the other gentleman who he recognized from the Embassy and his wife. They did not seem surprised to see Jacques, though they greeted him warmly.

"Our mutual friend, Edgar, made the arrangements for us to sail on this ship because he knew that you were going to America on this same ship. Unfortunately, no one in our group speaks English. Edgar suggested that we travel with someone who he knew could interpret for us. For this, we thank him," the gentleman said. "I am Mark Ivanov and this is my wife Raisa. These are my two daughters Alisa and Tatyana. You know Felix and this is his wife Valentina and their daughter Tamara. We are all going to Chicago. I have a cousin there."

The last of the group of passengers to enter the dining room was a Greek couple. They introduced themselves. Then the Steward requested that they be seated for dinner. During the meal the Captain gave a brief orientation of the ship. He suggested that they could use this room at any time except one hour before meals to allow the steward enough time to straighten out the room and set the table for the next meal.

"The other area of the ship that is strictly for the passengers use is a small lounging deck on the stern of the ship. There is a deck locker there with several lounging chairs for your use in nice weather," the Captain said. "I suggest that you use our pleasant lounging area as much as you can while we are in the Mediterranean Sea where the weather should be nice. Once we enter the Atlantic Ocean, you may not have an opportunity to use that area."

They all thanked Captain Walsh, and when the meal was over, he excused himself, and left the dining room. Soon after, the ladies excused themselves and went to their respective cabins while the four gentlemen stayed. They smoked and chatted for some time before they retired for the evening.

On the afternoon of the second day, the ship turned west to cross the Mediterranean Sea. The sea was calm and all ten passengers took Captain Walsh's advice to sit out on the deck in the warm sunshine under azure blue skies. Jacques noticed that the three teenaged girls were looking at him and whispering to each other until the youngest shyly came over to him and asked,

"Mr. Jacques. Would you teach us to speak English?"

Her mother immediately scolded her for making such an outrageous request. Jacques held up his hand to her mother not to scold any further and replied,

"You are Tatyana, and the only one brave enough to ask for help in learning to speak a new language. I think that you girls had a wonderful idea for this long voyage. English is not my native language but I will teach you as best as I can."

Then he whispered in Tatyana`s ear,

"Why not invite your parents to join us in the dining room for English lessons."

CHAPTER FORTY-THREE

The Martha Washington docked at Gibraltar to take on fresh food supplies to feed the passengers and crew on the long voyage across the Atlantic Ocean. They arrived on a high tide and were scheduled to depart on the next high tide. That gave the passengers almost twelve hours to get their land legs back, and do some shopping in the city market place. The three teenaged girls were told about the wild monkeys that inhabited 'The Rock', so they begged their parents to go and see them. They were told that the Gibraltar Macaques are actually not monkeys but the last free range apes in Europe.

"Be careful. The little villains are friendly but they like to steal things from tourists, especially jewelry, and do not try to pet them, because they have been known to bite people."

Back on the ship, that adventure was all the girls talked about for several days.

The open Atlantic was nowhere near as calm as the blue Mediterranean. There were several days of rain during the voyage and two storms that made most of the land-lubbers seasick, but in spite of that, the journey was uneventful. Jacques found the scenery very boring, to say the least. It reminded him of his journey across the Steppes in a snow storm.

His only salvation on this voyage was the English classes that he held daily for the three girls. He thought his Maman would be proud of him for giving these young people a head start in their new world. On the second day of the classes, Raisa, the mother of Alisa and Tatyana joined the class and by the third day, all four parents were sitting in while the young ladies took notes. By the fourth day, it was obvious that all four adults were studying the girl's notes. It turned out to be a three week crash course in

English with a French accent. It must have been God's will that made Jacques purchase that pocket version Anglais-French, French-Anglais Nouveau Dictionaire that he surprisingly found at a book store in Constantinople. There were a few words that were unfamiliar to him in English and the dictionary came in handy. Sometimes, the classes would last from the end of one meal to the beginning of the next. By the end of the second week, the girls were asking Captain Walsh questions in English. He was amused by the French accent Jacques had fostered on the girls, but he could understand what they were talking about, and was amazed by their progress.

On the morning of the 21st day of June, 1919 the Martha Washington began to slow down. It was a clear day with big white puffy clouds in the blue sky. Jacques was in his cabin when there was a knock on the door. He opened it to find three teenaged girls jumping up and down with excitement. They were all talking at once.

"Jacques, hurry! We arrive. Come see America. Captain Walsh say, soon we be in America. Come Jacques."

In unison, the three girls turned and ran up the ladder to a gangway that ran alongside the bridge of the ship. Jacques followed. The other adults were standing by the railing looking at two small islands ahead of them. A small boat headed toward them off in the distance. It carried the harbor pilot who was to guide the ship into Boston Harbor. Soon they could see the city rising above the horizon and the land on both sides

When the ship stopped midstream in Boston Harbor, a tugboat came to greet them, along with another small boat which was to take the passengers and their luggage to the newly built Boston Immigration Station. It was called the Ellis Island of Boston where all immigrants were to be registered. An officer of the Martha Washington went along in the small boat to deliver the 'Ships Manifest', the passenger list. The passenger's luggage was placed in a large cargo net and one of the ships booms lowered the net into the small boat. Then one by one, the passengers descended a ladder into the boat. The Immigration Officers in the small boat cast off the lines, and they were on their way to the Immigration Station.

At the Immigration Station's dock, the Greek gentleman, Mr. Pappas kneeled, kissed the ground and said,

"Thank you God for bringing us safely to our new home."

Then, each person picked up their luggage, and they were directed inside the building by the Ships Officer. They filled out their forms, had their bags searched, traded their gold for American money and were interrogated by an Immigration Officer. Jacques was asked to translate for the Russian group because there was no interpreter there that spoke their language. They had a start at learning their new language but were not proficient enough to understand all of the questions. Each family had a letter from the American Embassy in Constantinople signed by the Assistant Ambassador Edgar Sealander, but the process still took several hours.

Before they left the Boston Immigration Station, the five ladies kissed Jacques and thanked him in English for their lessons. He blushed and wished them well. Then Mark gave Jacques an address in Chicago where he could be reached and Jacques told them that his telephone number will be in the New York City directory as soon as he finds a place to live.

They hailed two cabs and Jacques told both drivers to take them to the Boston South Station on Atlantic Avenue and Summer Street in Dewey Square. Then he returned to the Immigration building to find out if there was any information on the Baratashvili`s arrival in the United States, or his sister Olga`s arrival. He was directed to the Ships Passenger Arrival Records desk and inquired about all the ships that came here from Athens. There were seven ships that arrived here in Boston from Athens, Greece in the past six months, but none of the immigrants registered came into the United States under the name of Baratashvili, or Vesery. Jacques was very disappointed. He thanked the clerk for his troubles, collected his bags and left the building. Perhaps he will find her records in New York at Ellis Island. God willing! He went to the taxi stand and asked the driver to take him to the Boston South Station on Atlantic

Avenue and Summer Street in Dewey Square. At the ticket counter Jacques said, "I would like to purchase a train ticket to go to Grand Central Station in New York City"

EPILOGUE

Four years later

Jacque was sitting on a park bench in Central Park. Today was a gorgeous Sunday afternoon in New York City. The sky was a clear azure blue with just a few puffy clouds floating by. A little girl in a yellow dress ran up to him and said, "Papa, we're back!" The little girl had beautiful azure blue eyes just like her mother.

"Where is your mother?"

"She is coming. Momma can't run as fast as I can."

"I am glad that your Momma didn't run as fast as you, in her condition."

"You mean with the baby in her belly, Papa?"

"Yes, my little chicken." She gave him a big hug.

Then Irena appeared slightly out of breath.

"It is getting harder and harder to keep up with Jacqueline these days. Jacques smiled.

"Did you tell Alfred to meet us in our regular spot in the park?"

"Yes, he said he would be here before two o'clock".

"That would give the children more than hour to play together in the park before your sister Olga gets out of work at the hospital." It was tradition that the Leach and the Vesery families have dinner together every Sunday!

ABOUT THE AUTHOR

Rene' B. Vesery operated and owned his own business in the printing line in New York City for many years. He is a machinist by trade and an artist by choice. He now resides in Mt. Pleasant, SC with his wife Anne. They have four grown children, eight grandchildren and an adorable Westie named "Dolly".

Retirement in the South has afforded him the time and opportunity to fulfill his life long dream of writing about his father Jacques' journey thru a Revolution and to America.

His novel is based on true stories told to him by his father when he was a child.

He now hopes to add "author" to his list of accomplishments.